Social Development of Handicapped Children and Adolescents

Patrick J. Schloss
Pennsylvania State University

AN ASPEN PUBLICATION®
Aspen Publishers, Inc.

1984

Rockville, Maryland
Royal Tunbridge Wells

Library of Congress Cataloging in Publication Data

Schloss, Patrick J.
Social development of handicapped children and adolescents.

Bibliography: p. 237
Includes index.
1. Handicapped children—Care and treatment.
2. Handicapped youth—Care and treatment. 3. Handicapped
children—Education. 4. Handicapped youth—Education.
5. Social Learning. 6. Behavior modification. I. Title.
[DNLM: 1. Handicapped—Psychology. 2. Social behavior
disorders—In adolescence. 3. Social adjustment—In infancy
and childhood. 4. Social behavior disorders—In infancy
and childhood. 5. Social adjustment—In adolescence.
WS 105.5.H2 S345s]
HV888.S34   1983   362.4'089054   83-11786
ISBN: 0-89443-886-7

Publisher: John Marozsan
Editorial Director: R. Curtis Whitesel
Executive Managing Editor: Margot Raphael
Editorial Services: Scott Ballotin
Printing and Manufacturing: Debbie Collins

Copyright © 1984 by   Aspen Publishers, Inc.

Library of Congress Catalog Card Number: 83-11786
ISBN: 0-89443-886-7

Printed in the United States of America

2 3 4 5

To Patrick David

Table of Contents

Foreword

The volume of research having a direct impact on services in special education has grown at an exponential rate in recent years. Among the developments has been the creation of a number of new journals in the field to absorb the many studies that are appearing. However, that research has not had the type of impact on practice that the researchers would desire. All data suggest that the gap between information and practice is continuing to widen.

One area of particular concern for special educators and parents has been discipline. Many advances have been made in the management of conduct problems. Despite the priority that community members place on such management, the necessary communication of these new strategies to the practitioner has not occurred. The current volume aims to bridge this gap.

Some of the points that receive particular attention are behavior modification techniques, social learning methods, and approaches to the habilitation of children. Emphasis is placed on training positive incompatible behaviors as one method of decelerating or maintaining decrements in aberrant behavior. This latter approach is continuing to obtain greater credence based on the mounting empirical research in this area. One goal of the current volume is to provide information that consumers, such as teachers and consultants, can readily apply to the classroom setting.

Schloss also provides important information on characteristics of various handicapping conditions such as speech and language impairments, visual and auditory difficulties, mental retardation and learning disabilities. As he rightly points out, all these disorders are likely to have physiological and environmental components that, when taken together, can result in devastating effects on the child. The relationship of these disorders to anxiety, self-perception, and other psychological constructs is also highlighted. All these concepts are very important and have been emphasized infrequently in the special education literature. This information is a unique and valuable contribution.

Another highly important area for discussion is the integration of traditional and behavioral methods. Considerable discussion on how to employ expulsions, suspensions, and other common school remediation programs in a systematic fashion is provided. Finally, self-control strategies are likely to be of great value for dealing with the problems of children. These approaches and the others discussed should prove quite valuable for the teacher.

The current volume demonstrates a sensitive balance between scientifically obtained knowledge and practical considerations for the care and habilitation of the handicapped child. On the one hand, information must not be so technical as to make the practical implications hard to determine, nor must professionals continue to present folklore as fact in habilitating the developmentally disabled. Through the manner in which topics have been presented, Schloss may help accomplish the task of informing and at the same time may make both the scientist and practitioner aware of the unique contributions each may provide the other.

Johnny L. Matson
Director, Office of Research
Department of Learning, Development,
and Special Education
Northern Illinois University

Preface

This volume addresses what may be the most emotionally provoking topic for educators yet the most critical area of development for handicapped students. This topic is the social development of exceptional children and youth. Social development can be defined as the acquisition of stable and predictable response patterns that are consistent with community expectations and that allow the student to gain satisfaction and/or avoid dissatisfaction from the environment.

Socially skillful behaviors allow the student to generate reinforcement from the environment in a manner that is mutually reinforcing to the student and others. The socially skillful individual is able to obtain the teacher's attention during class by smiling and raising his or her hand. A youth lacking social skills may obtain the teacher's attention by talking out. The socially skillful individual avoids punishment from his or her parents by studying in order to produce good grades. The individual with poorly developed social skills may cheat to produce good grades and avoid punishment.

The difference between the socially skillful individuals and the students lacking social skills in the preceding examples was not one of function. That is, both individuals were able to avoid punishment and gain teacher attention. The difference involved the nature of the behavior that served the function. Smiling and raising the hand in class meet the standard of consistency with community expectations, while talking out violates the community norms. Similarly, studying is the acceptable means of producing good grades, but cheating is in violation of community expectations. Unfortunately, behavioral topographies, or the observable features of a response, are not easily classified as being socially skillful or not socially skillful because not all community members hold the same expectations. The problem of subjectivity in defining social skills deficits will be considered in Chapter 3.

Social development as defined here goes beyond the isolated ability to exhibit socially skillful behavior. Stability and predictability are also critical dimensions of social development. Not only is a child or youth expected to be able to display socially skillful behaviors, but also these behaviors should occur consistently as target situations occur. The educator is able to predict that Julie will raise her hand when she wishes to be called upon. Bill consistently asks for the teacher's assistance when being harassed by another student. As will be discussed in subsequent chapters, it is not enough for a student to know how to behave. Educational efforts must encourage the child or youth to exhibit these behaviors repeatedly in appropriate social situations.

The scope of this book goes beyond traditional concepts of discipline or behavior management that are limited to the approaches educators may adopt to maintain control over a child's or youth's behavior in the classroom. The text provides techniques that have been demonstrated to be effective in producing pervasive and lasting changes in students' behavior. Behavior change is expected to occur not only in the classroom but also in all relevant settings. Such change should be evident not only through the child's or youth's school years but also on into adulthood.

Patrick J. Schloss

Acknowledgments

This volume seeks to provide an informative procedural guide for practitioners concerned with the social development of handicapped children and youth. As such, the information it contains has been shaped as much by the work of practitioners in the field as contemporary research literature. While researchers and theorists are often acknowledged by citations in books, influential practitioners often go unnoticed. I would therefore like to commend the work of the staff of the Tri-County Educational Program for residents of the Anna State Mental Health and Developmental Disabilities Center. The administrative staff, including Lyle Sparks, Larry Goldsmith, Jim Selinger, and Liz Gersbacher, shaped these views with the sense of reality for budgetary and scheduling restraints. The educators, Fred Barnes, Billie Buell, John Burke, John DeGryse, Peg Firth, Charles Frey, Cindy Jan, Beverly Kondritz, Sylvia Presswood, Carolyn Reed, Mary K. Reed, Sharon Smaldino, Maureen Smith, Scott Tenney, and Brenda Trexler, tempered the ideas with an enthusiasm and confidence that cannot be reflected on journal pages. The ancillary service personnel, Dr. Lonny Morrow, Sandra Delfer, Ann West, Betty Teska, and Scott Tenney, eagerly infused ideas from their various disciplines. I would also like to commend the paraprofessionals, Tom Aken, Kristi Benson, Larry Dancler, Mark Ford, Barrett Hargrave, Susan Hartline, Bobby Joe Hines, Kevin Kozlowski, Gina Lovitt, Howard Mann, Kendra Moore, Frank Myers, Rebecca Zdankiewicz, Scott Rhine, and Calvin Yates, whose willingness to be trained while facing daily classroom responsibilities served as a critical test of the relevance of these concepts.

I would also like to acknowledge the assistance of the adolescent staff of the mental health center: Monty Field, Gerald Clark, Dr. Edward Bellamy, Carol Blackman, Bill Balabas, William Daly, Walter Stocks, Lennard Russell, and Renee Lynn. Their concern for human development and their ability to cooperate in 24-hour-a-day programming have helped to extend the focus of this book outside of the traditional classroom.

Appreciation is also extended to Dr. Cindy Schloss, Karen Golla, and Beth Bohn who critically read the manuscript and to Janice Leitzell, Kathy Shomo, Pat Tate, Susanne Warner, Bonnie Wilson, and Sue Breon who assisted in typing.

I am indebted to Dr. Johnny Matson for the contribution of a Foreword to the volume. It is an honor to have a person of his professional standing review and commend this work.

Finally, my continuing appreciation is expressed to Professor William I. Gardner, my mentor. The ideas contained in this volume are closely tied to the training and experiences he provided through my doctoral training.

Chapter 1

Introduction

The purpose of this text is: (1) to provide educators with an understanding of how social behaviors develop or fail to develop among exceptional children and youth; (2) to identify the behavioral characteristics associated with the various handicapping conditions; and (3) to provide an educational framework for achieving social development objectives. The importance of this endeavor is emphasized by reconsidering the point made in the Preface. First, the social development of exceptional children and youths is the most emotionally provoking aspect of special education.

A large number of educators are frustrated and disillusioned with the teaching profession. These findings have been attributed to the burnout syndrome or emotional depletion. Burnout is described in the special education literature as emotional stress that results in physical and mental exhaustion (Weiskopf, 1980). Other authors have defined burnout as a painfully and personally destructive response to excessive stress (Mattingly, 1977); becoming exhausted as the result of excessive demands on energy, strength, or resources (Freudenberger, 1977); and emotional exhaustion resulting from the stress of interpersonal contact (Maslach, 1978). In each case, the burnout syndrome is identified as the inability of child care workers or educators to effectively cope with emotional stress. The ultimate results of this syndrome are the attribution of student problems to factors beyond the educator's control, cynicism and negativism toward the student, the excessive use of technical terms to describe students' limitations, and a paranoia in which the educator believes that peers and administrators are seeking to make life more difficult (Freudenberger, 1977). Maslach and Pines (1977) suggest that, in the extreme, burnout may result in alcohol abuse, drug abuse, marital conflict, chronic physical illness, mental illness, absenteeism, and impaired sexual and professional performance.

A number of events may promote stress among members of the helping profession, including the characteristics of the individual, workloads and

1

responsibilities, and extra organizational difficulties (Cooper & Marshall, 1976). However, authors in the special education   literature continually emphasize the impact of the behavioral features of handicapped students as being a paramount contributor to occupational stress. Weiskopf (1980) has suggested that the perceived (not real) inability of special educators to promote behavior change with handicapped students lowers their self-esteem, thereby limiting job satisfaction. This view is supported by writers in the child care literature (Collins, 1977; Daley, 1979; Proctor, 1979).

Weiskopf (1980) contends that the amount of time special educators must spend in direct supervision of their students adversely affects their attitudes and effectiveness. She contends that the special behavioral characteristics of exceptional children and youths require virtually constant supervision and attention in the school environment. This view is supported by the research of Maslach and Pines (1977) and Bensky, Shaw, Gouse, Bates, Dixon, and Beane (1980). Maslach and Pines (1977) have demonstrated that program structures that are ineffective in controlling children's and youths' emotional outbursts "exacted a greater emotional price from the individual staff members" (p. 109). Kadushin (1974) argues that child care workers (and educators) must provide emotional support to children and youths with behavioral deficits. In the absence of supportive services that allow educators to replenish their personal emotional needs, burnout occurs.

There is consistent acknowledgment that in-service training and advanced professional preparation that address   stress producing aspects of special education can alleviate the burnout syndrome (Bensky, et al., 1980; Dixon, Shaw, & Bensky, 1980; Weiskopf, 1980). Schloss, Sedlak, Wiggins and Ramsey (1983) have demonstrated that providing educators of severely behaviorally disordered/aggressive youths with training in progressive muscle relaxation skills not only increases the educators' ability to use effective social development techniques, but also reduces the stress that accrues from working with highly volatile youths. The stated purpose of this volume in part is to provide technical information that may be used as a foundation for preservice and in-service training. This foundation may then facilitate educators' effectiveness and increase professional satisfaction.

Second, the social development of exceptional children and youth is the most critical area of development. Research by Fitzgerald (1968) and Kidd (1970) has demonstrated that a large majority of handicapped individuals educated in the public schools obtain gainful employment as adults. Intelligence, specific handicapping condition, or academic achievement does not appear to be an intervening variable. Other characteristics, including personal adjustment, self-assurance, initiative, cooperative work habits, perseverance, respect of authority, social competence, and interpersonal skills, do appear to have a bearing on occupational success (Domino & McGarty, 1972; Fiester & Giambra, 1972; Neuhaus, 1967; Sali & Amir, 1971). A study reported by the Research Utilization Branch of the previously active Department of Health, Education, and Welfare (1969) demonstrated that social adjustment is the predominant variable associated with absenteeism and work failure. Zigler and Harter (1969) concur that social-emotional responses, including anxiety, dependency, envy, aggression, and a negative attitude toward authority, are the major factors leading to poor occupational adjustment of the mentally retarded. Goldstein (1972), in surveying the social adjustment of adult mentally retarded individuals in vocational settings, reported adjustment problems to be more a function of social behaviors than task performance. A survey of sheltered workshop entry requirements reported by Johnson and Mithaug (1978) concurred with this finding.

Kelly and Drabman (1977) and Rosenberg (1959) provide evidence that other people's reactions to the mentally retarded are adversely influenced by the social cues retarded persons exhibit. Kelly (1982) states that teaching social skills to the handicapped would facilitate their adjustment to normalized community settings. He proposes adopting social skills training to "reduce interpersonal cues or behaviors indicative of retardation and to increase more appropriate social skills, which would facilitate the client's development of relationships" (p. 2). With regard to emotionally disturbed individuals, Kelly (1982) argues that "difficulties in handling and establishing interpersonal relationships are reported by even high functioning clients seen in almost any counseling or treatment setting" (p. 3).

Recent research has emphasized the importance of social development strategies for young children. Reviews by Michelson and Wood (1980) and Kelly (1982) emphasize the importance of remediating social skill inadequacies in childhood. Aside from promoting positive self-concept, peer relations, and general social adjustment, early social skill development can promote the acquisition of new and more complex skills. Kelly (1982) suggests that early life skill deficits may promote continued isolation, which precludes the learning of advanced interpersonal skills. Supporting this view, a substantial body of literature has demonstrated a positive relationship between social deficiencies in childhood and a range of subsequent adjustment problems including delinquency (Roff, Sells, & Golden, 1972), dropping out of school (Ullmann, 1957), bad conduct discharges from military service (Roff, 1961), and community mental health services (Cowen, Pederson, Babigian, Izzo, & Frost, 1973).

Kagan and Moss (1962) have demonstrated that social skill deficits in childhood (e.g., withdrawal, family dependence, lack of temper control, anxiety, sex role identification, involvement in intellectual mastery, and specific sexual behavior patterns) are closely related to analogous response patterns in adulthood. Barclay (1966), Muma (1965, 1968), and Porterfield and Schlichting (1961) presented the converse that high social status in childhood is associated with interpersonal adjustment in adult life.

Strain, Shores, and Kerr (1976) have demonstrated that deficits in interpersonal responses of school-aged children are associated with depressed academic achievement. This association has been attributed to the importance of student-to-student interactions in the learning process (Hops & Cobb, 1973, 1974) and the observation that teachers interact more favorably with students who possess positive social behaviors. The research of Hops and Cobb (1973, 1974), Cobb and Hops (1973), Foss and Peterson (1981), and Walker and Hops (1976) has identified a basic set of social "survival skills" that predict and promote achievement across subject matter. Training in areas such as eliciting assistance from the teacher, trying to answer questions, smiling, being attentive, and requesting work assignments has been demonstrated by the researchers to have a positive effect on academic achievement.

SOCIAL LEARNING THEORY CONSTRUCTS

The practices described in this text are supported by broad-based social learning theory constructs (Bandura, 1977b; Miller & Dollard, 1941; Rotter, 1975). The basic assumption underlying this view is that both acceptable and deviant behaviors are learned through the individual's interactions with historic and contemporary environments. Rotter (1975) has advanced a derivation of the learning theory model that relies on four major determinants: expectancy for reinforcement; value of reinforcement; psychological situation; and behavior. The following formula describes the relationship of the variables:

Behavior potential = (expectancy and reinforcement value).

This formula denotes that the potential for a behavior to occur is a function of expectancy of reinforcement. A substantial body of literature has supported its utility in understanding and predicting behavior of the mentally retarded (Mercer & Snell, 1977), the learning disabled (Sabatino & Schloss, 1981), and the emotionally disturbed (Schloss, Kane, & Miller, 1981).

The formulation proposed by Rotter has major implications for the development of social behaviors in educational settings. Social-personal deficits of an individual may be generated and maintained by one or more of the following factors:

- limited expectancy for reinforcement following the demonstration of a positive social behavior
- limited preference for the expected reinforcer following the demonstration of a positive social behavior
- limited ability to select and/or utilize a positive social behavior that will produce a high preference reinforcer
- increased expectancy for reinforcement following the occurrence of a disruptive behavior
- increased preference for the expected reinforcer following the occurrence of a disruptive behavior

The term *reinforcer,* used above, includes both positively reinforcing events and negatively reinforcing events. A positive reinforcer is defined as an event that is pleasant in nature and that increases the likelihood that the individual will behave in a similar manner. A negative reinforcer is defined as the response-contingent removal of an unpleasant event that increases the likelihood that the adolescent will behave in a similar manner.

The following example shows the application of these principles. When faced with an aggression-provoking incident, an individual becomes disruptive because: (a) he or she has a high expectancy for support and assurance from the teacher (a positively reinforcing consequence); and (b) he or she expects to be removed from an unpleasant conflict situation (a negatively reinforcing consequence).

The value of a given reinforcer is defined as the degree of preference for the event given an equal expectancy that other reinforcers may occur. Social learning theory distinguishes between *internal* and *external* reinforcement in that internal reinforcement is identified as the individual's perception that an event has value in and of itself. External reinforcement refers to outcomes that have predictable value to a group or culture to which a person belongs. Internal reinforcers are considered to be under the control of the individual while external reinforcers are under the control of others in the environment.

Social development procedures based on these principles involve the systematic manipulations of contemporary environments so that new learning occurs. In the case of handicapped populations, it is apparent that exceptional learning and behavioral characteristics reduce the individual's ability to profit from traditional environments. Simple verbal messages from adults and peers that, for the typical learner, convey social values, may be confusing for exceptional children and youth. Limited sensory, cognitive, and/or physical abilities may impair the child's or youth's ability to receive social rules, to decode and understand their meaning, to integrate new learning with existing information, to store that information, and to alter future behavior as the result of new learning. In short, the general population may alter expectancies for reinforcement, the relative value of reinforcers, and subsequent behavior through infrequent verbal interactions (e.g., counseling, peer interactions, and family discussions). Because these procedures require cognitive skills often deficient in handicapped children and youth, more direct and concrete intervention tactics are required.

Social learning theory has produced a number of carefully researched principles that accommodate the learning and behavioral characteristics of the handicapped. In general, features that recommend the application of a social learning approach to the handicapped include:

- Specific intervention program designs are based on the careful assessment of the youth and his or her learning environment.
- Intervention programs are monitored continuously. Program changes occur as indicated by evaluative data.
- Social learning programs have a positive orientation. Behavioral deficiencies are viewed as being a function of learning environments that do not support social-personal growth. Behavior change occurs through new learning. Theoretical statements of internal pathology, which provide little relevant information for treatment, are de-emphasized.
- Behavioral characteristics are not viewed as being inherently pathological but simply more excessive (occurring more frequently or intensely) or deficient (occurring less frequently or intensely) than expected by significant people in the youth's environment. Specific excessive behaviors (e.g., crying, negative self-statements, restlessness, etc.) or deficit behaviors (e.g., social interactions, speech, sleep, etc.) become the targets of intervention.
- Intervention programs are conducted on a continuous basis by all relevant people in the youth's learning environment.
- Successful intervention approaches can be readily transferred to community-based agencies (e.g., community mental health, public schools, etc.) if the resources are available.
- An objective and reliable appraisal of the resources and time needed to provide effective services can be made.
- Social learning programs can be easily integrated with psychopharmacological interventions.

UNDERLYING PRINCIPLES

Social learning principles emphasize functional relationships between behavior and the environment. The study of these principles allows educators and parents to direct the most potent procedures available to the development of social behavior among handicapped learners. Many of the principles appear to be "good common sense" as they have been applied for centuries by parents and educators. The Premack Principle, for example, states that if a child is required to participate in an unpleasant activity prior to engaging in a pleasant activity, the child will participate in the unpleasant activity more willingly (Premack, 1965). Throughout history parents and grandparents have been encouraging children to eat liver by ending the meal with a special dessert (e.g., "When you eat your liver, then you can have some ice cream.").

Understanding and applying social learning principles with a high degree of precision may effect change with the handicapped learner when less intense or consistent applications have failed. Therefore, the careful application of the basic principles described here will provide educators with the greatest amount of power in influencing the social development of handicapped learners. The following section will present an overview of the underlying principles of a broad-based social learning approach. Subsequent chapters will develop these topics in greater detail.

Impact of Learning Histories and Environments

The first principle is that exceptional behavioral characteristics are, in part, the product of deficiencies in the learning histories and/or present learning environments of the individual.

While it is apparent that certain handicapping conditions are the result of biochemical, sensorimotor, neurological, or genetic errors (R.L. Miller, 1974; Ornitz, 1974; Rimland, 1964), it is also apparent that these deficits do not work in isolation to produce disruptive behavior (Gardner, 1977; Kauffman, 1981; Menolascino, 1977; Miller & Schloss, 1982). Rather, excessive disruptive or withdrawn behavior may be a function of the individual with limited biophysical capabilities not being able to benefit from natural learning environments. There is strong evidence that well-designed environments that accommodate the characteristics of the handicapped individual can produce effective changes in social, emotional, academic, and vocational abilities (Ayllon & Rosenbaum, 1977; Carr, Newsom, & Binkoff, 1976; Gottman, Gonso, & Schuler, 1976; Koegel & Rincover, 1974; O'Leary & Dubey, 1979).

Schloss, Kane, and Miller (1981), for example, reported a social learning approach to truancy intervention. The authors demonstrated the effectiveness of an engineered environment that increased the amount of satisfaction gained from going to school, decreased the amount of satisfaction gained by staying home, and actively taught social skills that enhanced the youth's ability to benefit from going to school. Specific environmental change strategies included reducing academic demands to increase the likelihood of success at school, fostering peer relations, providing frequent praise for work completion, frequently communicating success in school to parents, encouraging the parents to send the youth to bed at a reasonable time, sanctioning privileges (e.g., loss of television, confinement to room, dockage of allowance), and using a social skill training program during the school day.

In highly unique demonstrations, Wiltz and Gordon (1974) and Hanf and Kling (1973) constructed simulated apartment environments in a clinical setting. In each report the parents were taught to structure the home environment to reduce disruptive acts of children. Continuous feedback was provided to the parents through electronic devices by a psychologist observing behind one-way mirrors. The authors reported that environmental manipulations suggested by the psychologist and implemented by the parents had substantially reduced match lighting, food throwing, urination over toilet facilities, noncompliance, and other disruptive behaviors. Unfortunately, both studies failed to systematically evaluate the extent to which the parents' new skills and subsequent behavior change of the children generalized to the natural home setting. Informal data provided by the parents did, however, suggest sustained progress.

Interaction between Individual Characteristics and Environment

The second principle is that a student's behavior characteristics reflect unique physical and psychological variables interacting with the learning environment to produce current social and emotional characteristics.

Deficiencies in social development cannot be explained through simple statements of internal pathology or deficient environments as these variables continually interact throughout the individual's life. Gardner (1977) has emphasized that every individual is biologically unique. An environment that supports social growth for one learner may be ineffective for another. The relative impact of the environment on future learning is a function of the individual's biophysical characteristics. For example, gifted and talented youths benefit most from unstructured environments that encourage the application of critical thinking, higher level conceptual functioning, problem solving, creative abilities, abstract thinking, and independence (Walker, 1978). Conversely, the severely handicapped require high degrees of environmental structure in the form of a routine schedule, consistent cue and reinforcement conditions, functional activities, a task-analyzed curriculum, integrated therapy, and home-based intervention (Bates, Renzaglia, & Wehman, 1981). The environmental differences required for these two extreme groups are obviously a function of their learning characteristics. Less obviously, effective environments for any two gifted youths or two severely handicapped youths may be different as a function of more subtle learning differences.

In addition, the current social performance of a handicapped youth is not only a function of internal features and present environments but also previous environments or experiences. To exemplify this point, Mercer and Snell (1977) suggest that, because the handicapped often have a history of failure and nonreinforcement, their expectancy for success in future endeavors is decreased. The generalized expectancy for failure resulting from historic environments results in a reduced likelihood that the individual will approach challenging tasks in the future. This view is supported by the research of Chandler and Boroskin (1971) and Keogh, Cahill, and MacMillan (1972). The researchers demonstrate that the present learning and behavioral characteristics of the handicapped are influenced by previous environments.

In summary, the handicapped learner at any point in time exhibits unique characteristics that result from his or her biophysical environment, historical learning environments, and contemporary learning environments. Given the educator's obvious inability to impact historical environments and biophysical characteristics, he or she must be content to shape current environments. Knowledge of other factors that have contributed to the student's current characteristics is useful only in that it assists the educator in engineering current learning conditions.

Educational Objectives

The third principle is that educational objectives should be based on the needs and characteristics of the learner, should be functional, and should be developed concomitantly throughout school and living environments.

The objectives established by a multidisciplinary staff for the handicapped individual should result from the thorough understanding of the individual. A priori objectives established for groups of students may be useful in generating ideas for the present student's needs, but the actual objective must reflect the student's unique physical and psychological characteristics as they interact with the demands of his or her environment. Target objectives, or the small steps that collectively form the terminal objective, should be arranged in a logical sequence. The terminal objective should be functional in that the natural environment is likely to reinforce the terminal objective. Reading, for example, is a functional objective because it generally produces a higher salary potential, makes available a wider range of recreational activities, and provides information that helps individuals avoid unpleasant events.

Finally, objectives should be developed concomitantly throughout important environments. It is clear that definite social, personal, academic, and vocational characteristics interact to produce an individual's behavioral repertoire at given times. Lovaas and Koegel (1972) have emphasized the interaction between the deficit social characteristics of handicapped individuals and the subsequent delayed development of a diverse range of abilities. It is apparent, for example, that isolating social objectives to be developed in one setting and vocational objectives to be developed in another would not provide the greatest power in influencing a range of functional objectives. Rather, the learning environment must be engineered so that work toward one objective supports work toward another on an ongoing basis. Moore and Bailey (1973), for example, demonstrate an instructional procedure for the integrated development of social behavior and academic behavior of a behavior-disordered child. The investigation emphasizes the need for teachers to possess skills in engineering educational activities and classroom environments to accommodate multiple instructional objectives.

Lack of Positive Reinforcement

The fourth principle is that exceptional characteristics reduce the child's or youth's ability to meet the expectations of parents, teachers, peers, and so on, thereby reducing the availability of normative reinforcing events.

Ferster (1961) has argued that handicapped children are severely limited in their ability to engage in positive social behaviors. This limitation reduces the individual's ability to acquire satisfaction from the natural environment by engaging in interpersonal relationships. The result of repeated failure to acquire social reinforcement from others is a further weakening of the individual's social repertoire. Gardner (1977) further advances this position by suggesting that in the absence of social reinforcement from parents, teachers, and other authority figures, children and youths will seek to gain *any* available source of satisfaction. Reinforcers, in this case, often include peer support and recognition by authority figures for disruptive behavior. The major detrimental effect is that these forms of reinforcement are generally produced through socially maladjusted behavior. The individual is motivated to approach events that produce coercive forms of reinforcement by exhibiting disruptive behavior. In the meantime, the individual is less and less apt to seek appropriate forms of reinforcement by demonstrating acceptable behavior. The net result is an increased likelihood that the youth will engage in maladaptive behavior and a decreased likelihood that he or she will engage in prosocial behavior. The longer this process continues, the less able the youth becomes to meet the criterion for success by exhibiting prosocial behavior and the stronger the controlling influence of coercive forms of reinforcement must become.

Libet and Lewinsohn (1973), in a social learning analysis of depressive-like behavior, exemplify this position. Their research demonstrates that depressed individuals are less able to exhibit positive social behaviors that meet the expectations of others. As a result, they receive less reciprocal positive social reinforcement. Coyne (1976) has demonstrated that depressive reactions function to produce coercive forms of social reinforcement in the absence of appropriate reinforcement not attainable through adaptive behavior. Applied treatment studies reported by J. Butler (1980), Hersen, Bellack, and Himmelhock (1980), and Rehm, Fuchs, Roth, Kornblith, and Romano (1979) have demonstrated that providing experiences for social skill development and establishing an attainable criterion for success in social endeavors can reduce the likelihood that individuals will engage in depressive reactions. Similar views have been advanced and studied in the areas of aggression (Bandura, 1973), impulsivity, distractibility, and hyperactivity (Hallahan & Kauffman, 1976), immaturity and inadequacy (Kauffman, 1981), and truancy (Schloss, Kane, & Miller, 1981).

Reduction in Number of Reinforcers

The fifth principle is that exceptional characteristics may reduce the number of events that are reinforcing to the child or youth.

A range of secondary reinforcers is developed in children through their association with more primitive satisfying events or primary reinforcers. For example, the pairing of a mother's voice and touch with food makes her presence alone satisfying to the child. Over time, the mother's social interactions acquire strong reinforcing properties for the child. As a child grows into preadolescence and adolescence, numerous reinforcing events are developed through their association with other reinforcers. Grades, adult approval, special awards or recognition, peer approval, money, etc., all acquire reinforcing properties through their association with primary reinforcing events and other secondary reinforcers (e.g., mother's approval). The presence of a handicapping condition restricts the child's or youth's ability to experience events such as adult approval, good grades, and recognition. Therefore, there are fewer opportunities for these events to be paired with existing reinforcers. Given the paucity of these experiences, events such as adult approval or grades fail to develop as reinforcers for the individual. On the other hand, available events, such as peer approval or recognition for disruptive behavior, may acquire unusually strong reinforcing properties. This learning history explains why many children and youths seem to be indifferent to teacher approval or grades while peer approval exerts an extremely strong influence.

In a review of literature pertaining to the reinforcement characteristics of the mentally retarded, Harter and Zigler (1974) emphasized the role of motivational deficits in the handicapped. Based on R.W. White's (1960) concept of effectance motivation, they argued that social competence results from numerous interactions with the environment. The interactions begin at birth and become more complex into adulthood. People become more competent in interacting and benefiting from these events as they grow older. This process of refining individual abilities allows the person to control the environment as he or she reaches social or intellectual maturity. Effectance motivation, therefore, is the development of mastery in successively more challenging tasks as a secondary reinforcing event. Harter and Zigler (1974) clearly demonstrate that pleasure is derived from mastery of difficult tasks—the more challenging the task, the greater the sense of personal reward. Other reviewers have presented similar findings (Hunt, 1965; Piaget, 1952b).

The concept of effectance motivation has major implications for the handicapped. Fundamental to the paradigm is the notion that success in increasingly more challenging tasks motivates future performance; however, tasks that are excessively difficult result in feelings of frustration and failure. Conversely, repetitious tasks that are easily accomplished result in feelings of laboriousness and boredom. Zigler's (1973) research has demonstrated that individuals required to engage in excessively difficult tasks exhibit reduced motivational levels. Ollendick, Balla, and Zigler (1971) have reported a study that indicates the handicapped are more likely to approach events that offer a high probability of success.

Deficiencies in Self-Control Skills

The sixth principle states that students with exceptional characteristics are less likely to develop self-control skills that operate in the absence of external contingencies.

Self-control has been defined as the ability to govern behavior through an internal locus of control (Meichenbaum & Goodman, 1971; Thoresen & Mahoney, 1974). Meichenbaum and Goodman have proposed a developmental view of behavioral adjustment. During early developmental years a child is controlled primarily by the speech of others, usually adults. The child is viewed as having an "external locus of control." Later, as the child develops cognitively, overt speech begins to serve as a regulator of behavior, and still later the child's inner speech or covert speech assumes the self-regulatory role. This inner, covert speech that regulates and controls the child's behavior is described as the development of an "internal locus of control." Current literature indicates that children and youths labeled as behavior problems exhibit primarily an external locus of control (Meichenbaum & Goodman, 1971). These children do not exert individual control over their behavior and therefore are directed by others. Researchers hypothesized that if self-control training could facilitate a transfer of control from external (others) to an internal (self) locus of control, behavior problems and intellectual performance could be improved (Meichenbaum & Goodman, 1971).

The contemporary social learning literature emphasizes the development of self-control skills among handicapped populations (Gardner, 1977). Unlike previous concepts of will power or self-discipline, considered to be immutable features of the individual, learning theorists describe self-control as a set of learned responses (Thoresen & Mahoney, 1974). Behavioral psychologists argue that the development of self-control skills may promote durable and pervasive behavior changes (Reese, 1978). In effect, self-control skills are carried by the student from one setting to the next and remain a functional part of his or her behavioral repertoire over time. Having acquired the ability to self-manage his or her behavior, the child or youth may be less dependent on external contingencies that vary from classroom to classroom or occupation to occupation.

Self-control involves problem solving and awareness of means-end causality (Meichenbaum & Goodman, 1971; Thoresen & Mahoney, 1974). Other skills such as delay of gratification and reflectivity are also thought to be necessary for self-control. Based on these concepts, Meichenbaum and Goodman (1971) have developed a cognitive self-guidance model for training self-control.

The program was based on the transference of overt speech regulation of behavior to private, covert speech regulation. The treatment involved teaching a strategy of defining the problem, deciding on the best attack strategy to achieve solution, guiding oneself through the strategy with allowances for self-correction and self-reinforcement, self-evaluating the accuracy of the solution, and providing appropriate reinforcement. The training consists of the following sequential components: (1) the adult overtly verbalizes and models the procedure for the child or youth; (2) the child overtly verbalizes and then whispers the procedure with adult supervision; (3) the child covertly guides himself or herself through private self-verbalization. This training procedure has been used to improve academic task performance and social performance (Meichenbaum & Goodman, 1971; Reese, 1978).

A second general type of self-control strategy often incorporated by learning theorists focuses primarily on the differences between desired and undesired responses (Anderson, Foder, & Alpert, 1976). The procedure, outlined by Glynn, Thomas, and Shee (1973), initially involves assisting the child or youth to target the behaviors to be changed. This allows the student to better understand and clarify specific responses considered by others to be appropriate and/or inappropriate. The student is then taught to monitor and evaluate these behaviors, thus charting his or her own success or failure. Research indicates that self-recording alone may produce a desirable change in behavior (Reese, 1978). Then the student must be involved in choosing appropriate consequences. Research has demonstrated that giving students the option of choosing their own reinforcers or punishers increases the effectiveness of the contingency (Reese, 1978). Finally, the student must be taught to properly apply these reinforcers or punishers (Reese, 1978).

A number of investigations have emerged in the literature supporting the efficacy of self-control procedures with children and youth. Birkimer and Brown (1979) have reported the use of an operant self-control procedure in reducing disruptive classroom behavior of elementary school-aged children. The self-control program involved instructing the children to monitor their off-task behavior, matching their results to the teacher's. Accurate monitoring and a low rate of off-task behavior were accomplished through the use of self-delivered reinforcement. This study demonstrated the self-control procedure to be more effective than simply posting rules or teacher administered contingencies. Varni and Henker (1979) provided a similar demonstration of Meichenbaum and Goodman's (1971) cognitive training procedure in reducing the hyperactive behavior and improving the academic performance of elementary school-aged children.

Major Factors in Developing Effective Social Development Strategies

The seventh principle states that effective social development strategies involve intervention through three major entry points: the antecedents, mediating personal characteristics, and consequences associated with the behavior.

The initial phases of designing a social development program involve a careful assessment of the characteristics of both the learner and the setting. Three factors are emphasized in the analysis of social development deficits.

These are: (1) antecedent conditions, or events that precede a behavior and influence the likelihood of its occurrence (e.g., being confronted by staff often precipitates aggression); (2) mediating personal characteristics, observable or inferred features of the individual associated with the occurrence of a behavior (e.g., a youth's inability to stay calm is associated with disruptive outbursts); and (3) consequent conditions, defined as events that follow a behavior and influence the likelihood that it will recur (e.g., a youth's verbally abusive episodes are maintained by attention from peers).

A number of strategies have been described in the literature that address these factors. A cursory review of many texts may suggest that intervention approaches are selected indiscriminately. Contrary to this view, the underlying theme of a social learning orientation is the analysis of specific factors that influence the target behaviors. Intervention approaches are selected on the basis of data generated from the careful study of the student's behavioral characteristics in association with influencing factors. The practitioner who is familiar with these procedures is able to select from a range of intervention strategies on the basis of his or her understanding of the learner.

Intervention approaches that focus on antecedents involve the identification of events that are likely to cue or trigger a disruptive response and/or incompatible prosocial behavior. In the initial phases of a program, events observed to cue disruptive behavior (e.g., unstructured time, failing grades, specific authority requests, criticism, peer influences, didactic lessons, etc.) may be removed from the educational setting. Once the child or youth's disruptive behavior is reduced to acceptable levels, these events may be gradually reintroduced. Similarly, certain antecedent events may be observed to increase the likelihood that prosocial behaviors will occur (e.g., frequent feedback, positive peer models, high-interest activities, specially designed educational materials, special seating arrangements, involvement in classroom management decisions, etc.). In the initial phases of intervention, these events may be scheduled to occur frequently. Once desirable behavior occurs at the expected rate, they may be gradually withdrawn.

In short, antecedent control involves: (1) identifying cues for disruptive behaviors; (2) identifying cues for prosocial behaviors; (3) arranging for disruptive cues to occur less often while prosocial cues occur more often; and (4) gradually reinstating the original cue conditions commensurate with the student's demonstrated ability to self-manage his or her behavior.

Intervention approaches that focus on mediating personal characteristics involve teaching the child or youth to exhibit specific self-control skills that mediate between provoking antecedents and disruptive behavior. For example, a child may become agitated because he is not able to go to recess until all of his work is completed. The educator may teach the child to delay gratification, thereby reducing the power of the antecedent in provoking disruptive behavior. Similarly, relaxation skills may be developed to mediate between frustrating events and aggression.

Finally, intervention procedures that focus on consequences involve three major contingency arrangements. First, behaviors that consistently produce satisfying consequences are likely to reoccur. If calm hand raising is more effective in attracting the teacher's attention than talking out, calm hand raising will occur more frequently. If, on the other hand, talking out has a greater likelihood of gaining the teacher's attention, talking out will be more prevalent. In the first case, hand raising is positively reinforced by teacher attention. In the second case, talking out is positively reinforced by teacher attention.

Second, behaviors that consistently result in the avoidance or removal of unpleasant events are likely to reoccur. If studying diligently for a test results in the avoidance of a bad grade, studying is likely to occur more often. If cheating is used to avoid a bad grade, cheating will probably occur more often. In the first case, studying is negatively reinforced by the avoidance of a bad grade. In the second, cheating is negatively reinforced by the same consequence. Finally, behaviors that consistently produce unpleasant events are likely to diminish or cease. If swearing consistently produces the unpleasant consequence of a dockage of privileges, swearing is likely to occur less often. Similarly, if completing assignments repeatedly produces the unpleasant consequence of a bad grade and a subsequent dockage of privileges, assignment completion may be expected to occur less often. In the first example, swearing was punished by a dockage in privileges. In the second, assignment completion was punished by the same consequence.

Although the three entry points may appear to involve discrete program procedures, they are more effective when used in combination. The most powerful intervention programs involve the manipulation of antecedents to insure success for the student, developing mediating personal characteristics that result in the student's increased ability to self-manage his or her behavior when faced with provoking antecedents, and the structuring of consequences to ensure that the student recognizes the relationship between positive performance and satisfying outcomes.

Tactics To Promote Social Learning

The eighth principle is that a number of systematic tactics may be used to promote social learning and increase the consistency with which newly acquired behaviors are performed.

Prompting

Prompting suggests that educators arrange conditions that are likely to produce desirable behavior. For example, an educator may request that a student do homework. This prompt may then lead to homework completion, which may then be reinforced. Given that a verbal prompt may not be sufficiently strong, the teacher may use a note to parents as a prompt. Again, the prompt is used to encourage the completion of the activity so that the youth may be reinforced. In addition to verbal and physical guidance, a number of devices may be used as effective prompts. A timer, notebook, bulletin board, or a written schedule may all be used to cue behavior that may later be reinforced.

Observational Learning

Observational learning emphasizes that a child or youth's current behavioral repertoire may be influenced through his or her observations of others in the learning environment. In effect, a student need not be exposed directly to punishing or reinforcing consequences for his or her behavior to be changed. Behavior change may occur through the observation of others faced with these contingencies. For example, a child may begin swearing as the result of frequently observing her mother gain compliance by exhibiting profane language. Similarly, a youth may begin to speak very assertively because of television dramas in which the star obtains material wealth through a direct and persuasive verbal style.

Chaining

Chaining suggests that complex behavioral patterns can be developed by linking a number of simple responses already in the individual's repertoire. Ordering a meal at a restaurant involves the chaining of a series of simple behaviors that collectively produce the satisfying consequence of a meal. Chained behaviors may include greeting the waiter, requesting a menu, reading the menu, selecting from the menu, verbalizing the decision to the waiter, and so on. In a similar fashion, disruptive behaviors may result from a chain of basic responses. For example, a requirement to read words above a youth's ability level may be linked to frustration, covert verbal aggression, overt verbal aggression, physical aggression, and escape. The entire sequence is reinforced by the removal of the reading assignment. A single disruptive behavior may also exist in a chain or series of appropriate behaviors. For example, getting off the bus may be linked to running into school, knocking a student down, arriving in the classroom, and being seated prior to the bell. As should be apparent, the principle of chaining is used in social development programs to sequence basic behaviors into complex social responses; identify and remove individual disruptive behaviors that exist in a chain of appropriate responses; and intervene at the start of a chain of disruptive behaviors so that more intense adverse behavioral reactions are avoided.

Shaping

Shaping suggests that less than perfect performance may be reinforced early in the behavior change program. As the youth's ability to display the appropriate behavior increases, the teacher's criteria for reinforcement increase. In other words, initially the teacher may reinforce minimally acceptable behavior. As this behavior is performed more consistently, the teacher may require a closer approximation to the "perfect" behavior. Over time, the teacher may gradually increase his or her expectations for the youth's behavior by withdrawing praise and reinforcement from a lower level of performance and applying it to a slightly higher level.

Timing

Timing emphasizes that a reinforcer will have its greatest effect if provided immediately following a desirable behavior. Presenting reinforcing events immediately following desirable behavior helps the child or adolescent to understand the precise behavior that produces personal rewards. When a period of time elapses from the performance of a behavior and the positive consequence, the individual is less likely to associate his or her performance with the attainment of the reinforcer.

For example, many handicapped individuals are not aware that performance on a job produces a paycheck and possible promotion. This is because these consequences are far removed in time from the actual work behavior. Therefore, professionals in vocational programs may provide pay following each hour or day of work. This helps the individuals to learn that work produces money. Similarly, teachers often provide feedback immediately following each school assignment because the delayed feedback of a grade each nine weeks is often ineffective in teaching the relationships between work and grades.

Pairing

The principle of pairing states that more natural incentives (such as praise) should always accompany unnatural reinforcers (such as candy). For many handicapped individuals praise alone is not a sufficiently strong motivating event. Therefore, more powerful reinforcers are needed (e.g., free time, a special activity, cola). The need for these unusual reinforcers will be reduced as they are paired frequently with more natural incentives (e.g., praise, attention, grades, money). Therefore, the rule of pairing suggests that events that do not motivate the individual, but should, may develop reinforcer strength by being paired with less natural reinforcers.

For example, teachers may decide that praise alone is not a sufficiently strong reinforcer to encourage adolescents to complete class work. Therefore, they may provide the youth a one-minute bonus of time during recess for each day in which homework is completed. One of the educator's goals is to develop the strength of praise and reduce the need for recess in motivating homework completion. Therefore, each time the teachers award a recess extension, they praise the students for the work done. Pairing recess time with the praise will eventually result in increasing the effectiveness of praise as a motivating event.

Scheduling

The principle of scheduling suggests that the more frequently a reinforcer is given for a specific behavior, the greater the likelihood that the behavior will occur in the future. Children and adolescents are likely to engage in behaviors expected to produce reinforcement on every occasion. Behaviors are less likely to occur that do not produce continuous reinforcement.

When teaching or developing new behaviors, reinforcement should be provided on a continuous basis. That is, reinforcement should be provided each time the behavior occurs. Continuously reinforcing the child or youth's behavior is the fastest way to increase the performance of the new skill. Unfortunately, the natural environment seldom reinforces every occurrence of a child or youth's behavior. Therefore, while continuous reinforcement is used in the initial phases of a behavior change program, once the behavior is performed fairly consistently, the rate of reinforcement should be gradually decreased.

Moving from a continuous to a partial schedule of reinforcement increases the chances that the new behavior will become a lasting part of the youth's behavior patterns. Initially the schedule may be reduced from reinforcement for each occurrence to every nine of ten occurrences. Once the child or youth adjusts to this partial schedule, reinforcement may be provided for seven of ten occurrences and so on until reinforcement occurs on a schedule that is consistent with the natural environment.

To stress the point, in the initial phase of the behavior change program, reinforcement should be provided each time the behavior occurs. This is the fastest way to develop new behavior patterns. Once the new behavior occurs consistently, the frequency with which reinforcement is provided should be gradually reduced. The ultimate goal is to limit the rate of reinforcement to the level existing in the natural environment.

CONCLUSION

This chapter has served four major objectives. First, it has highlighted the need to go beyond traditional concepts of discipline and behavior management and provide educators with techniques that have been demonstrated to be effective in producing pervasive and lasting changes in handicapped students' behavior. The second objective is to emphasize a skill training orientation in which the educator not only seeks to punish or extinguish maladaptive responses but also to develop stable and predictable positive social response patterns. Particularly important are patterns consistent with community expectations and those that allow the student to gain satisfaction and/or avoid dissatisfaction from the environment. These socially skillful responses may be expected to replace disruptive behaviors that serve the same function. The third objective is to alert the reader to the importance of these issues. Social development is not only the most emotionally provoking area of concern for educators but the most critical area of development for the handicapped.

Finally, this chapter has provided an overview of the basic principles underlying the concepts and strategies that will be detailed in subsequent chapters. These social learning principles emphasize the following: the importance of an individual's interactions with historic and contemporary environments in shaping existing behavioral repertoires; the biological and experiential uniqueness of the individual; the importance of functionally integrated academic, social, and vocational objectives; the potential impact of a handicapping condition on a child or youth's social efficacy; potential entry points for social development programs; and systematic tactics that may be used to promote social learning.

Subsequent chapters will build from these themes an integrated social learning approach for developing a range of interpersonal skills with handicapped children and youths.

Chapter 2

Behavioral Characteristics of Exceptional Children and Youth

The preceding chapter emphasized that educators must be concerned with the development of a wide range of skills beyond simple or complex academic tasks. Assertiveness skills, conversational skills, proper etiquette, and a range of other social skills are equally important to the adaptation of the handicapped youth in independent living and work environments.

Students having difficulty reading printed materials or remembering academically related concepts may also have difficulty participating in relationships with teachers, parents, siblings, peers, employers, and other significant individuals. Educational activities must prepare the youth to engage in social behavior necessary for adjustment in adult life (Bryan & Bryan, 1977; Lerner, 1971).

A review of prevalent definitions for handicapping conditions emphasizes the variety of exceptional characteristics attributed to handicapped adolescents. Each of the major handicapping conditions can be associated with social performance problems that limit the child's or adolescent's ability to succeed in independent living and vocational environments. For example, mental retardation is defined in part by the individual's ability to adjust to his or her social environment (Grossman, 1973) and behavior disorders are defined by persistent unacceptable responses to environmental demands (Kauffman, 1981). Several authors have argued that the various areas of exceptionality may place an individual at risk for the development of social adjustment difficulties (Bryan & Bryan, 1977; Menolascino, 1977; Sanders, 1980).

Research studies reported by Bryan (1976), Bryan, Wheeler, Felcan, and Hanek (1976), and Bryan and Bryan (1977) have presented data that highlight the association between learning disabilities and social-personal deficits. Similarly, numerous authors have addressed the relationship between social-personal deficits and mental retardation (Heber, 1964; Rutter, 1971; Sternlicht, 1977). Menolascino (1977) has argued that the sensory, cognitive, and environmental limitations often associated with the mentally retarded diminish their ability to develop positive social and emotional characteristics. Other authors have discussed the relationship between auditory defects (Malkin, Freeman, & Hastings, 1976; Schlesinger & Meadow, 1971), visual impairment (W.H. Miller, 1970) and physical handicaps (Lewandowski & Cruickshank, 1980; McMichael, 1971) with social-personal adjustment difficulties.

The importance of activities that promote social personal development in educational settings cannot be understated. As Lerner (1971) has emphasized ". . . a lack of sensitivity to people and poor perceptions of social situations . . . affects every area of the child's (or adolescent's) life. This is probably the most debilitating learning problem the child (or youth) can have" (p. 247). This chapter will review research that addresses the behavioral characteristics associated with each of the major handicapping conditions. The following sections present general statements regarding the ways in which handicapped students differ from the general population. It would be a gross generalization to suggest that they describe all students with the particular handicapping condition. A subsequent chapter will present an approach that goes beyond categorical labels and into the study of differences between and within individuals.

AUDITORY HANDICAPS

The major effect of an auditory handicap is that the individual has difficulty in acquiring functional communication skills. Auditory handicaps, including a range of hearing loss in one or both ears, may substantially reduce an individual's ability to benefit from typical classroom activities. Social, educational, and career development may be adversely affected by the inability to communicate efficiently with others. The extent to which an auditory handicap impairs the individual's development derives from two major variables: (1) the age at which the hearing loss occurs; and (2) the severity of the hearing loss. These variables are specified in Connor, Hoover, Horton, Sands, Sternfeld, and Wolinsky's (1975) definition of deafness and hearing impairment:

> . . . the deaf are defined as those individuals whose hearing loss is so severe at birth or during the prelingual period that it precludes the normal acquisition of language comprehension and expression. The partially hearing are persons whose hearing loss, although significant in degree, was acquired either after the critical period of language acquisition, thus enabling the individual to

develop some communicative skills, or does not totally impair oral language development. (p. 242)

The age of onset and severity dimensions are further emphasized by the classification scheme of the Committee on Nomenclature, Conference of Executives of American Schools for the Deaf (1938). Their classification includes two populations with auditory impairments:

1. The deaf: those in whom the sense of hearing is nonfunctional for the ordinary purposes of life. This general group is made up of two distinct classes based entirely on the time the loss of hearing occurred. These include:
   - the congenitally deaf—those who were born deaf.
   - the adventitiously deaf—those who were born with normal hearing, but in whom the sense of hearing becomes nonfunctional later through illness or accident.
2. The hard of hearing: those in whom the sense of hearing, although defective, is functional with or without a hearing aid. (p. 2)

Current literature emphasizes the pervasive impact that a hearing impairment may have on a child or youth's social development (Altshuler, 1974, 1976; Herder, 1948; Rainer & Kallmann, 1969; Sanders, 1980). Although it is clear that there is as wide a range of behavioral characteristics among the hearing impaired as within the general population (Reivich & Rothrock, 1972), an auditory impairment may place a child or youth "at risk" for the development of minor or major behavior disorders (Kennedy, 1973). Vernon (1969) suggests that behavior disorders are of epidemic proportions among deaf children. He reports that as many as 10 or 12 percent exhibit severe emotional or behavioral disturbances. Rodda (1974) has presented data that indicate that in a three-state area (Ohio, Indiana, and Kentucky) 1,930 of 16,000 known hearing-impaired individuals exhibit behavior disorders of sufficient severity to warrant professional attention. The author argues that over half of the population experiences mild or transient behavior problems.

Personality disorders demonstrated to be associated with hearing impairment include: psychotic reactions (Myklebust, 1960); neurotic tendencies (Springer & Roslow, 1938); immaturity (Altshuler, 1962); and withdrawal tendencies (Knapp, 1968). The most common disturbances found among the hearing impaired are behavior disorders that include hyperactivity, irritability, aggression, social isolation, sleeping, and eating disturbances (Altshuler, 1974). Although these responses are common among most children and youths, they become cause for concern when they limit the person's ability to benefit from social or educational aspects of the environment (Gardner, 1977). In addition, Altshuler (1974) has emphasized that behavior disorders not ameliorated in early years can evolve into adult neuroses.

To date, causal relationships between the handicapping aspects of a hearing impairment and specific behavior disorders have not been empirically derived, though a number of hypotheses exist. Each relates to the cumulative effect of a child's or youth's inefficiency in decoding social cues. Altshuler (1974) exemplifies these positions by stating:

> Prima facie, [hearing impairment] must influence somehow the various developmental paths. . . . Precisely how it does so, the exact pathways for mediation of its effects, the weight to be assigned to each intermediate avenue, and the absolute residual influence that the handicap must impose are simply unknown. (p. 367)

The author further argues that a hearing impairment creates an alternate frame of perceptual reference. The response patterns of hearing-impaired individuals are best understood by considering a frame of reference partially or totally void of auditory input.

Meadow (1976) has suggested that impulsivity, egocentricity, and rigidity are common characteristics of hearing-impaired children and youths. She argues that these features result from the limited development or absence of early communication. Impulsiveness, defined as the absence of careful, coherent, advanced planning prior to action, results from a demand for immediate reinforcement as opposed to delayed gratification. Language deficits restrict the hearing-impaired child's or youth's ability to consider the advantages of future possibilities in lieu of short-term gains. Parents of hearing-impaired children and youths often reinforce this characteristic by giving in to short-term demands as opposed to explaining beneficial aspects of delaying rewards. The potential for the hearing-impaired individual to become frustrated and aggressive motivates the parents to comply with the demands for impulsive, immediate delivery of rewards. The hearing-impaired child or youth can learn to delay gratification only through frequent and consistent experiences in which significant others communicate and require the child or youth to experience the advantages of long-term efforts.

Egocentricity, described by Meadow (1976) as self-centeredness or unwillingness to consider the needs, opinions, and desires of others, is another response pattern influenced by a hearing loss. Normal development involves growing from self-centeredness to sensitivity toward the wishes of others. This growth results from communication of social norms and re-inforcement of compliance with those norms. Due to the difficulty in com-munication, parents often comply with ego-centered requests rather than express disapproval. Again, the threat of frustration and aggression may motivate significant others to comply with requests rather than to explain the ramifications of self-centered behavior on others.

The third characteristic, rigidity, is the inability of an individual to alter response patterns to conform to changing events. Meadow (1976) suggests that the hearing-impaired individual's inflexibility to a variety of social cues results from a failure of significant others to communicate the reasons for specific expectations. The child or youth applies a particular rule indis-criminately because of a lack of understanding of the basis for the social rule. In effect, significant others establish a basic set of social rules, never allowing the child or youth to learn or experience variations of the rule. The individual becomes unable to discriminate between social conditions that should elicit one set of responses and those that should elicit an altered set of responses.

VISUAL HANDICAPS

A visual deficit may affect the educational, social, and vocational de-velopment of an individual in a number of ways. Traditional educational practices rely heavily on the student's ability to perceive visual images. Colors, forms, sizes, textures, and actions are frequently used in instruc-tional presentations. The interpretation of these stimuli may be impossible or highly difficult for students with impaired vision. Acceptable social behaviors are also acquired in part through the use of vision. The visually impaired individual is less able to read and interpret cues necessary for the development of socially skillful behavior. One of the greatest limitations imposed on the visually impaired is reduced mobility. The effectiveness with which the visually impaired individual can move in his or her envi-ronment has been demonstrated to be the primary determinant of inde-pendence as an adult (Knowles, 1969).

Visual impairments may be the result of reduced visual acuity, a limited field of vision, defective color vision, or an external muscle imbalance. Visual handicaps have traditionally been classified by two major categories: (1) *partially sighted* in which visual acuity is better than 20/200, but worse than 20/70 in the better eye with correction; and (2) *legally blind* in which visual acuity is 20/200 or less for distance vision in the better eye, with correction; or visual acuity of 20/200 or more if the widest diameter of field of vision subtends an angular distance less than or equal to 20 degrees (National Society for the Prevention of Blindness, 1966). However, the range of vision emphasized by this classification has little utility for educators in the public schools. Students with visual acuity in the legally blind range may be able to read print under special magnification conditions. Bateman (1967) has proposed a functional definition of blindness that has direct implications for special educational provisions. She suggests that the visually impaired, partially sighted are those who can use their vision for reading when adaptations are made in the presentation of reading materials, while the blind must rely on Braille as a primary reading medium.

A substantial body of literature has demonstrated a relationship between the attitudes of significant others and the social characteristics of the severely visually impaired. In one such study, Sommers (1944) reported that emotional and behavioral disorders are more a function of the attitudes of people in the blind individual's environment than the actual sensory handicap. Sommers identified six adjustment patterns among the severely visually handicapped adolescents studied. These included wholesome competency reactions, hypercompensatory reactions, denial reactions, defensive reactions, withdrawal reactions, and nonadjustive behavior reactions. The author argues that while many of these response patterns are not approved of socially, only the last is distinctly maladaptive. The remainder have redeeming qualities in that they reduce stress by serving as adjustment mechanisms. Buell (1950) supported these findings by demonstrating that severely visually impaired children with overprotective parents perform significantly less well on gross motor tasks (The Iowa Brace Test) than visually impaired children neglected by their parents.

Whether the behavioral characteristics of the severely visually impaired can be attributed to the attitudes of significant others, or whether they result from the different perceptual reference that results from an inability to visualize daily events, researchers continue to report psychosocial features of the severely visually impaired that set them apart from the general population. In early studies, Brown (1938, 1939) found a higher incidence of "neurotic tendencies" among the blind than found in the seeing. McAndrew (1948) reported that the visually impaired exhibit greater degrees of rigidity than found in the general population. She also presented data indicating that the deaf are more rigid than the blind. She attributed these findings to the limited "life spaces" of the sensory impaired, suggesting that limitations in sensory input restrict differentiation in their personalities.

Land and Vineberg (1965) studied the locus of control of visually impaired and normal students using the Bialer-Cromwell Children's Locus of Control Scale. The scale measures the extent to which a child may be described as exhibiting an internal or external locus of control. Children with an internal locus of control are described as believing that they are instrumental in dictating outcomes of situations. Children with an external locus of control believe that some other agent is responsible for their success or failure. The author reported statistically significant differences between the severely impaired and sighted group, with the visually impaired falling on the external and the sighted group falling on the internal ends of the continuum.

Several studies reported relationships between anxiety and demographic variables of visually impaired children and adolescents. Hardy (1968a) administered the Anxiety Scale for the Blind that he developed (1968b) to 122 blind adolescents in two residential schools. He discovered that students with light perception and projection obtained significantly positive relationships between age and anxiety level. He also reported that more intelligent students were less anxious than less intelligent students. Miller (1970) supported these findings by demonstrating a higher anxiety level among eleventh- and twelfth-grade visually impaired students when compared to ninth- and tenth-grade visually impaired students. Bauman (1964) also concurred with Hardy's findings reporting significantly higher levels of anxiety and insecurity among the blind when contrasted with partially seeing students. Bauman's research further indicated that residential placement may be a factor in producing heightened states of anxiety and difficulty in emotional and social adjustment.

Cholden (1958) discussed ideologies that may heighten severely visually impaired students' anxiety and limit their acceptance of the handicapping condition. The author emphasizes that severely visually impaired children and youth are often preoccupied with: (1) their physical image, masculine strength in males and attractiveness in females; (2) the issue of developing independence as the youth grows into adulthood; (3) the exhibitionism often accompanied by the adolescent's desire for anonymity. Abel (1961) emphasized the special emotional needs of the severely visually impaired, including the need to be understood, to have questions answered, to participate in family and peer social interactions, to be optimistic toward the future, to gain mobility skills, and to obtain the best materials, equipment, and programs that education has to offer.

A considerable amount of research has focused on the self-concept of severely visually impaired children and youth. Davis (1964) and Jervis (1964) have argued that the development of a positive self-concept is central to the mental health of blind individuals. In a study of self-concept, Meighan (1971) administered the Tennessee Self-Concept Scale to 203 severely visually impaired adolescents. He concluded that the scores of the target group when compared to the norms were significantly different in a negative direction. Physical self, moral-ethical self-behavior scores, and identity were determined to be the basic dimensions of self-concept that were most deviant.

Scott (1969) has argued that the blind child learns a social role that is consistent with the expectations of society. Attitudes learned at childhood about stigmatizing aspects of a visual handicap and confirmed as the youth progresses into adulthood produce limited personal expectations and a general negative self-image. The research done by Mayadas (1972) and Mayadas and Duehn (1976) concurs with this view, revealing a strong positive relationship between the expectations of significant others, the subject's perception of those expectations, and the subject's self-expectations. No relationship was identified between the subject's role expectations and the expectations of strangers. The researchers interpret these findings as supporting the view that blind individuals are subject to sociocultural variables that have a dramatic effect on their self-concept and subsequent behavior.

PHYSICAL AND HEALTH DISORDERS

Children and adolescents with physical and health disorders represent a broad and diverse population. Specific handicapping conditions range from cerebral palsy to asthma. Because of the heterogeneity of this group, general statements regarding the cognitive, psychological, or affective characteristics of this population cannot be made. The severity of the handicapping condition, the age at which it was incurred, the nature of the condition, the visibility of the condition, and the support systems available may all contribute to the influence of the disability on the student's social development. As with other categories of exceptional children and adolescents, specific physical and health disorders do not exert a simple or predictable effect on the development of the student. Rather, the impact of a disability on the characteristics of the individual can only be understood through studying the complex interaction of physical, cognitive, and environmental variables.

The diverse nature of physical and health disorders and the resulting variability in associated behavioral features have led to broad descriptive definitions. Current definitions make few assumptions of common academic, social, or personal characteristics. Kirk (1972), for example, defines these students as:

> . . . those who are crippled, deformed, or otherwise physically handicapped (exclusive of the visually and auditory handicapped) and those who have health problems which interfere with func-

tioning in a regular classroom . . . comprise heterogeneous groups with varying disabilities, each a unique problem which limits the effectiveness with which a child can cope with the academic, social, and emotional expectations of the school and community. (p. 349)

Similarly, Sirvis (1978) has suggested that the physically handicapped are "individuals with functional limitations related to physical ability and medical conditions, such as strength and stamina" (p. 361).

In addition to educationally relevant definitions, physicians working through the American Medical Association have devised and refined an extensive system for classifying permanent physical impairments. Individual guidelines target anatomical features that may be affected by physical or health disorders. These include: extremities and back (1958); visual system (1958); cardiovascular system (1960); ear, nose, and throat (1961); central nervous system (1964); respiratory system (1965); the endocrine system (1966); and mental illness (1966). While these publications focus on the extent and nature of a disability or illness and facilitate medical interventions, they also provide a common conceptual foundation through which educators may understand physical or health disorders.

As with the visually impaired, there appears to be strong empirical support for the influence that significant others' reactions to the disability may have on the personality characteristics of the child or youth. There is considerable agreement that environments that do not meet the needs of the physically handicapped child or youth may be detrimental to later psychosocial adjustment. On the basis of a thorough review of available literature, Freedman (1967) concluded that environmental factors are as important, if not more important, than the handicapping condition itself in generating emotional disturbances. Fitzgerald (1951) and Allen and Pearson (1938) in separate investigations agreed that behavior disorders among the physically handicapped are closely related to parental attitudes. These findings are in variance with the position that behavior disorders result from the individual's inability to accept his or her physical limitations.

In studies involving cerebral-palsied children, Nussbaum (1962) and E.A. Miller (1958) demonstrate the impact that the parent-child relationship has on the youth's emotional adjustment. The latter report demonstrates a stronger relationship between the adjustment of the child and his or her parent's attitudes than the severity of the handicapping condition. The ability of parents to maintain a healthy attitude was brought into question by McMichael's work (1971). Her study suggests that parents and siblings of physically handicapped children face high levels of stress and emotional conflict that are coincidental to the presence of the handicapped child.

Studies that have sought to demonstrate a relationship between demographic variables, such as age of onset (Lange, 1959) and degree of disability (Dreikurs, 1948), and emotional disturbance have been inconclusive though there is a general consensus in the literature that these factors have a discernible impact on the mental health of physically handicapped individuals. The visibility of a disability does, however, influence the emotional adjustment of the individual (as well as the attitudes of others). Cruickshank (1952) compared cardiac children and other physically handicapped children with nonhandicapped children. On the basis of a sentence completion task, it was reported that the cardiac children were better adjusted to societal expectations than the other physically handicapped students. The researchers speculated that the cardiac condition was not apparent to society and therefore did not produce detrimental attitudes in others.

Harway (1952) demonstrated that physically handicapped students overestimate and are inconsistent in evaluating their personal attributes. Wysocki (1965), using Machover's Draw-A-Person Test, reported differences between physically handicapped and nonhandicapped children on the basis of expressions of inferiority, anxiety, and aggression. As with other studies, these findings are interpreted from within the context of the social system in which the child develops. Self-concept and emotional expression are viewed as learned responses that are influenced by the attitudes of significant others.

SPEECH AND LANGUAGE IMPAIRMENTS

Speech is defined as the ability to use oral symbols in a manner that conveys meaningful utterances to others. Speech requires the individual to develop sounds into words and words into sentences. Speech disorders result from deficiencies in oral production regardless of whether the individual is able to encode or formulate verbal messages. Language refers to the ability to express verbal messages (formulation or encoding). Speech is the production of the "sound" that the listener hears while language involves the convention or code by which oral symbols are organized. Language deficits are included within speech deficits since speech is comprised of both the organization of sounds and the production of the sounds.

Bankson (1978) emphasizes the differentiation between speech and language disorders in the following definition:

> The term speech impairment is used in a generic sense to refer
> to disorders of articulation (speech sound production) and fluency

(rhythm). Each of these parameters relates to the mechanics of producing speech. Language impairments, as defined by speech pathologists, usually refer to disorders in comprehending or verbally expressing the symbols and grammatical rules of language. (p. 389)

In one of the earliest studies of the relationship between speech defects and personality disorders, Wood (1946) administered a battery of psychological inventories to the parents of 50 children with articulation disorders. Based on the resulting data, the author concluded that a positive relationship exists between the emotional adjustment of a child's parents and the quality of the child's speech. Additional findings suggested that parental counseling is an adjunct to speech training alone in correcting articulation defects. Using parental attitude scales to compare parents of speech-impaired children with normal-speaking children Berlin (1958) and Darley (1955) provided further support for Wood's findings. Andersland (1961) in a similar investigation demonstrated that the parents of kindergarten-aged children with articulation problems resistant to change performed poorest on a measure of personality adjustment.

Though wrought with design flaws and limited by sample size, a number of studies have demonstrated an association between children's articulation deficits and personality maladjustment. Trapp and Evans (1960) reported significantly higher anxiety levels, using the Wechsler Digit Symbol Test, among children with severe articulation defects when contrasted with children with mild defects and normal-speaking children. Butler (1965) administered the Bender-Gestalt Visual Motor Test to 15 children with articulation defects and reported that over half exhibited a high degree of emotional disturbance. Based on parental interview data from 49 articulation-defective children and a matched control group of normal-speaking children, Solomon (1961) reported higher levels of tension and anxiety and poorer overall adjustment among the speech-defective children.

A number of studies have examined the relationship between self-perceptions and social acceptance of speech-handicapped students. Perrin (1954), using a sociometric technique, found that speech-defective students are more likely to be socially isolated. Lerea and Ward (1966) demonstrated a greater reluctance on the part of speech-defective children to interact with others. Sergeant (1962) reported that adults with articulation disorders are less self-confident and adjust socially less adequately than normal-speaking adults.

Of all the pathologies of speech, stuttering has received the greatest attention of personality researchers. Moncur's (1955) previous work identified nervousness and maladjustment to occur with greater frequency among stutterers than nonstutterers. Goodstein (1958) reported that stutterers exhibit a depressed level of aspiration and are more perseverative when compared to nonstutterers. Contradictory findings were reported in Emerick's (1966) study of goal-setting behavior and Wingate's (1966) study of general perseverative factors among stutterers. With regard to social role perception, Buscaglia (1962) has demonstrated that stutterers are less able to evaluate the roles of others than nonstutterers and Sheehan, Hadley, and Gould (1967) report a positive relationship between the frequency of stuttering episodes and the discrepancy between the perceived status of self and that of the listener.

SPECIFIC LEARNING DISABILITIES

Of all the handicapping conditions identified in this chapter, specific learning disabilities stand out as the most recent category of exceptional children and youths. Prior to the early 1960s, programs for learning-disabled students were virtually nonexistent. Even as late as the early or middle 1970s many educational systems in the nation did not recognize learning disabilities as a category of exceptionality. At the present time there is still considerable debate and confusion associated with the field. A review of the literature conducted by Clements (1966) revealed 38 labels that have been used to describe children and adolescents with characteristics subsumed by the label learning disabilities. Frequently cited labels have included minimal brain damage, cerebral dysfunction, specific reading disorder, perceptually handicapped, attention disorder, minimal brain injury, and dyslexia in hyperactive children.

In spite of the controversy surrounding terminology used in the field, there is little question that a group of children and adolescents exists who exhibit marked disabilities in one or more areas of academic achievement while performing within the normal range in others. With regard to the variability of performance, this represents the most heterogeneous group of exceptional children and adolescents addressed in this chapter. This fact may account for the diversity of professional views in the field. Cruickshank and Paul (1980) report literature that highlights deficits in discrimination, memory, sequencing, affect, motor inhibition, impulse control, gross motor functioning, figure-ground discrimination, visual motor functioning, visual perceptual functioning, auditory acuity, sensory integration, conceptual and abstract thinking, language usage, socioemotional functioning, self-concept, and body image.

Kirk's (1968) definition of learning disabilities emphasizes the broad range of characteristics associated with this group of exceptional individuals. Kirk defines learning disabilities as referring "to a specific retardation or disorder in one or more of the processes of speech, language, perception, behavior, reading, spelling, writing, or arithmetic" (p. 398).

Kirk's definition characterizes learning disabilities as deficiencies in a specific academic skill or ability in relation to general academic functioning. Kirk also distinguishes learning disabilities from mental retardation in that mental retardation implies a general deficit in all areas of academic functioning while learning disabilities are denoted by deficits in specific areas. For example, the mentally retarded adolescent is generally several years below grade level in all or most academic areas including reading, math, spelling, language, etc. The learning-disabled individual may be below grade level in but a few of the areas while the remainder are within the normal range. Thus, the mentally retarded individual exhibits a general deficit in academic performance while the learning-disabled person is deficient in a restricted range of academic skills.

Wepman, Cruickshank, Deutsch, Morency, and Strother (1975) have proposed an alternate approach to the definition of learning disabilities. Their definition proceeds from a psychoeducational orientation that emphasizes the underlying pathology presumed to result in a learning disability. In an expanded version of the Wepman Committee's definition, Cruickshank and Paul (1980) define learning disabilities as follows:

> Learning disabilities can be defined as resulting from perceptual processing deficits which are, in turn, the result of a malfunction in some aspect of the central nervous system. Learning disabilities may occur in a child or youth of any age, of any intellectual level, and be of widely diversified etiologies. (p. 503)

Cruickshank and Paul's definition is in sharp contrast to Kirk's in that an emphasis is placed on underlying neurological conditions. According to this position, learning disabilities may co-exist with other conditions, including mental retardation. The authors contend that perceptual processing deficits may occur in the mentally retarded, physically handicapped, behaviorally disordered, etc. From this frame of reference, learning disabilities are not restricted to individuals within the normal range of intelligence. Rather, learning disabilities are defined by the presence of a neurological disorder regardless of general cognitive functioning.

Hallahan and Kauffman (1976) have identified five common themes contained within most of the prevalent definitions of learning disabilities. While subtle deviations may be present in many of the current definitions, these points bring a degree of order to the search for a unified definition. The five major points are:

1. The learning disabled student is academically retarded.
2. The learning disabled student has an uneven pattern of development.
3. The learning disabled student may or may not have central nervous system dysfunctioning.
4. The learning disabled student does not owe his learning problems to environmental disadvantage.
5. The learning disabled student does not owe his learning problems to mental retardation or emotional disturbance. (Hallahan & Kauffman, 1976, p. 20)

A number of excessive and deficit social and emotional behaviors have been associated with the presence of learning disabilities. Anxiety, hyperactivity, emotional lability, rigidity, and distractibility have been used to describe learning-disabled populations by a number of writers (Auerbach, 1971; Berman & Siegal, 1976). Poremba (1974) has argued that the majority of delinquents in the United States were previously unserved learning-disabled youths. His view is supported by the research of Jacobson (1974) reporting 50 to 80 percent of delinquents to be learning disabled. Compton (1974), in assessing the incidence and types of learning disabilities, reported a pattern of 75 percent exhibiting sudden drops in achievement coupled with a high rate of truancy.

From one theoretical orientation, Johnson and Myklebust (1967) argue that a neurological dysfunction may result in deficits in social perception. The authors suggest that social perception deficits may impede a student's ability to adjust to common social demands of the environment. The four characteristics of a social perception deficit as enumerated by Lerner (1971) are: (1) poor performance in independent activities; (2) poor judgment of moods and attitudes of others; (3) insensitivity to the behavioral expectations of a given social setting; and (4) repeated inappropriate overt motor and verbal behavior.

Tannis Bryan and her colleagues have highlighted the impact of social and emotional deficits on peer relations of learning-disabled youths. Bryan (1974a) utilized a sociometric technique to measure social attraction and rejection of learning-disabled students and matched comparison children. Her results indicated that learning-disabled students are more likely to be accepted by peers. A one-year follow-up replicated these findings indicating that peer relations were stable over time (Bryan, 1976). In similar investigations, Bryan (1974b) demonstrated that learning-disabled children are more likely to be rejected by their teachers and that individuals who meet learning disabled students for only a short period of time judge them less favorably than nondisabled children.

Bryan and Bryan (1977) offer two explanations for the coexistence of learning disabilities and behavior disorders. First, either disorder can produce the other. Second, children who have difficulty understanding printed material may also have difficulty in understanding people. Bryan, Wheeler, Felcan, and Henek (1976) and Bryan and Bryan (1977) have presented data that support these contentions. Their research has demonstrated: (1) that learning-disabled children are not good people readers; (2) that their responses in social interactions reflect an insensitivity to the feelings of others; and (3) that learning-disabled children are often disliked by their peers.

Auerbach (1971) has described an approach to learning disabilities that emphasizes the social context in which the child develops. He argues that effective intervention with the learning-disabled student must concentrate on the ecosystem in which the child or youth functions. This approach is expected to increase the child's, parent's, teacher's, and professional's frustration tolerance and ability to manage stress. Attention to task, flexibility in social endeavors, and emotional stability are seen by Auerbach as being essential components of any successful treatment plan for the learning-disabled child.

Sabatino and Schloss (1981) in reviewing literature pertaining to the self-concept of learning-disabled children and youths produced the following generalizations:

1. Lowered self-esteem or a more negative self-concept does appear to characterize learning disabled children in contrast to those not so disabled. Self-concept does seem to be a highly unstable measure, especially for first and second graders.
2. Self-concept seems to be fixed toward school tasks by third grade and remains fairly stable after that.
3. Information on one's condition seems to raise self-concept.
4. There seems to be little relationship between specific academic underachievement factors and specific views of self.
5. In sum, self-concept and academic achievement share a modest relationship with identifiable learning disabled populations. The meaning of that relationship is only speculative at present. However, initial research would indicate that the variables that have an impact on self-concept also may affect several other critical factors such as age of recognition of the problem, information on the problem, and the amount of control children feel they have in given situations. In short,

self-concept may reflect social learning for a task with regard for the people involved. (p. 466)

MENTAL RETARDATION

Mental retardation refers to a developmental delay associated with intellectual and adaptive functioning that is substantially deviant from the general population. Because of the varying degrees by which functioning can be impaired across academic, social, personal, and career vocational skills, mental retardation designates a highly heterogeneous group of individuals. Numerous classification systems have been proposed to establish homogeneous subgroups. The public schools categorize retarded students as mildly or educably mentally retarded, moderately or trainably mentally retarded, and severely or custodially mentally retarded.

Telford and Sawrey (1972) have identified five common characteristics that warrant the use of mild mental retardation as a functional label. First, the subgroups in the mild range are virtually indistinguishable based on socially and educationally relevant variables. Second, they represent an arbitrarily established low end of the normal distribution curve of intelligence. Third, subnormal intellectual functioning is typically the result of an interaction between constitutional and environmental factors. Fourth, while research data indicate that this group is statistically below average in physique and general health, individual members within this group are not perceptibly different from the general population. The majority of individuals within this population can compete successfully in physical endeavors with individuals of normal and above normal levels of intelligence. Fifth, most mildly mentally retarded individuals are identified only after a thorough and intensive assessment of intellectual and adaptive functioning. Additionally, research has indicated that once the mildly retarded leave school and enter careers, their adjustment to the demands of society is only slightly less adequate than that of peers of the same age and socioeconomic status.

In general, the mildly mentally retarded represent a group of children and adolescents whose general intellectual capabilities limit their ability to benefit from the typical classroom structure. This group frequently includes students who are considered culturally disadvantaged or educationally handicapped.

Unlike the mildly mentally retarded, the severely retarded can often be distinguished from the general population by their physical characteristics. Severe mental retardation is often attributed to: (1) chromosomal aberrations such as Down's Syndrome, Klinefelter's Syndrome, and Turner's

Syndrome; (2) biochemical anomalies such as phenylketonuria (PKU) and Tay-Sach's disease; (3) endocrine disturbances, the most prevalent of which is cretinism; (4) cranial anomalies of genetic origin such as microcephaly; (5) syndromes resulting from environmental insult, including hydrocephaly, epilepsy, infection of the brain, and cerebral palsy. It is important to note that the preceding conditions do not presuppose the coexistence of mental retardation.

Mental retardation has been classified and defined from a psychological and educational frame of reference. The American Association on Mental Deficiency (AAMD) sixth revision of the *Manual on Terminology and Classification in Mental Retardation* (Grossman, 1973) defines mental retardation as follows: "Mental retardation refers to significantly subaverage general intellectual functioning existing concurrently with deficits in adaptive behavior, and manifested during the developmental period" (p. 5).

Kirk (1972) has proposed an educationally sensitive definition for educable and trainable mentally retarded students. He suggests that the educable mentally retarded individual is one who may achieve:

(1) minimum educability in the academic subjects of the school, (2) social adjustment to such a point that he can get along independently in the community, and (3) minimum occupational adequacy to such a degree that he can later support himself partially or totally at the adult level. (p. 191)

According to Kirk, the trainable mentally retarded child is one who, because of subnormal intelligence, is not capable of learning in classes for the educable mentally retarded but who does have potentialities for learning "(1) self-care, (2) adjustment to the home or neighborhood, and (3) economic usefulness in the home, a sheltered workshop, or an institution " (p. 221).

The literature regarding the association of mental retardation with emotional disturbance seems to cluster around several major topics, including incidence, range of disturbance, etiological connections such as differential diagnosis and pseudoretardation, and treatment. The present discussion will focus on the first five areas, and a discussion of treatment will be presented in a later section.

Beier's (1964) review of behavioral disturbances in the mentally retarded concluded that there is a higher incidence of emotional disturbances among the mentally retarded than would be found in the general population. Numerous other authors have supported this claim (Blatt, 1958; Heber, 1964; Robinson & Robinson, 1976), although methodologically sound research evidence is severely lacking (Gardner, 1966; Menolascino, 1977;

Rutter, 1971). The major problem with studies that have sought to quantify the incidence of emotional disturbance among the mentally retarded has been the inappropriate generalization of data drawn from institutional samples to the general population. It is likely that a high rate of emotionally disturbed individuals are found in institutions because of the inability of community programs to work with the severely disturbed (Menolascino, 1977).

Menolascino (1965) investigated 600 potentially mentally retarded children who were referred to the Nebraska Psychiatric Unit for clinical suspicion of mental retardation. Assessment based on individual psychiatric examination and standardized playroom interviews revealed an incidence of emotional disturbance of 31 percent. Menolascino also found that the frequency of emotional disturbance tended to increase sharply in children over four years of age and that boys displayed almost a twofold increase in the number of psychiatric problems as compared to girls. These findings must be considered cautiously in light of a number of limitations in research design that resulted in a sampling bias.

Rutter (1971), in a comprehensive study of behavioral disturbances among the retarded, accounted for many of the limitations of Menolascino's study. Rutter reported that 42 percent of the mentally retarded school-aged children living on the Isle of Wight were emotionally disturbed as compared to 10 percent of the educationally normal children. He also showed that maladjustment in the retarded sample was associated with low socioeconomic status.

With regard to range of disturbance, Sternlicht and Deutch (1972) state that all of the major and minor behavioral disorders can and do occur in combination with mental retardation. This position is emphasized by the most recent revision of the terminology and classification manual of the American Association on Mental Deficiency (Grossman, 1973). Categories of the medical classification system referring to psychiatric disorders require the diagnostician to use the current classification scheme of the American Psychiatric Association (1980). Thus, no special psychiatric disorders are recognized as uniquely associated with mental retardation.

It is important to note that the incidence of severe psychotic reactions in the mentally retarded is probably extremely low. Wolfensburger (1960) has suggested that the mentally retarded are incapable of creating a fantasy world. Their delusional systems are actually attempts to make sense of their world.

As defined by Grossman (1973), mental retardation refers to significantly subaverage intellectual functioning existing concurrently with deficits in adaptive behavior. Adaptive behavior is the degree to which the individual exhibits behaviors that contribute toward social adaptation and personal independence. These behaviors may be identified as being motivational, affective, intellectual, social, motor, and so on.

A more detailed explanation of the function of adaptive behavior is advanced by Leland, Nihira, Foster, Shellhaas, and Kagin (1968). They suggest that adaptive behavior is an indication of an individual's ability to cope with the immediate environment. Three abilities are considered to be subsumed by adaptive behavior. The recognition of strengths and weaknesses in any of these facets is an important starting point for teachers wishing to devise successful programs for retarded adolescents. These three abilities are independent functioning, personal responsibility, and social responsibility.

Independent Functioning

In general, independent functioning refers to the individual's ability to successfully reach closure on age-appropriate tasks that are expected by community members. Deficits in independent functioning lead to a dependence on more socially competent people in the environment. While a reliance on others may be functional in some instances, a pervasive dependence on others may limit the extent to which all adolescents can benefit from and contribute to educational and vocational experiences.

Personal Responsibility

Personal responsibility may be viewed as the person's ability to control his or her personal behavior and assume the responsibility for its outcome. In addition, personal responsibility refers to the person's willingness to engage in behaviors that he or she is capable of performing. This area underlies the person's decision-making process.

Social Responsibility

Social responsibility involves the ability of the individual to conform to standards inferred from his or her peer group. It also includes social adjustment, emotional maturity, and the acceptance of civic responsibility that ultimately leads to a degree of economic independence.

Educators cannot assume that independent functioning, personal responsibility, and social responsibility will develop adequately in mentally retarded individuals independent of special environmental influences. Numerous studies have demonstrated that the retarded do not develop these attributes commensurate with their age group (Leland, Shellhaas, Nihira, & Foster, 1967). This is explained in part by the retarded individual's relative inability to interpret and respond to environmental influences in a way that will promote new learning. Limited learning diminishes the number of positive social responses acquired by the individual that may be exhibited when faced with demanding situations. The result may be that the individual behaves inappropriately as the result of an inability to identify and/or use adaptive behaviors that others acquire without special learning experiences.

People become socially competent as the result of numerous interactions with their environment. These interactions begin at birth and become more complex through adulthood. People become more competent in interacting with and benefiting from the environment as they become older. This process of refining individual abilities allows the person to control the environment as he or she reaches social or intellectual maturity (White, 1960).

The motive underlying this process has been termed *effectance*, which can be described as satisfaction gained from the successful completion of a challenging task. Effectance encourages attention to and experimentation in subsequent tasks that require greater skill. The result of this hierarchical process is a continual growth in competence. Effectance motivation is facilitated by the satisfaction gained from a history of successes and failures across many areas. A review of the literature pertaining to effectance motivation by Harter and Zigler (1974) clearly demonstrated that pleasure is derived from mastery of difficult tasks. Also, the more challenging the task, the greater the sense of personal reward gained from its completion. Other reviewers have presented similar findings (Hunt, 1965; Piaget, 1952).

The concept of effectance motivation has strong implications for the mentally retarded. Fundamental to the paradigm is the idea that success in increasingly more challenging tasks motivates future performance. Tasks that are excessively difficult result in feelings of laboriousness, frustration, and ultimate failure. It has been shown that individuals who are required to engage in excessively difficult and frustrating tasks exhibit reduced levels of effectance motivation (Zigler, 1973).

The retarded are generally expected to perform at a level commensurate with their chronological age peers. The tasks that are deemed challenging for others are often overwhelming for the retarded. Because retarded persons find little enjoyment in accomplishing these tasks, future endeavors of a similar nature are not intrinsically motivating.

The mentally retarded are also characterized by a limitation in events that are reinforcing (Gardner, 1977). In effect, there are fewer functional incentives that a teacher may offer to promote achievement. Natural reinforcers that elicit the efforts of normal children are typically not effective with the mentally retarded (Levy, 1974). The limited range of reinforcement is influenced by several factors. The major detriment can be viewed in terms of the social learning theory advanced by Rotter (1954). Rotter's formulation follows from the premise that people approach objects or events in which they have a high expectancy for success and reinforcement. Social behavior may then be predicted by examining the individual's learning history in relation to goal or threat objects.

Because the retarded are subjected to an increased frequency of failure experiences, their expectancy for failure in future endeavors is increased (Cromwell, 1963). The generalized expectancy for failure and nonreinforcement reduces the likelihood that the individual will approach the event in the future (Chandler & Boroskin, 1971; Keogh, Cahill & MacMillan, 1972). The reinforcement properties of the event are, as a result, reduced. Thus, events typically viewed as being reinforcing for the average student may not be reinforcing for the retarded because of the generalized expectancy of an aversive or neutral outcome.

Further complicating this effect is the fact that the mentally retarded individual generally is not exposed to the variety of pleasant activities and events encountered by the average student. The lack of exposure to diverse reinforcing conditions inhibits the individual from forming positive associations with those activities or events. The retarded person does not anticipate the reinforcing qualities of an event because of the lack of experiences that would lead to an expectancy of reinforcement.

Activities and events typically applied in educational settings as incentives and goals may not be effective with the mentally retarded. Further, a disproportionate number of events in the educational environment may have acquired aversive properties through the person's learning history. The final result is that the mentally retarded person may actively avoid events that other children consider to be intrinsically reinforcing. Another hypothesized effect of frequent failure experience is the development of a negative self-concept. Unfortunately, research to date has failed to produce clear findings with regard to the self-concept of the mentally retarded (Lawrence & Winschel, 1973).

Locus of control is a construct that has been derived from the social learning theory literature and applied to the mentally retarded (Rotter, 1954). As discussed previously, reinforcement may be viewed as being a consequence of the person's own actions (internal) or as a result of an outside influence (external) such as the influence of others. It is important to recognize that locus of control is considered to fall on a continuum with external at one extreme and internal at the other.

Lawrence (1975) has proposed that the external-internal continuum may be described by a five-stage process. In the first stage, children attribute events that affect them to forces beyond their control. This is particularly

true of failure experiences. In the second stage, the child begins to inter-
nalize success. Failure remains externalized, though it begins to fade. The
maturing child becomes essentially internal in the third stage. Self-responsibility for success is the principal focus of this stage. In the fourth stage,
self-responsibility for success becomes tempered by a sense of modesty.
Also, internality for failure becomes strongly established. Finally, the individual becomes genuinely self-reliant and accepts the responsibility for
successes and failures equally.

Lawrence suggests that mentally retarded adolescents frequently do not
progress beyond the first two stages. This is attributed to numerous frustration and failure experiences resulting from subnormal intellectual ability.
Fox (1972) has demonstrated that the mentally retarded cluster at the
second and third stages, and relatively few obtain the fourth and fifth stages.
These findings indicate that the mentally retarded have a limited capacity
for self-reliance and independence. Therefore, they may not be effective
agents in promoting their own development. If educational programming
is to have a durable and generalized effect, the students must assume
control of the contingencies that shape their behavior. Unfortunately, externally directed individuals perceive reinforcement as being under the
control of others.

The mentally retarded often have difficulty in making fine distinctions
based on relevant social cues (Gardner, 1977). This is evidenced by the
fact that individuals frequently have adaptive behaviors in their repertoire
but are unable to use them at appropriate times. For example, the mentally
retarded student may know how to shake hands but not know the conditions
under which it is appropriate to greet a person in this manner. In effect,
environmental cues that assist individuals in identifying appropriate behaviors may not have a strong and reliable influence for mentally retarded
persons.

Discrimination deficits have a major influence on the atypical behavior
of the retarded. Not only is it important that an appropriate behavior be
matched with a given social setting, the intensity, duration, and magnitude
of the chosen behavior must be discriminatively selected based on the
relevant social cues. For example, moving quickly from one class to the
next between periods is generally rewarded, but running to class is punished. Playing hard at recess is rewarded while being aggressive is punished.

Another major discrimination problem is the imitation of inappropriate
behavior exhibited by poor models. The functional person is able to discriminate between good models and poor models in a number of settings.
The retarded individual may not have this ability. For example, a behavior
displayed out of the view of teachers by the "class clown" may be imitated
by the retarded adolescent in view of the teacher.

This problem is further complicated in that some individuals may be excellent models of some behaviors but be poor models of others. The adolescent may observe a professional football player making numerous touchdowns and thus choose to emulate his play. The player may also have a reputation for fighting. The student must learn to discriminate between good play and fighting behavior, modeling only the good play.

BEHAVIORAL DISORDERS

The behaviorally disordered may well be the most difficult group of adolescents to work with in general educational settings. Without question, they represent the group of students for whom social development interventions are most critical. Frequent verbally and physically aggressive outbursts, self-abusive behavior, withdrawn behavior and/or irrational verbalizations are not only a problem for the behaviorally disordered individual, but also other students in the classroom. A behavior disorder differs from a specific or general learning disability in that a learning disability, in and of itself, does not interfere with the learning of others. An aggressive adolescent's disruptive behaviors may limit the ability of all students to benefit from the learning environment. Further, disruptive responses may be emotionally provoking for both the teacher and other students. Thus, the behaviorally disordered adolescent becomes a catalyst for disruptive behavior on the part of other students.

Characteristics associated with behavior disorders range from frequent excessive disruptive behavior, including physical aggression, verbal aggression, self-abusive behavior, and noncompliance, as well as withdrawn or depressive-like behavior. Excessive or inappropriate emotional reactions such as anxiety, fear, and hostility are also characteristic of the severely behaviorally disordered adolescent. Current literature emphasizes that behaviorally disordered adolescents do not vary from the general population on the basis of the specific types of behaviors that they exhibit. Rather, differences exist in the strength of specific responses.

The fact that behaviorally disordered adolescents exhibit aggressive behaviors does not, in and of itself, distinguish them from their peers. It is the frequency, magnitude, or duration of the aggressive behaviors that sets the adolescent apart from other students. For example, an adolescent that cries in class may not be considered to have an affect disorder unless crying occurs substantially more frequently than would be expected with the average student. Prevalence studies provide highly variable estimates of the number of students exhibiting behavior disorders. Froomkin (1972) has reported 2 percent; Bower (1960) 10.5 percent; Kelley, Bullock, and Dykes

(1977) and Salvia, Schultz, and Chapin (1974) 20 to 24 percent. Variability in prevalence estimates results from differences in definition and measurement.

As with the other areas of exceptionality, there is little agreement in the professional literature on precisely how behavior disorders should be defined. Hewett and Forness (1974) have identified nine definitions that have appeared over the past 20 years. The authors emphasize the association of specific definitions with the theoretical orientation of the writer.

Kauffman (1977) has proposed an educational definition with four important features: (1) it recognizes the social context in which behavior occurs; (2) it recognizes the student's perceptions of his or her own behavior; (3) it emphasizes the role of education in altering deviant behavior; and (4) it emphasizes the use of educationally relevant criteria in identifying severity levels of behavior disorders. Kauffman's definition is as follows:

> Children with behavior disorders are those who chronically and markedly respond to their environment in socially unacceptable and/or personally unsatisfying ways, but who can be taught more socially acceptable and personally gratifying behavior. Children with mild and moderate behavior disorders can be taught effectively with their normal peers (if their teachers receive appropriate consultative help) or in special resource or self-contained classes with reasonable hope of quick reintegration with their normal peers. Children (and adolescents) with severe and profound behavior disorders require intensive and prolonged intervention and must be taught at home or in special classes, special schools, or residential institutions. (p. 23)

Current classification schemes in the field of behavior disorders follow two major orientations. The first is an internal deviance or mental illness position; the second is an environmental adaptation or social competence approach. The internal deviance orientation views behavior disorders as being symptoms of a presumed underlying pathology. This position suggests that aberrant behaviors are the visible signs of hypothesized mental illness. In order to understand the overt behaviors, the therapist or educator must study and diagnose the underlying mental illness. Treatment then focuses on remediating the pathological condition that produces the aberrant behavior. From this point of reference, the overt behaviors are useful only in that they may facilitate the diagnosis of the illness.

Classification schemes that have evolved from this orientation, the most notable of which are the *Diagnostic and Statistical Manual* of the American Psychiatric Association (1952, 1968, 1979) and the Group for Advancement of Psychiatry Categories (1966), have been criticized in recent literature. Quay (1972) and Werry (1972) have argued that the classification of an adolescent's behavior may vary over time as a function of environmental conditions, the evaluator and/or the evaluation procedure. Phillips, Draguns, and Bartlett (1975) have reviewed literature, which suggests that specific categories tell very little about the treatment or prognosis for an individual. Phillips et al. (1975) summarize current misgivings of medically oriented classification schemes as follows:

> Some of these categories are based on a presumed psychodynamic etiology for a disorder; others reflect disapproval of a given behavior; others are listed in simple descriptive terms. Other problems with the present scheme concern the inadequate fit between an individual's behavior and the category to which he is assigned. (p. 30)

Empirical classification schemes, typified by the work of Quay (1972, 1975), have used complex statistics to identify problem behaviors that cluster together. Based on Quay and his colleagues' work, four stable behavior classes have been identified:

1. Conduct disorders are characterized by behaviors including defiance, disobedience, irritability, attention seeking, negativism, bullying, uncooperativeness, etc. These response patterns have been labeled by others as socialized aggressive and psychopathic.
2. Personality problems, or anxiety withdrawal behaviors, are described as hypersensitivity, shyness, feelings of inferiority, lack of self-confidence, self-consciousness, tendency to be easily upset, fearfulness, anxiety, and so on. These response patterns have also been labeled neurotic, overinhibited, and overdependent.
3. Inadequacy or immaturity refers to children and youths who are inattentive, sluggish, disinterested, preoccupied, reticent, drowsy, and so on.
4. Socialized aggressive behaviors include gang activities, cooperative theft, and other acts that reflect participation in a delinquent group.

Research over the past two decades has supported the validity of this view of children and adolescents' behavior disorders (McCarthy & Paraskevopoulos, 1969; Quay, 1975; Quay, 1979; Quay, Morse, & Cutler, 1966; Von Isser, Quay, & Love, 1980).

SUMMARY AND CONCLUSIONS

The handicapped represent a highly diverse population. Variability between groups of different handicapping conditions and within groups of the same handicapping conditions preclude general statements of the relationship between handicaps and social and emotional characteristics. It must be emphasized that the research reviewed in this chapter describes *groups* of handicapped individuals. Conclusions indicate, for example, that the learning disabled, as a group, are accepted less by their peers. This finding cannot be generalized to a specific case as it results from a group mean. Some learning-disabled individuals may be highly popular while others are socially isolated. Confident statements of the relationship between an individual's handicapping condition and social/personal features can only be made after studying the individual. Guidelines for undertaking this investigation are presented in following chapters.

An additional limitation of the existing literature is that it provides a crude description of the handicapped without examining etiological or treatment variables. For example, research indicates a higher prevalence of maladjustment among the hearing impaired, yet little is known regarding the cause or treatment of this phenomenon. In reviewing five volumes of the VOLTA Review and American Annals of the Deaf, Schloss (1982) reported a paucity of applied treatment research.

With regard to etiology, four major relationships between social-emotional adjustment and a specific handicapping condition may exist: (1) a specific handicap results from social-emotional maladjustment (e.g., stuttering results from insecurity in social situations); (2) a specific handicap leads to social-emotional maladjustment (e.g., stuttering produces high levels of anxiety); (3) a specific handicap and social-emotional maladjustment are independent of each other (e.g., stuttering results from an anticipatory speech reaction while social-emotional deficits result from poor peer and adult models); and (4) etiological relationships previously described may occur in combination. For example, Figure 2–1 illustrates a potential relationship between learning disabilities and social-emotional maladjustment. In this example, academic deficits produce social-emotional maladjustment that further diminishes academic performance levels.

Having emphasized the limitations of research pertaining to the social-emotional adjustment of handicapped children and youth, a number of conclusions can be drawn:

1. In all cases the social-emotional characteristics of handicapped children and youth differ in degree but not kind from the general population. All of the major and minor behavior disabilities found among

Figure 2–1 Learning Disabilities and Social-Emotional Maladjustment

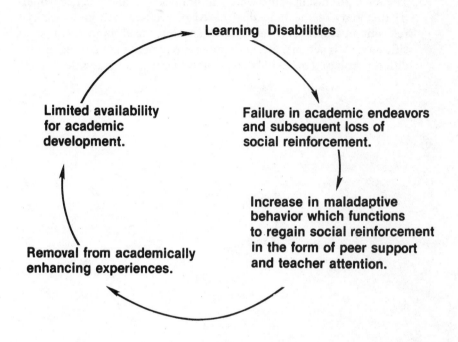

the general population occur in handicapped populations. Yet, no new or unique behavior typologies have been identified in the handicapped.

2. Social-emotional deficits appear to occur more often among the handicapped as a group when compared to the general population. When considering the individual, differences may be substantial, indiscernible, or nonexistent.

3. There appears to be a significant positive relationship between the attitudes toward the handicap and personal adjustment of the handicapped individual's parents and his or her own social-emotional adjustment.

4. Although specific handicapping conditions may place a child or youth "at risk" for the development of minor or major behavioral disturbances, specific etiological relationships cannot be assumed. A handicap may produce behavioral disorders; it may result from behavioral disorders; a handicap and behavior disorder may coexist as a result

of common etiological factors; or they may result from independent causal agents.

5. The most promising approach for future research and practice would be the study of the individual based on well-defined and socially relevant measures (e.g., aggressive behavior, social competence, specific anxiety reactions, etc.) as opposed to identifying between-group differences based on global personality constructs such as adjustment.

Chapter 3

Identification and Classification of Social Development Deficits

The preceding chapter has identified the major groups of handicapped students and their associated behavioral characteristics. The data emphasize the importance of educators' awareness of social development deficits that are associated with the various handicapping conditions. Knowledge of general social and emotional characteristics of the handicapped will enhance the practitioner's ability to benefit from the professional literature. Current research demonstrates the relationship between various handicapping conditions and constituent students' social learning styles, behavioral repertoires, and environmental histories (Cromwell, 1963; Cruickshank, 1975; 1980; Jacob, O'Leary, & Rosenblad, 1978; E.A. Miller, 1958; Offord, Abrams, Allen, & Proushinsky, 1979; Patterson, 1975; Swap, 1974).

The educator must be sensitive to current classification practices. This information allows for more effective communication with other professionals relative to broad issues or social development deficits among the handicapped. The practitioner's awareness of these trends, research implications, and the resulting program structures has as its foundation knowledge of the behavioral characteristics associated with each handicapping condition.

Beyond the educationally relevant classification of major handicapping conditions, recent efforts have focused on the development of systems of nomenclature that identify a wide range of social, personal, and emotional disorders. These nosological schemes seek to establish clear relationships between a disability and its nature, origin, or prognosis. The most widely popularized of these systems has been the American Psychiatric Association's *Diagnostic and Statistical Manual of Mental Disorders,* referred to as DSM-III (American Psychiatric Association, 1980).

The classification scheme provides five major headings for childhood and adolescent disorders as follows:

1. Intellectual—mental retardation
2. Behavioral (overt)—attention deficit disorder, conduct disorder
3. Emotional—anxiety disorders of childhood or adolescence, other disorders of childhood or adolescence
4. Physical—eating disorders, stereotyped movement disorders, other disorders with physical manifestations
5. Developmental—pervasive developmental disorders, specific developmental disorders. (pp. 35–36)

If an appropriate diagnosis cannot be drawn from this set, the clinician is instructed to select from diagnoses listed for adults. Adult categories appropriate for children include organic mental disorders, substance use disorders, schizophrenic disorders, affective disorders, schizophreniform disorders, anxiety disorders, somatoform disorders, personality disorders, psychosexual disorders, adjustment disorders, and psychological factors affecting physical disorders.

In addition to the preceding categories, DSM-III provides a description of the essential features of the disorders, associated features, age of onset, sex ratio, prevalence, usual course, familial pattern, impairment, complications, predisposing factors, and criteria for diagnosis. This system has undergone three revisions since the publication of DSM-I in 1952. Yet it has been widely criticized and is unlikely to be adopted in educational settings (Kauffman, 1981).

DEFICIENCIES OF CURRENT CLASSIFICATION SCHEMES

Probably the major limitation of DSM-III and other contemporary classification approaches is an overreliance on the diagnostic-prescriptive or medical model (Albee, 1968; Begelman, 1971; Szasz, 1960; Ullmann & Krasner, 1969). It has been argued that existing systems for classifying deviant human behavior rely on an assumption that behavioral descriptions provide relevant information for treatment. While the empirical classification of disease in the medical profession has provided diagnostic-prescriptive relevance, disorders of cognitive functioning are not subject to the same empirical scrutiny. As may be expected, these systems have been demonstrated to be highly unreliable and offer few substantive implications for treatment (Achenbach & Edelbrock, 1978; Dershowitz, 1974; Harris,

1979). Further, these descriptions provide limited information with regard to prognosis or the expected course of the disorder.

Even if treatment-relevant information could be extracted from these diagnostic systems, numerous authors and researchers have been critical of their reliability in identifying psychological disorders (Blashfield, 1973; Cohen, Harbin, & Wright, 1975; Hersen, 1976). There is a consistent acknowledgment in the literature that when individuals are diagnosed by independent clinicians, the resulting rate of agreement is woefully low (Frank, 1969). Studies in which independent psychiatrists diagnose the same client report inter-rater agreements ranging from 20 percent to 67.4 percent (Ash, 1949; Sandifer, Pettus, & Quade, 1964). Other researchers have demonstrated that psychological diagnoses are influenced by factors extraneous to the behavioral characteristics of the client (Cohen, Harbin, & Wright, 1975; Reiss, Levitan, & Szyszko, 1982).

Similar objections have been raised with the traditional classification scheme used to identify or label various handicapping conditions in special education. A recent study by Gollub and Sloan (1978) suggests that diagnostic labels are frequently assigned on the basis of socioeconomic status as opposed to school performance. Rivers, Henderson, Jones, Lodner, and Williams (1975) have argued that exceptional labels are often applied to minority children as the result of inappropriate testing practices. The authors stress that inappropriate labeling has had an adverse influence on the social, economic, educational, political, emotional, and cognitive aspects of black youths' development. Franks (1971) provides further data supporting the influence of race and social class on the exceptional label as identified by school personnel. The author reported that in 11 Missouri school districts providing services for both mentally retarded and learning-disabled students, black students comprised 34.21 percent of the students in mentally retarded classes but only 3.22 percent of the students in learning disabilities classes. The data clearly indicated that race and/or socioeconomic status had a biasing effect on the exceptional label assigned to the learner.

Data reported by Schloss and Miller (1982) demonstrate that public school teachers have differing expectations for educational services of adolescents having been labeled "institutionalized" vs. those labeled "regular school students." Despite the fact that both populations were identified as exhibiting exactly the same behavioral and learning characteristics in the school environment, the educators identified a more restrictive and exclusionary educational placement for the student identified as having been institutionalized. This finding was reported to be consistent with the thesis of MacMillan, Jones, and Aloia (1974) that labels have a significant and potentially adverse influence on the expectations of teachers.

Reynolds and Balow (1972) have suggested that professionals attribute characteristics to an individual that are overgeneralized from an exceptional label. The authors contend that these characteristics are often not reflected by an assessment of the individual. Overgeneralization from an exceptional label may set into place a "self-fulfilling prophecy" described and studied by Rosenthal (1966). Rosenthal and Jacobson (1968), though criticized for methodological limitations, have demonstrated that educators who expect low performance levels from students based on an exceptional label will often obtain low performance. On the other hand, teachers expecting superior performance will obtain high performance. Thus, a student's exceptional label may encourage teachers to establish expectations that are contrary to the best educational practices for the individual. In effect, the authors argue that deviant labels "create" deviance.

A related issue is that exceptional labels typically emphasize limitations of the individual without recognizing characteristics that may be within the norm for the general population. A review of definitions presented in the preceding chapter indicates the negative bias of current classification schemes. Mental retardation is defined by deficits in intellectual functioning and adaptive behavior; specific learning disabilities result from a specific retardation or disorder in one or more processes of speech, language, perception, reading, writing, or arithmetic; and behaviorally disordered individuals chronically respond to their environment in socially unacceptable ways. In the definitions presented in Chapter 2 there is a distinct paucity of positive characteristics associated with any handicapped group. When positive characteristics are identified, the emphasis is generally placed on how they are a symptom of underlying pathology as opposed to being an asset for the individual.

Another limitation of current categorical approaches is the misconception held by many professionals and the general public that exceptional characteristics are static and that once a child or adolescent is diagnosed as being handicapped, he or she will remain handicapped. This issue is exemplified by the concept of pseudomental retardation. This label was applied to individuals originally diagnosed as being mentally retarded who progressed to the degree that their intellectual functioning and/or adaptive behavior fell within the normal range. The assumption made by professionals was that mental retardation cannot be remediated. Thus, individuals who perform beyond previously anticipated levels are assumed to be misdiagnosed (Bialer, 1966). Beyond definitional issues, Ysseldyke and Foster (1978) have demonstrated that professionals in the field are reluctant to reevaluate and alter an individual's exceptional label as his or her behavior changes. Additionally, the researchers have demonstrated that the exceptional label, independent of the student's behavior, biases teachers' expectancies.

Research conducted by R.L. Jones (1970, 1972) emphasizes that exceptional labels and class placement may have an adverse effect on the self-esteem of the adolescent. Two separate investigations demonstrated that: (1) the exceptional adolescents avoided disclosing that they were enrolled in the special classes; (2) they complained of being ridiculed and made to feel different as a result of their placement; and (3) they felt that being enrolled in a special class limited their chances for later job placement. Rivers, Henderson, Jones, Lodner, and Williams (1975) suggest that exceptional labels are psychologically harmful in that "the lifelong labeling process militates against the individual's developing and sustaining a healthy conception of self" (p. 217).

CHARACTERISTICS OF A FUNCTIONAL CLASSIFICATION SCHEME

Millon and Millon (1974) have identified three major efforts to overcome the problems inherent in current classification approaches. These are: (1) recommending their total abolition (Laing, 1967; Sarbin & Mancuso, 1970); (2) substantially altering their form and content (Cautela, 1968; Hayes-Roth, Longabaugh, & Ryback, 1972; Kanfer & Saslow, 1965; Miller & Schloss, 1982; Millon, 1969); and (3) continuing to refine current systems (Lorr, 1966; Overall & Gorham, 1963; Spitzer, Endicott, Cohen, & Fleiss, 1974). It is clear that the field of special education could not continue to pursue vigorous research and development efforts without a common classification approach. However, it is equally apparent that current approaches to the classification are ineffective and often detrimental.

The deficiencies of current classification schemes have been highlighted in the writings of numerous authors. The effect of exceptional labels in removing students from positive learning environments (Bruininks & Rynders, 1971); the limited evidence that special class groupings facilitate performance for slower students (Bartel & Guskin, 1980; Dunn, 1973); the stigmatizing effect that special class placement may have on students (Bloom, Hasting, & Madaus, 1971); the impact of exceptional labels on teacher expectations (Schloss & Miller, 1982); and the limited information that exceptional labels provide with regard to treatment and/or prognosis (Bartel & Guskin, 1980) emphasize the need for alternative strategies to the diagnosis and classification of exceptional characteristics. This chapter presents an alternative for the special educator—the characteristic specific classification scheme.

The Characteristic Specific Classification Scheme

Classification of Behaviors Rather Than Student

The major difference between the proposed classification scheme and contemporary classification approaches is that the emphasis is placed on intra-individual differences as opposed to inter-individual differences. In effect, the characteristic specific system seeks to describe the strengths and weaknesses of the student across relevant behavioral dimensions in contrast to DSM-III, which describes how a person is different from presumably normal individuals. The present approach avoids gross comparisons between individuals on the basis of one or two measures, such as IQ and adaptive behavior. Rather than establishing a stigmatizing label that isolates the student from his or her peers, the present scheme identifies the student's strengths and weaknesses, providing direct implication for educational intervention.

To emphasize the point, intra-individual differences refer to the comparison of one or more of the individual's skills and abilities with other personal attributes. This leads to an understanding of discrepancies in performances within the individual. Subsequent program recommendations may be based on an understanding of the student's performance in one area that relates to his or her performance in other areas. Thus, the practitioner goes beyond the recognition of group differences and emphasizes the study of the individual characteristics that are pertinent to a specialized social development program.

Recognition of the Complexity of the Individual

It has been emphasized throughout this chapter that current labeling or classification practices in special education and psychology give the practitioner very little useful information about the learning and behavioral characteristics of the individual. A major reason for this is that current classification schemes identify and label individuals on the basis of one or two deficit characteristics without consideration of the total behavioral repertoire of the individual. This position is supported in the writings of Telford and Sawrey (1972) who have noted that many exceptional individuals exhibit exceptionality in more than one area. Some students labeled as learning disabled may exhibit problems associated with visual perceptual deficits, behavior disorders, and speech impediments. Other more severely handicapped individuals may exhibit sensory deficits, poor motor coordination, and no oral language skills.

The characteristic specific classification system recognizes that in order for the educator to develop an effective social development plan for a student, the educator must be sensitive to both the skills and deficiencies of the individual across a broad range of response requirements. The exceptional individual cannot be programmed for on the basis of one or two relevant pieces of information. Rather, all of the relevant learning and behavioral dimensions must be identified and evaluated prior to developing the social development program.

Emphasis on the Development of Positive Characteristics

Gardner (1977) has noted that "if the child does not learn academic skills at a rate or level expected, or if he does not behave emotionally or socially as expected, too frequently it is assumed categorically that the fault lies within the child" (p. 10). Kauppi (1969) recognizes the potential circularity of attributing behavior or learning deficits to presumed causes within the child. He argues that children's learning deficits are frequently attributed to mental retardation, not the educational system that failed to measure and meet their other needs.

Phillips, Draguns, and Bartlett (1975) have argued that current classification schemes employed in psychology and psychiatry are somewhat distant from the person's actual behavior in typical environmental situations. Further, these classification approaches provide little useful information. Similarly, classification schemes used in special education have little to do with actual classroom behavior and tell the teacher very little about the actual characteristics of the individual. The characteristic specific system delineates educationally relevant characteristics for each student. Rather than identifying the student as behaviorally disordered, the system produces a detailed description of characteristics that influence the student's adjustment in relevant settings. The identification of these characteristics provides a target for specific educational procedures.

The characteristic specific classification system removes blame for deviant characteristics from the individual while highlighting specific target behaviors. In this way, the identification of specific social skill deficits is the foundation of an effective behavior change program. Factors unrelated to the direct instructional and management process are no longer considered important. Thus, the circularity of attributing behavior problems to mental retardation, behavioral disorders, learning disabilities, etc. which are subsequently defined by the presence of the same exceptional characteristics is avoided.

Empirical Foundation

Empiricism, or the reliance on objective and reliable data to generate program decisions, is central to the rationale of the characteristic specific classification system. The system requires the educator to identify specific exceptional behaviors that may influence the student's adjustment in educational, vocational, living, and recreational settings. The behaviors targeted are a function of directly observable events. Rather than identifying a student as being autistic, the educator would identify specific performance problems that can be reliably observed and measured. These behaviors then become the focal point of the teacher's social development strategies. Because they are observable and measurable, the impact of the educational program can be evaluated by monitoring these behaviors.

Measurement procedures proposed for use with the classification system involve monitoring and evaluating classified behaviors directly. Direct measurement avoids the presumption of covert processes or internal events. The educator/evaluator is not concerned with a theoretical underlying process that may or may not be valid but the overt behavior of the adolescent; that is, the discrepancy between what the individual does prior to intervention and what is expected following intervention.

Recognition of the Validity of Learning Principles for All Students

A popular notion in special education research over the past two decades has been that various groups of individuals learn best through different teaching approaches. For example, mentally retarded adolescents achieve best in programs designed for the mentally retarded while learning-disabled adolescents achieve best in programs for the learning disabled. Similarly, auditory learners acquire information most effectively through auditory presentations while visual learners benefit most from visual presentations. The aptitude treatment interaction (ATI) assumption, as it is referred to in the literature, has been highly criticized in recent publications (Gardner, 1977; Ysseldyke, 1973). The general consensus of the literature is that while future investigation of aptitude by treatment interactions in education may be fruitful, the clear association between curriculum treatments and individual variables has yet to be demonstrated.

On the other hand, a common set of principles associated with social learning has been validated with individuals exhibiting a diverse range of characteristics. The learning theory principles involve viewing behavior along various skill dimensions. Complex behaviors are considered to be comprised of component behaviors that are chained together. Educational programs involve directly teaching and chaining component skills until a terminal objective is met. In using these principles, the teacher systematically arranges the learning environment to produce the desired behavior change. A more detailed discussion of how these principles may be used to teach new behaviors, strengthen existing behaviors, reduce excessive behaviors, and influence the persistence of behaviors will be provided in subsequent chapters.

Facilitation of the Identification of Educational Goals

Just as traditional classification systems tell very little about the specific characteristics of the individual, they tell very little about expected outcomes of educational interventions. Knowing that an adolescent is behaviorally disordered tells the teacher very little about the goals or objectives he or she may establish for the individual. Goals relating to specific behaviors, such as the reduction of aggressive outbursts, the increase of positive self-statements, the development of assertiveness skills, etc., are not easily identified from the diagnostic label. The speed at which goals may be achieved and settings in which the new behavior(s) will be exhibited are even less easily discerned.

The characteristic specific classification system provides a direct link between classification and performance expectations following the educational intervention. Target behaviors identified in the system may result in more global goal statements. For example, the goal of developing more positive interaction skills with authority figures may be established for an individual with specific behavioral deficits in making complimentary statements to others, using appropriate greetings, initiating conversations, and so on.

Recognition That Exceptional Characteristics Are Not Stable over Time

The general purpose of any educational intervention, regardless of the severity of the learner's handicap, is to improve the extent to which the adolescent adapts to current and future social environments. Educational interventions, maturation, or changes in environmental demands often result in the increased adaptability of the individual across specific behavioral dimensions. A classification system must be sufficiently flexible to account for these changes (Cromwell, Blashfield, & Strauss, 1975). Traditional classification systems that require the diagnostician to determine that the adolescent does or does not have an attention deficit, eating disorder, pervasive developmental disorder, etc. are limited in that they do not account for the educator's demonstrated ability to facilitate behavior change across functional skill areas. In addition, research has demonstrated that once an individual is placed in a traditional exceptional category, teachers are reluctant to change the exceptional label as his or her behavior changes (Ysseldyke & Foster, 1978).

Similarly, it has repeatedly been argued that characteristics that may be designated exceptional are as much a function of the environment and the observer as the identified individual (Bartel & Guskin, 1980; Kauffman, 1981). This view is exemplified in Rhodes' (1967) conceptualization of behavior disorders. He states that "what is considered deviant, how it is designated, interpreted, and treated is viewed as much a function of the perceiver as the behavior." A functional classification system must account for the differing expectations of individuals in various environments. A student may have a behavioral disorder in the school setting as defined by the teacher, but be a model worker on the job as viewed by the employer.

The characteristic specific classification system accounts for these limitations by objectively evaluating specific behaviors in association with relevant environments. A student's profile within the classification system can be periodically evaluated and reevaluated to reflect change associated with the educational objectives and intervention approaches. In short, rather than saying that an individual is behaviorally disordered through his or her high school career, specific exceptional behaviors are identified. As these behaviors are remediated, they cease to be identified as exceptional. An individual is not viewed as being behaviorally disordered across settings. Rather, specific behaviors he or she exhibits in specific settings are identified as being excessive (occurring too often) or deficit (occurring too seldom) in relation to the expectations of people in those settings.

Assumptions of Common Etiology and Treatment

It is generally understood that a variety of causal agents may produce specific learning disabilities, mental retardation, behavioral disorders, and so on. For example, the *Manual on Terminology and Classification in Mental Retardation* of the American Association on Mental Deficiency (Grossman, 1973) identified infestations and intoxications, trauma or physical agents, postnatal gross brain disease, unknown prenatal influence, chromosomal abnormality, gestational disorders, psychiatric disorder, and environmental influences as being potential etiological agents of mental retardation. Similarly, Kauffman (1981) has identified family, biological, and school factors that may be associated with the development of behavioral disorders. Although potential etiological agents have been enumerated for each exceptional category, recent literature estimates that 80 percent of all educable mentally retarded children have unknown etiologies, and etiological agents are less seldom identified for behaviorally disordered and learning-disabled youths (Hallahan & Kauffman, 1976).

The characteristic specific classification system avoids assumptions of common etiology and treatment by emphasizing the reliable observation of current conditions that influence the specific target behaviors. It is acknowledged that historic events (e.g., parental neglect, brain injury, trauma, malnutrition, etc.) may have produced the adolescent's current behavioral characteristics. However, educational approaches that deal directly with the student's current characteristics and contemporary maintaining conditions offer the most promise for effective intervention and treatment. To emphasize, the characteristic specific classification system is primarily concerned with the identification of specific exceptional behaviors. Explanations of these behaviors rely on identifying the influence of contemporary events. For example, Robert is mentally retarded as the result of a chromosomal abnormality, and his genetic structure cannot be altered. Thus, the teacher must seek to identify events in the current environment that will influence Robert's positive development. In short, knowing that Robert has a skill deficiency in small part assembly that may be remediated through systematic instruction and that Robert is highly motivated by infrequent praise from a supervisor is far more important than knowing that he is mentally retarded as a result of the translocation of the 21st chromosome.

THE CHARACTERISTIC SPECIFIC CLASSIFICATION SYSTEM*

The characteristic specific classification system facilitates the identification of exceptional social characteristics within the individual rather than categorizing an individual as exceptional. The system provides for three general response classes: (1) excessive disruptive responses; (2) deficit interpersonal responses; and (3) alternative prosocial responses. Within each class is a set of exemplary behaviors. The classes are identified because skills within these areas are closely associated with adjustment in educational, independent living, leisure, recreational, and vocational settings. The excessive disruptive response and deficit interpersonal response classes highlight behaviors that an individual may exhibit that limit his or her adjustment in these settings. The objective of intervention is to reduce the frequency or magnitude of the occurrence of the behaviors.

Behaviors within the alternative prosocial response class are intended to provide socially skillful behaviors that may be developed to replace the responses identified in the initial classes. The objective here is to teach and motivate alternative responses that may be substituted for extinguished

---

* This represents an adapted version of "The Characteristic Classification System" presented in Miller, S.R., & Schloss, P.J., *Career vocational education for handicapped youth.* Rockville, Md.: Aspen Systems, 1982.

disruptive or deficit behaviors. For example, verbally aggressive behavior may be targeted for reduction from the excessive disruptive class while ignoring interruptions from others is taught and reinforced from the alternative prosocial response class. Any time a behavior is identified for reduction in the first two classes, one or more incompatible behaviors from the alternative prosocial response class should be targeted for development.

Specific behaviors provide more precise descriptions of intervention areas. The responses identified in the classification system are somewhat arbitrary and by no means exhaustive. Because they represent only a small sample of the range of behaviors that may comprise a response class, open spaces are provided so that additional responses may be enumerated.

Along with the classification of specific behavioral excesses or deficits, the system encourages the identification of a number of variables that are associated with the performance or nonperformance of the specific behaviors. These performance factors add a greater understanding to the nature of the student's behavior. They also may suggest potentially effective educational strategies. The following section will discuss each of the performance factors with respect to behaviors identified in the characteristic specific classification system.

Performance Factors

The major performance factors addressed in the system are: (1) the degree of the exceptional characteristic; (2) the nature of the exceptional characteristic; and (3) the contemporary events that influence the exceptional characteristic. These performance factors are a critical component of the system because information they provide is essential to developing and evaluating an effective social development program. Simply knowing that a student does not comply with teachers' requests tells us about the student's current behavior, but very little about how to change the behavior and, therefore, falls short of the criteria of a functional classification established earlier in this chapter.

Information provided through the performance factors indicates: (1) the degree of the discrepancy between what the student does and what he or she is expected to do; (2) the relationship between the student's behavior and his or her skill, discrimination, and motivational characteristics; and (3) events in the learning environment that influence the student's exceptional characteristics. These data, as will be explained in the following chapters, provide the foundation for understanding how the learner's characteristics interact with potential social development strategies.

Degree of Exceptional Characteristics

The degree of exceptional characteristics indicates the extent to which the child or adolescent's current behavior deviates from what is expected by others. This is accomplished through a three-step process. First, a reliable measure of the student's current performance is obtained. Procedures for obtaining these data may include systematic observations, criterion-referenced tests, norm-referenced tests, a measure of permanent product, self-report, or parent interviews. Second, a decision is made regarding what is expected of the student. Ideally, this decision results from a multidisciplinary staff meeting in which all individuals concerned for the student's social development contribute. Finally, the discrepancy between the student's current performance and the expected performance is computed. This discrepancy becomes one of the terminal objectives of the social development program.

Exceptional characteristics may be either excessive or deficit. An excessive characteristic occurs more often than expected, while a deficit characteristic occurs too seldom. Physical aggression, for example, may be considered excessive because it occurs more often than is viewed acceptable by significant people in the adolescent's environment. In-seat behavior, on the other hand, may be considered deficit because the rate of the response is below the expectations of the teacher.

For example, it may be determined through systematic observations that an individual greets classroom visitors 60 percent of the time. Because the individual desires to be an appliance sales person and social amenities are an important skill on the job, the teacher, student, and parents agree that he or she should greet visitors 100 percent of the time. Therefore, the resulting exceptional characteristic is a deficit of 40 percent in greeting visitors.

Similarly, a student may be observed to swear on the job from 4 to 20 times an hour. Since the student works as a waiter and excessive swearing may lead to dismissal, a multidisciplinary staffing may agree to an expected level of swearing of zero times an hour while on the job. Thus, the exceptional characteristic is an excess of 4 to 20 swear words uttered an hour while on the job. In this example, specific alternative prosocial responses would also be targeted for development.

Nature of the Performance Factors

The discrepancy between what an adolescent does and what he or she is expected to do may result from any or all of the following three deficits: (1) skill deficits; (2) motivational deficits; and (3) discrimination deficits.

The recognition of how these factors influence the student's current behavior is essential to developing an effective social development program. Performance problems resulting primarily from skill deficiencies would be most strongly influenced by a skill training approach. Performance problems resulting primarily from a discrimination deficit would be most responsive to procedures that teach the student specific conditions under which the behavior is expected to be performed.

In the case of a skill deficit, the student does not have the prerequisite behavior in his or her repertoire. Skill deficits are assessed by observing whether or not the student has ever performed the desired behavior. If the student has not, it is reasonable to assume that he or she does not have the skill. For example, a student may fail to phone in sick prior to being absent from work. Recognizing that the student has never been observed to use the phone may indicate that he or she has a skill deficiency in this area. A similar evaluation strategy would be to provide strong incentives for using the phone as desired. If the student fails to use the phone even though the motivational conditions are very strong, the performance problem probably results from a skill deficiency.

In the case of a motivational deficit, the student does not desire to perform the behavior although the prerequisite skills are in his or her repertoire. Motivational deficits are assessed by determining whether or not the student has ever been observed to perform the behavior. If he or she has, then the skill is in the individual's repertoire, but the present motivational conditions are not sufficiently strong. If the student in the previous example had, on occasion, called in sick, it would be clear that the student possessed the necessary skill but that he or she was not motivated to call the employer. In the present example, the educator would develop a motivational strategy to increase the likelihood that the individual would call the employer, while in the previous example the educator would teach phone usage skills.

With a discrimination deficit, the individual does not know under what conditions to exhibit the desired behavior, although the prerequisite skill is present. Discrimination deficits may be assessed by observing if the student consistently performs the desired behavior, but under the incorrect stimulus conditions. For example, the student may repeatedly call the employer at all hours of the day; thus, he or she has the skill and would appear to be highly motivated. However, the student is not able to discriminate times at which calling the employer is considered acceptable from times that it is considered a nuisance. In this case, the educator may wish to teach and motivate the individual to phone the employer only under specific conditions (e.g., prior to being absent from work).

Two points must be emphasized. First, different exceptional characteristics may result from different performance factors. For example, a student may not do his math homework because he would rather watch television (a motivational deficit), while he may not do his piece work on the job for which he is paid very well because he does not know how (a skill deficit). Second, the performance factors may influence a specific behavior in isolation or in combination. A student may behave aggressively toward a peer because it produces compliance from the peer and status from other peers (a motivational deficit). Additionally, he may behave aggressively because he does not have the ability to gain compliance and status through positive social behaviors (a skill deficit). In this case, the educational approach would consider both the motivational factors and skill factors.

Influencing Events

Data on influencing events further delineate conditions that may be associated with exceptional characteristics. In effect, the influencing events describe cue and motivational conditions that have been observed to increase or decrease the likelihood that the expected behavior will occur. The influencing events category is broken down into two sections. The first requires a description of antecedent events associated with the occurrence of the expected behavior, and the second requires a description of consequent events associated with the occurrence of the target behavior.

Antecedent events are defined as conditions that precede the occurrence of the target behavior and influence (i.e., increase or decrease) the probability of its occurrence. For example, failure on an excessively difficult assignment may be observed to precede truancy and increase the likelihood that the student would be truant. Therefore, difficult assignments may be recorded as an antecedent that increases truancy. Consequent events are defined as conditions that follow a target behavior and influence (i.e., increase or decrease) the probability of its occurrence. For example, it may be observed that once a student is truant, the teacher withdraws the assignment with no unpleasant consequence to the student. As this occurs, the rate of truancy increases. Thus, the removal of the assignments following an absence may be a consequence that increases truancy.

Antecedents and consequences that are recorded may be associated with increasing the strength of deficit exceptional characteristics or decreasing the strength of excessive exceptional characteristics. In either case, identifying the conditions that tend to result in exceptional behavioral characteristics is an important part of understanding the learner and his or her environment. With this information the teacher not only knows whether skill training, discrimination training, or motivational procedures are indicated, but also understands which events currently influence the behavior.

In summary, the characteristic specific classification system serves four major functions. First, it facilitates the identification of specific behaviors that may be considered excessive or deficit. These behaviors become the target of the career-vocational education program. Second, it assists the multidisciplinary team in identifying terminal objectives or the expected level of the identified behavior following successful educational intervention. Third, it encourages the educator to consider the relative impact of skill, motivational, and discrimination factors on the identified behavior. Finally, it emphasizes the assessment of conditions in the environment that cue and consequate the identified behaviors. Each of these elements is critical to establishing an effective social development program for the handicapped. Table 3–1 shows the interrelationship between performance factors.

Table 3–1 Characteristic Specific Classification System

Cluster: Excessive Disruptive Responses

Sample Behaviors	Degree		Nature			Influencing Events	
	Current Level	Expected Level	Skill Deficit	Motivation Deficit	Discrimination Deficit	Antecedents	Consequences
Physically aggressive toward authority							
Physically aggressive toward peers							
Physically aggressive toward objects							
Physically aggressive toward self							
Verbally aggressive toward authority							
Verbally aggressive toward peers							
Verbally aggressive toward self							
Aggressive gestures toward authority							
Aggressive gestures toward peers							
Noncompliant toward authority requests							
Negativistic							
Refuses directions							
Jealous toward others							
Steals							
Fails to accept blame							
Fails to accept criticism							
Is dishonest, lies							
Makes excessive noise, boisterous							

PERFORMANCE FACTORS

Table 3–1 continued

Cluster: Excessive Disruptive Responses

PERFORMANCE FACTORS

Sample Behaviors	Degree		Nature			Influencing Events	
	Current Level	Expected Level	Skill Deficit	Motivation Deficit	Discrimination Deficit	Antecedents	Consequences
Irritable							
Dominates others							
Tardy							
Truant							
Quarrelsome							
Hyperactive							
Anxious							
Distractible							
Pouts							
Rationalizes							
Has tantrums							
Impertinent							
Uncooperative with peers							
Uncooperative with authority							
Seeks excessive attention from peers							
Seeks excessive attention from adults							
Is associated with members of a gang							
Engages in excessive disruptive behaviors with others							
Stays out at night							
Daydreams							

Cluster: Deficit Interpersonal Responses

Underachieving

Withdrawn

Exhibits frequent mood swings

Inflexible

Poor personal hygiene

Adult dependency

Irrational talk

Shy or timid

Reticent

Aloof

Overly sensitive

Easily hurt

Easily embarrassed

Negative view of self

Limited confidence

Preoccupied

Short attention span

Poor coordination

Passive

Drowsy

Bored

Lacks perseverance

Messy

Table 3–1 continued

Cluster: Alternative Prosocial Responses

Sample Behaviors	Degree		Nature			Influencing Events	
	Current Level	Expected Level	Skill Deficit	Motivation Deficit	Discrimination Deficit	Antecedents	Consequences
Raises hand to gain teacher's attention							
Uses "please" and "thank you" when making requests of others							
Asks for help when confronted with difficult task							
Asks permission to leave a certain area of the room or room itself							
Finishes assignments before asking for privileges							
Keeps track of own books and lessons							
Keeps personal work area neat							
Assists the teacher when asked							
Participates in classroom activities							
Works cooperatively with other students on projects							
Uses free time constructively							
Uses good posture when sitting at desk							
Follows rules for emergencies							
Asks peers for help							
Encourages other peers to join in (table games, projects, etc.)							
Shares materials with peers							
Volunteers answers to questions							
Is attentive during movies							

PERFORMANCE FACTORS

Is attentive to guest speakers

Listens to directions

Uses pleasant tone of voice

Follows rules of the classroom when teacher is absent

Asks permission before leaving an area

Waits for acknowledgment from teacher before speaking out

Asks for help before giving up

Ignores interruptions from others

Accepts punishment without becoming upset

Stays seated during instructional time

Maintains a neutral disposition following a failure episode

Apologizes when wrong

Accepts ideas that may be different

Reacts positively to authority figures

Adapts to changes in routine

Participates appropriately in larger groups

Responds to questions asked

Reports emergencies as directed

Displays appropriate manners (social amenities) saying:
"Good morning!"
"Hello, how are you today?"
"Thank you!"
"Would you mind if I . . . ?"
"Goodbye!"
"See you later!"

Uses friendly gestures, including:
opening doors
giving right-of-way to others in hall, sidewalks, etc.
assisting those with physical incapabilities

Responds appropriately to affection

Table 3-1 continued

Cluster: Alternative Prosocial Responses

PERFORMANCE FACTORS

Sample Behaviors	Degree		Nature			Influencing Events	
	Current Level	Expected Level	Skill Deficit	Motivation Deficit	Discrimination Deficit	Antecedents	Consequences
Responds to introductions by shaking hands							
Introduces himself or herself to another							
Introduces two people							
Initiates a conversation							
Talks before a small group							
Displays appropriate affect:							
smiling							
nodding agreement							
inquisitive expression							
expression of displeasure							

Source: Adapted from Miller, S.R., & Schloss, P.J. *Career vocational education for handicapped youth.* Rockville, Md.: Aspen Systems, © 1982.

Chapter 4

Beyond Traditional Disciplinary Views

The preceding chapter has defined social development problems as excessive or deficit social responses to environmental cues. The classification system avoids identifying the child or youth as being "disruptive" or socially maladjusted. Rather, it identifies specific responses that later may become the focus of intervention. At this juncture the critical reader may be poised to argue that these issues are not germane solely to handicapped populations. Chapter 2 presented data indicating that while a handicapping condition may place a student "at risk" for the development of minor or major social deficiencies, the range of problems is no more broad or narrow than those found among the general population. Chapter 3 argued that broad labels identifying handicapping conditions are of limited utility to educators in the classroom. Chapter 1 suggested that a common set of learning principles may be used to describe and modify *all* human behavior, regardless of age, sex, race, or exceptional labels.

Since handicapped students experience the same social development problems, the specific exceptional labels provide little useful data, and the same treatment approaches are applicable. The scope of the book may be broadened to all children and youth with one qualification. Social learning practices may be prioritized on the basis of "power." Power here may be defined as the relative ability of approaches to alter behavior. Chronic and severe behavior problems that are highly resistant to change require high-power strategies, while mild, transient problems may be ameliorated through low-power strategies. Verbal reprimands from the teacher are generally effective in reducing many disruptive behaviors among typical primary grade students. Reprimands, however, may not be sufficiently strong to influence the disruptive behavior of a few "special needs" children. These children require a more powerful strategy (e.g., note home to parents, loss of privileges, etc.). The scope of this book, then, involves special needs children and youth for whom "more powerful" approaches are required.

This rationale is supported by the unprecedented cry from school administrators for teacher training institutions to promote preservice educators' skills in managing chronic and severe classroom behavior problems (Duke, 1978). Beyond the concern of school officials, 11 of 12 Gallup polls between 1969 and 1980 report that Americans consider discipline to be the major problem in public schools. These are particularly critical concerns in view of federal legislation and litigation requiring even children with identified learning behavior disorders to be educated in the "less restrictive settings," often interpreted as the regular classroom (Abeson & Zettell, 1982; Dybwad, 1982).

As will be discussed later, Public Law 94-142 and the Rehabilitation Act of 1973 restrict the use of expulsion and suspension as disciplinary techniques for handicapped children. The child finds provision of the law, as well as other existing state and federal mandates, requires local educational agencies to actively promote school attendance of children or adolescents who would previously have been encouraged to "drop out." At the same time, it has become clear to many educators and administrators that traditional low-power disciplinary techniques are marginally effective with severely behaviorally disordered individuals. As evidence, a child may spend half of his or her school career in the corner, hallway, or principal's office but show no improvement in behavior, only more disdain for school authority figures.

In short, there is an increased demand for all educators to develop skills in managing the most chronic and severe conduct problems. Disciplinary tactics must go beyond traditional low-power practices destined to failure with many special needs students. The purpose of this chapter is to present a comprehensive model for teaching and motivating positive social behavior. Prior to describing this model, the chapter will examine the limitations of the traditional disciplinary model.

THE TRADITIONAL DISCIPLINARY MODEL

Figure 4–1 illustrates a simplified version of the disciplinarian model. Within this view, behavior that violates the expectations of the teacher produces aversive consequences that are expected to deter the future occurrence of the behavior. A child who talks out in class may be reprimanded by the teacher. The reprimand is expected to reduce the probability that the student will talk out in the future. Similarly, doodling on a desk may result in a requirement by the teacher to write lines out of the dictionary. The teacher, in this case, seeks to deter the child from future doodling.

The traditional disciplinary model may be said to be effective for a student if three outcomes become apparent. First, the behavior targeted

Figure 4–1 The Traditional Disciplinarian Model

Behavior   ⟶ *Aversive Consequences*

Behavior that	Unpleasant condition
violates the	expected to deter
expectations of	the future occurrence
the educator	of the behavior

by the educator must occur substantially less often following the presentation of the aversive consequences. Second, the reduction in rate should be pervasive across all relevant settings (e.g., other classrooms, lunchroom, bus, etc.) and durable over time (e.g., through school age and into adulthood). Third, alternative prosocial behaviors must be demonstrated that replace the disruptive behavior. While these criteria are frequently met for the general population, they are often violated in efforts to discipline handicapped youth. These criteria will be considered separately.

Reduction in the Target Behavior

Azrin and Holtz (1966) define punishment as an event that, presented as a consequence of a behavior, reduces the likelihood that the behavior will recur. The authors emphasize the functional relationship between a consequence and specific response rate. An event is punishing *only* if its presentation results in a reduction in the target behavior. Additionally, punishment must be identified with reference to a precise behavior. An event that effectively diminishes a youth's failure to comply with requests may have little impact on episodes of verbal aggression. Therefore, the event is punishing only when applied to noncompliance but is not punishing when applied to aggression.

This definition emphasized the importance of the educator's knowledge of the individual student. It encourages precision beyond general statements identifying detention or extra work as punishment. To be accurate, the statement must specify the behavior to be punished and evaluate the effectiveness of the procedure (Sabatino & Schloss, 1981). Detention may be said to punish noncompliance only if noncompliance occurs less often in the future. If noncompliance occurs at the same rate, detention is not considered to be a punishing event. Azrin and Holtz's definition provides a framework whereby effective punishment procedures may be identified.

Unfortunately, Azrin and Holtz also suggest that not all behaviors of all students can be punished through traditional consequences. A recent informal survey of members of the Illinois State Dean's Association (administrators concerned for discipline in junior and senior high schools) by this author identified four extreme consequences of disruptive school behavior: (1) detention; (2) in-school suspension; (3) home suspension; and (4) expulsion. The deans suggested that these consequences were generally effective in suppressing target behaviors for a majority of students but were ineffective for one or two percent of the students. Criterion one for the effective use of the disciplinarian model is satisfied if the target behavior is suppressed as a result of the presentation of aversive consequences. When it is not met, alternatives identified later in this volume should be considered.

The Effect Is Pervasive and Durable

These criteria suggest that not only should the punishment procedure have an initial impact on the target behavior(s) but: (1) behaviors similar to the target behavior should be suppressed; (2) the effect should be apparent in settings other than the one in which punishment was administered; and (3) the effect should be maintained over time. These criteria emphasize that the traditional disciplinary model is effective only when it produces a change in the child or youth's behavioral repertoire across settings and over time. Thus, punishment procedures applied to an individual that suppress behavior under highly restricted stimulus conditions (e.g., for specific teachers) or that have temporary effects do not fulfill the second criteria for the effectiveness of the traditional disciplinarian model.

The goal here is to adopt motivational approaches that have a generalized and prolonged effect. Meichenbaum, Bowers, and Ross (1968) report a highly structured behavior management program that effected an improvement in the classroom behavior of adolescent delinquent girls. However, the same report failed to demonstrate that the effects of the program carried over to other classroom settings. Similarly, Pendergrass (1972) demonstrated the effectiveness of a two-minute time out in reducing undesirable behavior of two withdrawn children. Once the procedure was removed, the disruptive behavior reappeared. As such, these approaches were limited in their ability to promote a pervasive and durable change in students' behavior patterns. Alternative strategies that may promote generalization and maintenance of a behavior change will be discussed in following chapters.

Developing Alternative Prosocial Behaviors

The primary goal of education is to influence the development of positive social, emotional, academic, and vocational characteristics. Although punishment may be effective in reducing or eliminating a range of excessive disruptive responses, it does not teach or reinforce positive social characteristics. This view is emphasized by Gardner (1978):

> A punishment procedure does not teach a child what to do. It suppresses or controls behavior, but when used in isolation, the procedure does not provide a more appropriate mode of behavior as a replacement. It merely serves to reduce (typically on a rather temporary basis) the likelihood that the punished behavior will be repeated under similar circumstances. (p. 254)

Bandura (1973) has emphasized that children and youths exhibit disruptive behavior in an attempt to gain satisfaction from their environment. Consequences that support the disruptive behavior may include: (1) the avoidance of unpleasant events (e.g., truancy allows the child or youth to avoid unpleasant aspects of school); and (2) the acquisition of pleasant events (e.g., verbal aggression produces compliance from peers). Isolated punishment procedures may not remove the natural function of the behavior. For example, punishing the youth for being truant does little to help him or her to gain satisfaction from the school environment and/or make home less satisfying during school hours (Schloss, Kane, & Miller, 1981). Additionally, punishment does not insure that the child or youth has the ability to gain satisfaction through prosocial behaviors. Punishing a youth for being truant does not teach the child or youth responses that will make school more pleasant (Schloss, et al., 1981).

Thus, while punishment may temporarily suppress truancy, it is ineffective in providing alternative responses to replace school avoidance behavior. While many children and youths have the ability to independently identify alternative responses to the response being punished, many special needs students are unable to identify and use alternative positive social behaviors (Bryan, 1974; Bryan, Wheeler, Felcan, & Henek, 1976; Chapman, Larsen, & Parker, 1976; Schloss & Sedlak, 1982). Therefore, beyond suppressing norm-violating behaviors, disciplinary strategies must insure that alternative prosocial behaviors are developed.

The special education literature has identified a number of negative side effects of the excessive or isolated use of punishment with handicapped children and youths. Each of these effects limits the extent to which the preceding criteria may be fulfilled. The negative side effects will be considered prior to a discussion of alternatives to the traditional disciplinarian model.

NEGATIVE SIDE EFFECTS OF PUNISHMENT

Few other topics in behavioral psychology have received as much attention as the potential pitfalls of the unwise use of punishment. Existing data suggest that although punishment may produce a temporary change in behavior, the adverse effects that may result from the punishment procedure may offset the therapeutic effects of the procedure (Blackham & Silberman, 1980). The negative side effects discussed in this literature have major implications for the use of the traditional disciplinarian model in the education of handicapped children and youth.

The frequent use of punishment may cause a child or youth to withdraw. Empirical data suggest that a child's or youth's inability to discriminate between a punishing stimulus (e.g., a specific teacher) and other associated stimuli (e.g., all adults) may result in a generalized suppression of responses (Lovaas, Schaeffer, & Simmons, 1965). If a sufficient number of conditioned punishers are developed, the youth may become unresponsive in virtually all interpersonal interactions. The child's or youth's inability to discriminate between a punished response (e.g., talking in class) and other associated responses (e.g., talking in social situations) may have a similar effect. Seligman, Maier, and Solomon (1971) have demonstrated, through an experimental analogue, that depressive-like reactions may occur from the punishment of motor responses. Initially, the specific behavior being punished is suppressed, but response suppression becomes generalized as an increasing number of responses becomes associated with the aversive event. Ultimately, the child or youth learns that all behaviors produce noxious stimuli, and therefore they become helpless (Seligman, 1974; Seligman & Groves, 1970).

The child or youth may engage in negative emotional behavior to avoid or escape the punisher. Bandura (1969, 1973) has argued that individuals may engage in high rate aggressive behavior in order to escape aversive consequences. As an example, a number of researchers have described a process whereby an authority figure presents an aversive consequence, and the child or youth retaliates with his or her own aversive stimulus (e.g., verbal or physical aggression). The coercive process escalates until one individual withdraws his or her aversive stimulus, thereby negatively reinforcing the other individual (Patterson, 1975; Patterson & Cobb, 1971). Schloss (1982) has presented data that suggest that depressive-like reactions on the part of mentally retarded subjects result in the avoidance or removal of authority demands. Blackham and Silberman (1980) suggest that punishment may be an antecedent to escape behaviors including lying or running away. Schloss, et al. (1981) have identified truancy as behavior that functions to allow youths to escape aversive aspects of school.

The punisher may serve as an aggressive model. Lefkowitz, Eron, Walder, and Huesmann (1977) have demonstrated that aggression in children and adolescents may often be associated with highly punitive and inconsistent parental control. Bandura (1973), in a review of research, has emphasized that children and adolescents imitate behavior observed of others. High-status models including educators, parents, and peers are more likely to be emulated, and observational learning is more likely to occur when the behavior is reinforced.

These data suggest that students observing teachers (high-status models) obtain compliance (reinforcement) through aversive control techniques are likely to engage in similar behaviors in order to produce compliance. Heron (1978) cautions mainstream educators of the effect of observational learning on the behavior of general students toward handicapped youths. The author emphasizes that the educator who employs punishment procedures excessively with handicapped children is:

> . . . modeling a particular approach to problem solving. The teacher, therefore, should not be too surprised when children imitate her behavior. Specifically, if the teacher repeatedly criticizes the mainstreamed child . . . the regular children will use the same technique in their interactions with exceptional children.
> (p. 251)

The child may develop verbal concepts of himself or herself associated with the frequent use of punishment. Cognitive and behavioral psychologists alike agree that the life experiences faced by individuals shape the view they have of themselves (Ellis, 1973; Mahoney, 1974; Rogers, 1969). Gardner (1977) has argued that children and youths who are frequently criticized and punished develop compatible verbal labels for themselves. Further, these verbal labels govern future behavior. In effect, they become a part of the self-fulfilling prophecy in which the child's or youth's performance is limited by his or her expectations.

A substantial body of empirical literature has demonstrated the association between a child's or youth's verbal behavior and actual performance (Lovaas, 1961, 1964; Risley & Hart, 1968). Children who are frequently criticized or otherwise punished for deviant behavior may begin to limit their personal expectations. Ultimately, the individual may acquire a failure avoidance as opposed to a success striving disposition.

LEGISLATION AND LITIGATION

Recent legislation has restricted the use of traditional disciplinary procedures with handicapped students. Public Law 94-142, The Education for

All Handicapped Children Act, provides federal aid for state and local educational agencies for a portion of the excess costs of providing special education services to the handicapped. States become eligible for funding through the submission and acceptance of a plan insuring that all handicapped students residing in the state are provided a free, appropriate education. Specific procedural due process safeguards are required in evaluation and placement decisions, hearings, and appeals. Section 504 of the Rehabilitation Act of 1973 requires that no otherwise qualified handicapped individual shall, by reason of the handicapping condition, be restricted from participation in any program receiving federal financial assistance. As Public Law 94-142, the regulations include requirements for identification, evaluation, and placement; provision of a free, appropriate education and nonacademic services; and procedural safeguards.

Public Law 94-142 and Section 504 of the Rehabilitation Act of 1973 make it illegal to suspend or expel handicapped students under certain conditions. It has been argued that contrary to the provisions of these laws, suspension and expulsion may deny the handicapped student's right to: (1) a free and appropriate education; (2) have any change in placement occur only through a multidisciplinary staff conference; (3) an education in the least restrictive environment with maximum possible interaction with non-handicapped peers; (4) continue the current, educational placement pending a hearing or appeal or further diagnostic and evaluative work; and (5) obtain benefits, aids, or services as the result of a handicap.

A substantial body of litigation has supported these positions. *Stuart v. Nappi* (1978) resulted in an injunction being issued prohibiting the expulsion of a learning-disabled youth with a history of behavior problems. The court ruled that exclusion from school related to the handicapping condition and deprived the student of her right to an "appropriate education." *Goss v. Lopez* (1975) directed that students facing possible suspension are entitled to a due process hearing. The court ruled that when an emergency situation justifies a delay in normal hearing procedures for a suspension, a preliminary hearing must be convened as soon as practical. In no case should the hearing be later than 72 hours after the removal of the student from the regular educational placement. The suspension can be extended only as long as the emergency situation exists. The child or youth may not be suspended for an aggregate of ten days or more in a school year. *Mattie T. v. Holladay* (1977) provides that a child or youth may be removed from a special education placement for behavioral reasons when the individual's behavior represents an immediate physical danger and constitutes a clear emergency in the school. Such removal can be no longer than three days and must result in a formal review of the individualized educational program.

Stuart v. Nappi (1978) ruled that expulsion of handicapped students violates the provisions of Public Law 94-142 for procedural guidelines in changing the placement of exceptional children and youth. The court found that a change in placement results from expulsion or any other exclusion for more than ten days in a school year. In accordance with Public Law 94-142, any change in the placement of a handicapped student must be made through a multidisciplinary staff conference with parental participation. As discussed previously, this ruling does not preclude the suspension of handicapped students in emergency situations.

Placement in "the least restrictive environment" has also served as a basis for enjoining disciplinary procedures that exclude handicapped students from the school setting. *Stuart v. Nappi* (1978) noted that expulsion would limit educational services to homebound tutoring unless a special school placement was provided. Homebound instruction would restrict the girl's participation in socially enhancing experiences, thereby perpetuating a vicious cycle in which disruptive behavior is sustained. The court ruled that the school must provide a continuum of placements that match the characteristics and needs of handicapped individuals, while maximizing interactions with nonhandicapped peers. Expulsion was ruled as denying the student the right to interact with nonhandicapped peers. The court stressed, however, that the needs of the handicapped student are not being met in the regular classroom if a handicapped student is sufficiently disruptive so as to significantly impair the education of other students. Therefore, a multidisciplinary staff conference should be used as a vehicle to identify a more restrictive placement that meets the student's needs.

A similar issue is that P.L. 94-142 assures handicapped children and youth the right to continue in their current educational placement pending the results of a multidisciplinary staff conference. Therefore, disciplinary procedures that remove a student from the placement specified in the initial individualized education plan (IEP) for an extended period of time violate this right. To be in compliance with the federal mandate, school personnel must reconvene a multidisciplinary staff conference for the purpose of evaluating and modifying the current placement (*Howard S. v. Friendswood Independent School District,* 1978).

In *Frederick L. v. Thomas* (1976) and *Stuart v. Nappi* (1978), the courts ruled that the schools are obliged to provide an educational program appropriate to the student's social-emotional needs. Antisocial behavior that results from an inappropriate placement may not result in a disciplinary process that includes exclusion from the school setting. The court in *S-1 v. Turlington* (1979) ruled that the handicapped (e.g., behaviorally disordered youths) cannot be excluded from their educational programs as the result of actions that result from the handicapping condition (e.g., disruptive behavior). In each case, the courts ruled that an appropriate, educational program that minimizes the extent to which youths are disruptive should supplant the disciplinary process.

Although the focus to this point has been on students identified as handicapped, P.L. 94-142 and Section 504 of the Rehabilitation Act suggest that all students with a history of chronic and severe behavior problems fall under the protection of due process. Focal educational agencies are required to identify and evaluate handicapped children residing in their districts.

A child or youth whose disruptive behavior is sufficiently chronic or severe to warrant repeated exclusions from the regular educational program is arguably being treated as if he or she were behaviorally disordered. An argument can be made that unless the child's or youth's behavior is highly disruptive and chronic, long-term exclusions may be a violation of state statutes (i.e., compulsory education laws) that emphasize the responsibility of public schools to educate all children. A disparity between the offense and resulting consequences may be a violation of substantive due process. If, however, the student's disruptive behaviors are sufficiently severe to warrant the harsh penalty, the student may be argued to be behaviorally disordered as defined in P.L. 94-142. Therefore, although the student has not been formally classified as being behaviorally disordered, the school's treatment of the individual implies that he or she is behaviorally disordered.

The legislation and litigation cited here clearly limit the use of suspension and expulsion as disciplinary tools for the handicapped. A student may be suspended for no more than three successive days and a total of ten days in a school year. Suspension even then may only be for emergency purposes and must trigger a meeting of the multidisciplinary staff conference to evaluate the effectiveness of the current placement. Even students not identified as handicapped may come under the protection of these guidelines if there is evidence that they have had a history of chronic and severe behavior problems.

By way of summarizing these data and providing a transition to their practical application, Exhibit 4-1 provides a model disciplinary policy for handicapped students. It should be noted that, in the ideal case, these principles would be integrated with procedures used with all students. In effect, the guidelines established for the handicapped may be equally beneficial to all students.

Both the technological and legal issues emphasize a degree of care and planning that must accompany any decision to adopt a disciplinary procedure. It is important to recognize that viable alternatives exist to suspension and expulsion. Further, when used properly, other punishment procedures need not have undesirable side effects. The social learning

Exhibit 4–1 Model Regulations for the Discipline of Handicapped Students*

The following policy shall apply to all students who have been identified as handicapped under P.L. 94-142 and Section 504 of the Rehabilitation Act of 1973 and to students who have been referred for evaluation pursuant to those rules and regulations.

General Procedures

1. The student's individualized education plan (IEP) shall include a description of disciplinary procedures deemed to be appropriate if at the time of the IEP meeting it is known that the student exhibits social development deficits.
2. Educators responsible for the supervision and care of special education students or students awaiting special education evaluation shall receive written instructions with respect to advisable disciplinary approaches for each student. These instructions shall contain:
   - the student's name;
   - the names of any persons anticipated to employ the disciplinary procedure;
   - the forms of discipline appropriate for the student;
   - the disciplinary procedures to be followed; and
   - a recording procedure that may be used to evaluate the effectiveness of the procedure.
3. If an educator concludes that the advised forms of discipline for a student have been unsuccessful in modifying the student's behavior, that teacher shall, without delay, bring that information to the attention of a school administrator who has the power to convene a multidisciplinary staff conference. The parent will immediately receive notice of the meeting and be encouraged to attend.
4. The multidisciplinary staff in association with the parents and student (when appropriate) will work to develop a more effective means of managing the student's behavior. This may include an alternative, more restrictive placement. Agreement between parents and the school is required before a substantial program change may be made. The terms of the modified program will be written into the student's IEP. If there is no agreement, the parents or the district must make a request for an impartial due process hearing for the purpose of resolving the disagreement.

Suspension

1. Except in situations where the student's presence poses a danger to the student, other students, or school staff, appropriate school staff shall determine prior to the suspension of a student whether or not the misconduct is the result of the student's handicapping condition as defined by the rules and regulations governing the administration and operation of special education. Such determination shall be made by the staff members who are familiar with the student's handicapping condition and educational program. Such information shall be noted on the student's individualized education program.
2. If the student's misconduct is the result of his or her handicapping condition, then the student shall not be suspended except as provided by paragraph three below. Rather, the student's program shall be reviewed in a multidisciplinary staff meeting consisting of staff members familiar with the student's handicapping condition and educational program and the student's parents. The multidisciplinary staff meeting shall be conducted within three school days of the misconduct. The parents of the

Exhibit 4–1 continued

student shall be notified by telephone and mail to establish a time and date mutually agreeable. Whenever possible, the student should be included in conferences to maximize his or her involvement and subsequent change. Any decision to alter the program shall be made by the appropriate staff. Recommendations should be written into the IEP. If the parents disagree, their rights to an impartial due process hearing can be pursued.

3. The local district may suspend the student, even if the misconduct is the result of the student's handicapping condition, if the student's presence poses a danger to the student, other students, or school staff, or if the student's conduct is so disruptive over a lengthy period that normal classroom activities cannot continue. In addition, this ongoing threat of injury or disruption will be judged to be not amenable to change by less exclusionary means. If an "emergency situation" is determined, a student may be suspended up to three days, but any student with an IEP or pending evaluation will not be suspended for more than ten days cumulatively in a school year. A multidisciplinary staff meeting must be reconvened with student's parents to determine whether the placement has been appropriate, what interim services must be provided during the period of suspension (e.g., assignments or direct instruction), and what future services must be provided.

Expulsion

1. Prior to the expulsion of a handicapped student or a student who has been referred for evaluation, appropriate staff members shall determine if the misconduct is the result of the student's handicapping condition as defined by the rules and regulations that govern the administration and operation of special education. Such determination shall be made by the school staff members familiar with the student's handicapping condition and educational program in a multidisciplinary conference with the student's parents.

2. If the misconduct is not determined to be the result of the student's handicapping condition, the appropriate school staff shall, during the multidisciplinary conference, propose alternative services to be provided. The student and his or her parents shall be advised of their right to a due process hearing under the rules and regulations referred to above.

3. If the student's misconduct is the result of his or her handicap, he or she shall not be expelled. In such cases, the student's program shall be reviewed in a multidisciplinary staff conference that shall include appropriate staff members and the student's parents. The student may be placed in a more restrictive environment or a more therapeutic environment or other services may be provided to reduce or eliminate the misconduct. All due process protection must be accorded the child or youth through these proceedings.

* Appreciation is expressed to Mrs. Catherine Black of the Guardianship and Advocacy Commission for the State of Illinois for assisting in the development of these guidelines.

principles and procedures highlighted in this volume are intended to: (1) overcome the limitations of traditional disciplinary approaches; and (2) minimize negative side effects that often result from the unwise use of punishment. The multifaceted social development model provides a series of entry points and decision rules that overcome the limitations of traditional disciplinary approaches.

THE MULTIFACETED SOCIAL DEVELOPMENT MODEL

The social development model is illustrated in Figure 4–2. The multifaceted model includes three major entry points as well as the specific target behavior. The entry points are designated as antecedent conditions, related personal characteristics, and consequences. The intervention process involves identifying the antecedents, related personal characteristics, and consequences that influence the strength of the target behavior. Once identified, those factors that maintain disruptive behavior will be removed while those that support alternative prosocial behaviors will be presented. It should be noted that the multifaceted intervention model does not preclude the use of punishment or traditional disciplinary approaches. In many instances, these procedures may be selected in the consequence entry point. The major departure from the traditional disciplinarian model discussed earlier is the consideration of antecedents and related personal characteristics as controlling variables.

Addressing behavior problems by altering the antecedents that cue the behavior adds a greater degree of power to the intervention approach. A punishment procedure that is ineffective once a student becomes highly volatile may be strengthened by structuring antecedents so that the youth is not likely to become highly aggressive. This is illustrated in the case study of a hearing-impaired behaviorally disordered youth in Exhibit 4–2. Prior to intervention when presented with certain antecedents (e.g., "no,"

Figure 4–2 Relationship among Antecedents, Associated Characteristics, the Target Behavior, and Consequences

Antecedent $\longrightarrow$	Related Characteristics $\longrightarrow$	Target Behavior $\longrightarrow$	Consequences
conditions that precede the target behavior and influence the probability of its occurrence	observable and inferred characteristics of the individual that influence the target behavior	behavior that the intervention program is intended to strengthen or weaken	conditions that follow the target behavior and influence the probability of its future occurrence

Exhibit 4–2 Multifaceted Social Development Program for Bob A*

Bob is a white adolescent aged 14 years and 11 months. He is 5' 7" tall, and weighs 184 pounds. He possesses several personal characteristics that impact programming. These characteristics include: (1) a profound bilateral hearing loss that greatly reduces his ability to perceive and understand social situations, develop appropriate patterns of behavior, and develop speech and language skills; and (2) concomitant behavior disorders in the form of limited motivational development, limited social interaction skills, and a high rate of disruptive behaviors.

The demonstrable lack of success with general classroom approaches, the increasing risk of injury to himself as a result of the target behaviors, and the poor prognosis for success in any less restrictive setting are cited as justification for the adoption of this more restrictive approach.

Three objectives have been established:

1. The student will reduce the number of instances of spitting behavior.
2. The student will engage in progressive muscle relaxation through verbal and visual cues, thereby developing the abilities to display a positive alternative response to heightened emotional arousal.
3. The student will develop the ability to delay gratification by expanding the time between the performance of a positive behavior and the presentation of verbal/physical/tangible reinforcers.

A sheet with a grid of 15-minute intervals along the left side and the five target behaviors along the top will be used to record data that may be used to evaluate the effectiveness of the program. Should any one of the five targeted behaviors be observed, a mark is to be made under the appropriate heading in the time interval during which it occurred. The total frequency of each targeted behavior will be tallied and transferred to a graph.

Components Focusing on Antecedents

A factor identified as contributing to the likelihood of disruptive behavior was Bob's inability to predict when natural positive consequences would occur; therefore, he was unable to maintain a positive disposition in anticipation of pleasant events. Also, he was not motivated to cease disruptive behavior so that he could return to a routine that assured him of pleasant activities. Therefore, the following three strategies will be followed:

1. Staff members will develop and maintain a highly structured schedule that will be altered only under extreme circumstances.
2. Staff members will alternate pleasant activities with aversive activities so that the consequence of participating in an unpleasant activity will be the initiation of a pleasant activity.
3. If Bob disrupts the schedule through disruptive behavior, he will be reminded of the pleasant activities that he will miss as the result of remaining disruptive.

In order to assist in developing and maintaining positive emotionality in anticipation of pleasant events, a small card upon which one to ten circles have been drawn will be displayed. Upon completion of a specified interval during which no inappropriate behavior has been displayed, a hole will be punched and a reinforcer provided. In order to assist Bob in distinguishing between socially acceptable and unacceptable behavior, a card with a happy picture of himself on one side and an unhappy picture of himself on the other will be used. The happy side will be displayed during intervals of appropriate behavior and will be turned over to the sad side following inappropriate behavior.

Exhibit 4–2 continued

Components Focusing on Related Personal Characteristics

Motivational features will be developed by pairing primary reinforcers with secondary reinforcers on every occasion. Bob's ability to delay gratification will be enhanced by expanding the time between appropriate behavior and the awarding of the reinforcer. Social skills will be taught by identifying and reinforcing conversational alternatives to spitting. These will be developed through modeling and behavior rehearsal procedures. Finally, progressive muscle relaxation training will be conducted daily.

Components Focusing on Consequences

1. As described previously, Bob will receive a tangible reinforcer every two minutes as measured by an egg timer. Delivery of the tangible will follow punching a single hole in a slip of paper or a small card.
2. The egg timer will be started, and Bob will work on the assigned task. The punch card, hole puncher, tangible reinforcer, and Bob's happy face picture that says "Good work, Bob!" will be in view. After two minutes of appropriate behavior that consists of not spitting, a hole will be punched in his card and exchanged for a tangible reinforcer and a verbal reinforcer ("Good work, Bob! You are working on _____ (subject) quietly.") If inappropriate behavior occurs (i.e., spitting), the card will be destroyed, tangibles removed from view, and he will be told, "No, wrong!", and the sad face side of the card with "No, wrong!" will be displayed. Bob will be instructed to sit relaxed for 30 seconds as measured by a stopwatch. If during this time he again displays inappropriate behavior, the staff member will repeat, "No, wrong," point to the sad face, restart the egg timer. When he is behaving appropriately, the staff member will give the verbal reinforcer and turn the picture back to the happy side.

* Appreciation is expressed to Maureen Smith, Sharon Smaldino, Monty Field, Bob Shreve, and Renee Lynn for assisting in the development and implementation of this program.

"stop," and "wrong"), the youth would become highly aggressive and self-abusive. The most intrusive forms of punishment were used with no effect in reducing the disruptive behavior.

The multifaceted intervention approach involved altering the antecedents, related personal characteristics, *and* consequences. The antecedents that provoked disruptive behavior were withdrawn while antecedents that were associated with a positive mood were introduced. The youth was taught alternative ways to gain satisfaction and avoid displeasure. Finally, an elaborate system for reinforcing positive social behaviors and punishing aggressive behaviors was adopted. Any one facet of this program used in isolation would probably have been ineffective, but the integrated components had a dramatic effect as illustrated in the accompanying graph. It can be noted that once the aggressive behavior was under control, the provoking antecedents were gradually reintroduced, and the unnatural consequences were faded.

Antecedent Conditions

Antecedent conditions are defined as events that precede the occurrence of the target behavior and influence the likelihood of its occurrence. Antecedents can either cue a desirable response (e.g., a pleasant greeting from the teacher prompts a polite response from the student); cue an undesirable response (e.g., a poor test grade results in the student being truant from class); fail to cue a desirable response (e.g., asking a student the answer to a question results in withdrawal behavior); or fail to cue an undesirable response (e.g., the student sits quietly when teased by others rather than using his previous behavior of swearing).

Systematic observations of the individual (see Chapter 8) allow the educator to generate hypotheses regarding potential antecedents. Using the antecedent entry point involves altering events expected to provoke disruptive behavior. Often these events can be replaced by cues for positive behavior, thereby reducing the likelihood that disruptive behaviors will occur. For example, being criticized by a teacher may be identified as an antecedent to verbal aggression. The antecedent entry point is used by providing an expectation for success that reduces the rate of failure and subsequent criticism from the teacher. In this example, criticism is replaced by praise for less rigorous work. Once the student learns to respond appropriately to mild and infrequent criticism, the educator may gradually raise his or her expectations.

If it is observed that a naturally occurring event that should cue a positive social behavior does not serve this function, the event may be developed as a cue, thereby increasing the strength of the behavior. For example, systematic observations of a youth may reveal that she seldom says "thank you" when complimented by others. Intervention may develop others' complimentary statements as an antecedent for her saying "thank you."

Related Personal Characteristics

Related personal characteristics are defined as observed or inferred features of the individual that are hypothesized to mediate between antecedent or cue conditions and target responses.

A characteristic that may be associated with depressive-like behavior, for example, may be mediational responses that promote feelings of helplessness (Beck, 1972). While an intervention program may focus on the antecedents and consequences of depressive-like episodes, it may also be important to develop mediational statements that help the student to assert his or her control over the environment. For example, an antecedent to withdrawal may be the receipt of a poor work evaluation. A mediational response that the student may develop could be, "I didn't do well on this evaluation, but if I work harder, I'll do well on the next one." It is expected that the development of this and other verbal mediational responses would decrease the probability that the student would withdraw following subsequent experiences of a similar nature.

Similarly, specific social skills could be identified as related personal characteristics that, if developed, would reduce aggressive outbursts. For example, observations may demonstrate that verbal confrontations by peers are antecedents to aggressive behavior in the absence of more acceptable assertiveness skills. The student may be unable to exhibit assertive behavior that would allow him or her to avoid harassment from others without being disruptive. In this example, assertiveness may be developed to reduce the likelihood that the individual will become aggressive.

Consequent Conditions

Consequent conditions are defined as events that follow the target behavior and influence the probability of future occurrences. Specific consequences can either strengthen, maintain, or reduce a target behavior. Observing the student may help to generate hunches as to the function of specific consequences. If it is known that a specific consequence increases the likelihood that an undesirable behavior will occur, the reinforcing consequence may be removed. If it is known that there are few positive consequences associated with a desired social behavior, favorable consequences may be established.

Consequences can be described as being positively reinforcing, negatively reinforcing, or punishing. Positive reinforcers are events that follow a behavior and increase the probability that the behavior will recur. Although positive reinforcers are generally pleasant to the individual, sometimes consequences perceived by the teacher to be unpleasant may be positive reinforcers. For example, if it is observed that the frequency of aggressive outbursts increases after one-day suspensions, it may be concluded that the suspensions positively reinforce aggression. Negative reinforcement involves the removal of an unpleasant event following a behavior, thereby increasing the probability of the occurrence of the behavior. For example, a teacher's observations may reveal that being late for school often results in the adolescent not having to take quizzes in first-period civics class. If tardiness continues, it can be said that the avoidance of quizzes negatively reinforces tardiness. Finally, punishment is defined as a reduction in the strength of a behavior that results from the presentation of an unpleasant consequence. For example, if incorrectly completing a work assignment results in a poor grade and subsequently the number of incorrectly completed assignments decreases, the incorrect work was punished through the assignment of a poor grade.

The contingency relationships previously described occur over time as a part of the student's natural learning history. The sum total of an individual's experiences determine, to a large extent, the individual's current performance under certain antecedent conditions. Behaviors that have been consistently positively reinforced probably are a strong part of the student's repertoire. Behaviors that are consistently punished become weakened and eventually drop from the individual's response pattern.

The multifaceted intervention model is used to identify the natural contingency arrangements under certain antecedent conditions. Intervention, as illustrated in Exhibit 4–2, involves creating modified contingency arrangements until the student acquires more appropriate response patterns.

CONCLUSIONS

It should be clear that the model that underlies the social development process is not *different* than procedures found to be effective for average children and youths. Rather, the multifaceted intervention model illustrated in this chapter provides increased "power" that accommodates the learning and behavioral characteristics of many handicapped children and youths. The merits of the procedure become clear when considered against the criteria established early in this chapter. First, the flexibility and empirical nature of the approach emphasize the continuous search and validation of an effective procedure. If progress toward the predetermined objectives is not apparent (i.e., a reduction in specific disruptive responses and in increase in alternate prosocial behaviors), procedures within the entry points should be altered. Second, the self-control that results from the development of related personal characteristics that mediate between provoking antecedents and alternative prosocial responses may be an effective technique for promoting generalization and maintenance (Wehman, Abramson, & Norman, 1977). Applying the procedure consistently in all relevant environments will increase the likelihood that the behavior change will be pervasive and durable. Adoption of the related personal characteristic entry point insures that the student learns and practices alternative prosocial behaviors. The differential reinforcement of these behaviors across relevant settings may develop them as a permanent part of the student's behavioral repertoire. Third, these procedures attempt to offset the negative side effects associated with punishment. Negative emotional arousal that results from punishment procedures may be diffused by presenting antecedents that insure success and reward. The likelihood that the child will withdraw and/or avoid the punisher is minimized by positive components of the approach (i.e., the differential reinforcement of prosocial behavior). Finally, the multifaceted intervention model may encourage students to develop verbal labels for themselves associated with newly acquired prosocial responses.

In conclusion, the present approach offers a positive yet directive approach to reducing disruptive behaviors and increasing prosocial behaviors of handicapped students. The procedure reflects the limited cognitive abilities and behavioral repertoire associated with many handicapping conditions. While initially the approach may be somewhat time consuming, the achievement of pervasive and durable behavior changes may offset the initial effort. The following chapters will consider specific social learning tactics that may be employed in each entry point.

Chapter 5

Antecedent Control

Antecedent control involves identifying and altering events that are hypothesized to precipitate disruptive behavior. Frequent failure experiences, public reprimands, and peer taunts have been identified as events that lead to norm-violating behavior among the general population (Jones & Jones, 1981). As such, they may be viewed as general antecedents for disruptive responses. Antecedent control involves structuring classroom activities so that the child or youth is not exposed to these events.

When antecedent control involves removing stimuli that the student will be expected to face in subsequent environments, other entry points (e.g., developing related personal characteristics or altering consequences) may be used to teach the student to act appropriately when faced with the antecedents. However, to promote initial success, the educator may remove naturally occurring events with the intent of gradually reintroducing them as the student's social skills develop. The relationship of these factors is shown in Figure 5–1.

Figure 5–1 Relationship among Antecedents and Other Intervention
Facets

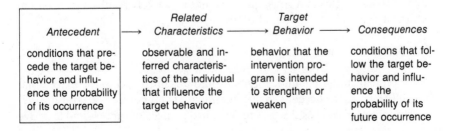

Antecedent	Related Characteristics	Target Behavior	Consequences
conditions that precede the target behavior and influence the probability of its occurrence	observable and inferred characteristics of the individual that influence the target behavior	behavior that the intervention program is intended to strengthen or weaken	conditions that follow the target behavior and influence the probability of its future occurrence

The terms *antecedent control*, as used here, and *prevention* are synonymous. By altering provoking antecedents the educator prevents the occurrence of disruptive behavior. Antecedent control may be viewed as a humane approach to behavior management as it involves removing the student from situations that have previously resulted in aversive consequences. Rather than requiring John to complete three workbook pages (an event that is often frustrating) John may be asked to complete only one. The result is that John becomes frustrated, verbally aggressive, and noncompliant substantially less often. The positive aspect of this treatment is that, because John is seldom disruptive, he is exposed to aversive consequences less often.

When viewed in a broader sense, antecedent control may be less than humane when used in isolation. Children and adolescents learn to adapt to their environments by facing and mastering successively more challenging tasks (White, 1960). In this developmental process, society gradually introduces more challenging demands as a child gains greater social competence. If social expectations are withdrawn at any point, the child or youth will not be motivated to acquire more complex skills. Yet, at some point, society may reintroduce expectations at a level commensurate with the individual's chronological age. At this time, the youth may be so far behind that the likelihood of developing efficient social skills is substantially reduced. This process is exemplified by the misuse of homebound instruction for behaviorally disordered youth. Not attending school minimizes the student's exposure to antecedents that may provoke disruptive reactions. Unfortunately, the child or youth has little opportunity to develop social skills that enable him or her to work through these provoking events.

Barring unusual circumstances, antecedent control should only be adopted as an isolated intervention strategy (i.e., without attention to related personal characteristics or consequences) when the events that are withdrawn will not be faced by the child or youth in subsequent environments. A youth may be removed from advanced math class where the performance demands often result in noncompliance if he or she is not expected to face similar demands in the future. Conversely, removal of a child from a lunchroom setting should be accompanied by intervention in related personal characteristics and consequences that ultimately result in the gradual return of the child to the lunchroom.

The 80 Percent Rule

For typical students, antecedents should be controlled to the extent that the child or youth succeeds in social endeavors 80 percent of the time. As the student experiences the favorable consequences of success and aversive consequences of failure, the individual's rate of prosocial behavior under the controlled antecedents should increase. At some point, slightly more provoking antecedents may be introduced. The student should again gain control through these events, and a slightly more rigorous set of antecedents may then be established. This process may continue until the original set of antecedents is in place and the youth is succeeding at a rate commensurate with his or her peers.

Antecedents should be controlled so that the criterion for success in social endeavors does not drop below 80 percent. This criterion may be lower if the antecedents are uncontrollable as in the case of some general school rules or standards. The criterion for success may necessarily be maintained at an extremely high rate (e.g., 99 percent) when the disruptive behavior may be injurious to self or others. Having considered the criterion for adopting antecedent control as an entry point, the remainder of this chapter will consider specific antecedent control procedures.

TEACHER-STUDENT RELATIONSHIPS

Interpersonal interactions between students and teachers often have been described as influential factors in the social performance of children and adolescents. An overemphasis on relationship building, however, to the exclusion of contingency management and skill development approaches, has led to widespread criticism. Probably the greatest limitation of an overreliance on interpersonal skills as a social development strategy for the handicapped is the importance of complex and abstract language structures. Research evidence presented in Chapter 2 emphasized the limited language capabilities associated with the major handicapping conditions. Language-oriented therapies (e.g., psychotherapy, client-centered counseling, rational emotive therapy, and group process) advocate the use of interpersonal relationships as primary change agents. Unfortunately, many handicapped individuals experience great difficulty in processing, internalizing, and subsequently reflecting the verbal messages of the therapist or teacher. Therefore, empirical support for the efficacy of these approaches with the handicapped is lacking.

In spite of this acknowledgment, a critical goal of the social development process advocated in this book is to promote overt and covert language as a controlling mechanism for the handicapped individual. Interpersonal interactions, as discussed here, are not isolated therapeutic techniques. Rather, they are components of the multifaceted intervention model. In short, it is not incongruous to establish an open relationship while working toward the attainment of specific social development objectives and managing consequences to promote those objectives.

The importance of this view was emphasized to this author in the case history of Tom. Tom was a twelve-year-old student in my junior high school special education class. He was also a client whom I saw during a counseling internship. I was carefully schooled in the use of client-centered therapy and thought myself to be quite adept in the humanistic psychotherapy process. One weekend Tom broke into a series of churches in town, causing considerable damage with spray paint. Immediately following these acts, he stole a car from a used car lot and drove 140 miles to Chicago. Once in town he sideswiped several cars. A while later, the city police observed him making a U-turn, and Tom was arrested. Tom was returned to school the next day. At the next counseling session, Tom was encouraged to reflect on the series of events. When pressed to identify an alternative way of behaving, he suggested that he would be certain to avoid making U-turns in the city of Chicago.

The point here is *not* that the counseling process was misguided, simply that it was incomplete. Tom was spared of any aversive consequences for his disruptive acts by correctional officials. Very little was done to develop related personal characteristics that would provide Tom with an alternative approach to gaining satisfaction. The sum total of the isolated counseling tactic was that it provided Tom with an opportunity to verbally rehearse a very exciting set of events.

Theoretical Perspective

Interpersonal relationships have been stressed as a part of the social development process by numerous authors. Lewin (1948) emphasized the role of individuals' perceptions in the social development process. He argued that youths are likely to perceive situations differently than adults. It is only through direct communication between adults and adolescents that the youth can be provided necessary information from which to channel future efforts. Lewin viewed the communication process as a means by which adolescents can clarify and resolve their conflicts with adult expectations. He argued that open communications between adolescents and adults can diffuse frustration that results from adult demands.

Other theorists, including Rogers (1965, 1969), Maslow (1968), and Coopersmith (1967), emphasize the importance of interpersonal interactions in the development of a positive self-regard. The authors assume that a sense of security in the form of being understood, respected, and supported is necessary for effective social functioning. Requisite to the development of these feelings are stable interaction patterns characterized by a sincere interest in the individual's ideas and expectations. This view is supported by the research of Baird (1973), Brookover (1945), Costin and Grush (1973), Dixon and Morse (1961), and Elmore and LaPointe (1975). Aspy (1969), Hefele (1971), and McKeachie and Lin (1971) further advance this position by demonstrating a relationship between the supportive interactions of teachers and academic performance gains of students. Conger (1977) summarizes these data by stating:

> . . . adolescents in our culture tend to prefer and to respond more favorably to teachers who are warm, possessed of a high degree of ego strength, enthusiastic, able to display initiative, creative, reactive to suggestions, poised and adaptable, able to plan, interested in parental and community relations and aware of individual differences in children, and oriented toward individual guidance. In contrast, teachers who are hostile or dominating generally appear to affect pupil adjustment adversely. (p. 375)

The interpersonal responses exhibited by a teacher can be identified as sending skills or receiving skills. Sending skills are defined as the act of communicating a message to the student. Receiving skills are those abilities that facilitate the assimilation of the message.

Sending Skills

A number of authors have identified various sets of sending skills. Each delineates techniques that help the student to become aware of the teacher's viewpoint and increase the likelihood that the child or youth will respond to the message in a socially skillful manner.

The teacher should speak in concrete terms. Concrete messages are particularly critical because of the handicapped student's limited language capability. Speaking concretely involves several facets. The first is talking in the present. Information is most likely to be exchanged when it relates to currently existing circumstances. Discussions about events that occurred weeks, days, or even hours hence are less concrete than those that center on a present event. The time to discuss emotional reactions to a potentially provoking event is immediately before, during, or shortly after that event. Waiting for a weekly counseling session is certain to reduce the impact of the interaction.

Second, the teacher should carefully select vocabulary and syntax to reflect the receptive language skills of the student. Short sentences comprised of easily understood words are more likely to be received than complex sentences including words not commonly used by the student. The teacher should avoid words or phrases with multiple or vague meanings such as, "I was *tickled* by your work," "That's a *funny* way to *look* at it,"

"Your *grandiose* statement was *absurd*," or "You seem *high strung* today." Statements should be both clear (in that they leave little room for personal interpretation) and complete, including all relevant information. Following potentially confusing statements with multiple concrete examples may result in increased comprehension. This tactic may also increase the likelihood that the original statement will be understood in the future.

Finally, social learning tactics such as modeling and behavior rehearsal may be used to make verbal expectations more concrete. Suggesting to a preschooler that he play less roughly in the sandbox may be accompanied by the teacher modeling a more desirable way to play. The child may also be guided through a rehearsal of the new behavior.

The teacher should tell the student what he or she is doing improperly and tell others what the student is doing correctly. Many handicapped students are cautious about adult relationships. Students who are made aware of their inadequacies "through the grapevine" as opposed to through direct interactions with the educator are likely to intensify this distrust. Little, if any, good can come of discussions with other students or unrelated staff about the problems of a particular student. Not only may it have an adverse influence on the student involved, but it also may lead the listeners to question how the educator describes them when they are not present.

A related issue is that the educator who talks about individuals' problems in a public forum serves as a negative role model. It is likely that children and adolescents may learn from the adult that talking about their "friends" behind their back is an acceptable social behavior. Later, the educator may be in the untenable position of arbitrating disputes that arise between students as the result of this activity. The unfortunate message sent to the students may be that they must learn from what the teacher says, not from his or her example.

A final adverse influence involves the negative expectations toward the student that may be developed. A substantial body of literature describes the impact that teacher expectations have on children and youths (Foster & Keech, 1977; Foster, Ysseldyke, & Reese, 1975; Gottlieb, 1974; Schloss & Miller, 1982). An overemphasis on a student's problems in discussions with others is likely to adversely influence their expectations of the youth. This phenomenon may cause teachers who know the student through reputation alone to avoid the individual or become overly directive. This response style may well be an antecedent for the student's disruptive behavior, thereby creating the self-fulfilling prophecy.

Conversely, talking directly to the student in an adult manner allows the educator to convey expectations and feedback without potentially confounding intermediaries. Initially, direct interactions may be more time consuming and unpleasant for the educator as he or she must deal immediately with the student's response. The long-term consequence of this style may be a relationship in which the student expects direct and honest feedback from the educator. The student can then learn to manage his or her feelings in relationship to these interactions.

In summary, talking to others about a student has the immediate benefit (to the teacher) of diffusing anxiety associated with the student's performance. Over time, however, this response style may confuse the student and generate or maintain a level of distrust. Further, it may have an adverse influence on the way other students and professionals approach the child or youth. Although talking directly to the youth may be unpleasant initially, it holds the potential of developing a relationship in which the student may expect and learn to respond appropriately to both complimentary and corrective feedback.

The teacher must balance the rate of socially enhancing interactions with the rate of corrective feedback. Educators who continually correct students run the risk of becoming a conditioned cue for negative emotional reactions. The repeated pairing of the teacher with unpleasant and anxiety producing interactions may result in the teacher alone eliciting anxiety. This conditioning process may limit the educator's ability to serve as a socially reinforcing agent. An additional negative side effect is that the student may actively avoid interactions with the teacher. These occurrences are incompatible with the educator's objective to establish a supportive relationship in which the student is encouraged to approach the teacher for feedback and guidance. Finally, negative feedback that occurs at an excessive rate may lose its ability to promote more adaptive responses. The student may conjecture, "What is the point of trying? I'm going to get yelled at regardless of what I do." Or, the student may think, "She yells at everyone. Why should I care if she yells at me?"

In order to offset the association between the teacher and corrective (anxiety producing) interactions, the teacher must engage in a higher rate of socially enhancing interactions. This is best accomplished through the guideline, "Look for good behavior." Educators should be alert to student performance, abilities, or attributes that may be socially reinforced. Classroom activities should be structured so that students are able to succeed at a high rate (remember the 80 percent rule), and the teacher is able to provide social reinforcement for success-producing behaviors. This approach will strengthen the impact of the corrective statements made the 20 percent of the time that success is not achieved.

Finally, the extension of simple amenities may favorably influence the student's perceptions of the teacher. Courtesies, such as "Please," "Thank you," "Good morning," "How are you today?," may place the teacher in a stronger position to influence the development of prosocial behaviors.

Beyond developing a positive association between the teacher and student, the student is also likely to emulate the teacher's responses in interactions with others.

The teacher must be aware of nonverbal language. Students are often as likely to respond to *the way* something is said as to *what* is said. The teacher's voice inflection, gestures, and general posture should corroborate his or her verbal message. Statements of concern for the student's welfare are best accompanied by direct eye contact and a forward posture. Interactions that are intended to calm a student should be delivered in a low, slow-paced tone of voice. Calming gestures may accompany these interactions. Statements intended to motivate performance should be delivered enthusiastically and at a relatively quick pace. It is often possible for a teacher to control the pace and tempo of a classroom activity simply by his or her gestures and intonation.

Beyond these more subtle, nonverbal cues, more obvious statements can be made through the teacher's overt behavior. Circulating among the students' desks and minimizing the use of the teacher's desk as a permanent station demonstrates an interest and involvement in the students' activities. Walking around in the classroom makes the teacher more available to "catch the students being good." Pats on the back, friendly handshakes, and other tactile reinforcers are delivered easily when the proximity between student and teacher is reduced.

The teacher should provide objective feedback and evaluation. Handicapped children and youths require immediate and frequent feedback regarding their performance. Often this feedback takes the form of an evaluation, though some authors have argued that evaluative statements are detrimental to the social development process as exemplified by Carl Rogers (1961):

> I have come to feel that the more I can keep a relationship free of judgment and evaluation, the more this will permit the other person to reach the point that he recognizes that the locus of evaluation, the center of responsibility, lies within himself. (p. 55)

Research evidence has left little doubt that evaluative statements can have a favorable effect on students' social performance (Mahoney & Thoresen, 1974). The manner in which feedback is delivered and the form of the feedback can have an impact on its effect.

First, the teacher must specify the behavior that is being evaluated. If the specific activity cannot be described objectively, feedback is either unnecessary or will have little positive impact. Telling a youth that he or she has a "bad attitude" will do very little to change his or her behavior.

Conversely, telling the student that "it is inappropriate to tell jokes about the problems of another individual" may have a favorable effect. The handicapped individual is not likely to be able to identify specific responses to change in the first example. The student is more likely to become aware of specific offensive acts through the second example.

Objectivity is more easily achieved if the number of activities subject to evaluative feedback are limited. The handicapped student will find it very difficult to assimilate and respond to a wide range of evaluative statements from the teacher. On the other hand, he or she is more likely to succeed if evaluative statements center on several (three to five) well-defined responses. Once the initial set of activities that were subject to evaluation is within the expected range of performance, additional responses may be added. This principle will assist the educator in maintaining the 80 percent success rate.

Receiving Skills

Effective receiving or listening skills are critical tools for controlling the antecedents of disruptive responses. Simply having someone to talk with may reduce the likelihood that a student will engage in maladaptive behaviors. By listening carefully, the educator may assist the child or youth to diffuse anxiety associated with aggression and withdrawal. In the process the teacher may also gain information that allows him or her to structure future classroom activities for the student.

Many times handicapped children and youths are able to process solutions to their own problems. If an educator quickly produces a solution without allowing the child or youth to seek his or her own solution, the educator short-circuits what may be an important learning experience. The process of identifying relevant pieces of information, organizing that data, and producing the best possible solution may be as important as the actual change in the target behavior. The educator should assist the student through this problem-solving process, providing only the amount of direction required to produce a satisfactory result.

Paraphrasing has been suggested by several authors as an approach to facilitating this process (Gordon, 1970, 1974; Johnson & Johnson, 1975a; Raths, Harmin, & Simon, 1966). Paraphrasing or active listening as described by Johnson and Johnson (1975b) involves seven major facets as follows: (1) restating the student's stated position as understood by the teacher; (2) preceding the reiteration with, "You think . . .," "Your position is . . .," "You believe that . . .," and so on; (3) remaining nonjudgmental by avoiding expressions of approval or disapproval; (4) maintaining a posture and affect that reflects the teacher's interest; (5) stating the student's position as accurately as possible, including statements describing his or her feelings and attitudes; (6) not adding or subtracting from the student's information; and (7) trying to empathize with the student.

Reflective questions may be asked by the teacher to assist the student to clarify his or her beliefs and feelings. These perception checks also assist the educator in evaluating the extent to which he or she is understanding the student's message. Reflective questions should be nonjudgmental yet directive in that they provide a structure from which the student's next line of discussion may proceed. Reflective questions may include, "It seems as if you . . .," "Your belief if . . .," "It seems as if . . .," and "You are saying that . . . ." These statements or questions keep the responsibility for determining a solution to the problem with the student. Additionally, they serve to clarify or emphasize a line of thought.

If an interpretation offered by the teacher is rejected, he or she may respond by paraphrasing the student's response. In this way additional information on the student's position can be acquired. Once the student restates his or her position, the teacher may again wish to formulate a more accurate interpretation. This process may continue until the handicapped student arrives at an acceptable solution or until the child or youth embarks on an irrational or obviously nonproductive line of reasoning. At this point the educator may become more directive and, to some extent, supply alternative statements.

Directive Interactions

A major assumption held in this book is that the handicapped student should actively participate in formulating his or her social development program. Further, the methods used to promote social development should be as minimally intrusive as possible while still being effective. Reflective interactions, as described in the preceding sections, place the responsibility for producing a solution in the hands of the student and, as such, meet these criteria.

Unfortunately, many troubled, handicapped children and youths do not possess sufficient information to arrive at a reasonable solution and/or are motivated to engage in a circular or unproductive line of reasoning. In these cases, the efficacy criteria may not be met. Therefore, a more intrusive approach that removes a degree of responsibility from the student is required. Directive interactions may serve this function. Directive interactions involve telling the student what to think, reinforcing the student for expressing the more appropriate thought process, and extinguishing statements that reflect an inappropriate line of reasoning.

Ellis (1973), a major proponent of directive counseling, emphasizes that irrational verbalizations may be a major influence in promoting and sustaining emotional disturbance. He argues that insight therapies that reflect rather than challenge irrational beliefs simply reinforce the destructive thought process. Ellis (1963) summarizes the therapists' (educators') role in the social development process as follows:

> The rational therapist (educator) believes that sustained, negative emotions—such as intense depression, anxiety, anger, and guilt—are almost always unnecessary to human living, and that they can be eradicated if people learn consistently to think straight and to follow up their straight thinking with effective action. (p. 52)

Ellis (1963) suggests that the directive educator "constantly, frequently keeps questioning, challenging, and reindoctrinating (students) until they are ready to give up their dysfunctional behavior patterns and replace them with more functional philosophies and behaviors" (p. 52). The importance of this active, directive role in working with the handicapped cannot be overstated. Many handicapped students do not have the cognitive ability or desire to independently seek appropriate solutions to social-personal problems. The reflective mode, previously discussed, simply encourages the student to rehearse and possibly be reinforced for an irrational thought process. Ellis' view encourages educators to interrupt the child or youth and redirect the line of reasoning.

Guidelines for Effective Interactions

Having discussed a range of student-teacher interaction approaches, a number of general guidelines can be established:

1. The educator must be continually aware of his or her interpersonal relationship with the student. The goal of the social development process is that, to the extent possible, overt and covert language assumes a controlling influence over the student's behavior. To promote this goal verbal interactions between the teacher and student should become an integral part of every facet of the educational program.
2. It is not inconsistent for the educator to maintain well-defined performance expectations and manage consequences while maintaining an open relationship.

3. Warmth, involvement, enthusiasm, creativeness, initiative, receptiveness, poise, and interest are characteristics of an effective teacher-student relationship.
4. Interpersonal interactions should reflect the language abilities of the handicapped student. Educators should speak in concrete terms, talk to students not about students, carefully balance the ratio of corrective to reinforcing interactions, be aware of nonverbal cues, and stress objectivity in feedback and evaluation.
5. The educator should be careful to gain as much information as possible from the student prior to forming a judgment. Paraphrasing and perception checks may be used to structure the student's interaction.
6. Discussions in which the child or youth engages in an irrational or circular line of reasoning should be redirected. There is little value in allowing the handicapped individual to practice dysfunctional interactions.
7. When necessary, the educator should question, challenge, and provide alternatives to irrational statements.

CLASSROOM STRUCTURE

The actual structure of academic activities can be antecedents for prosocial or disruptive behavior. Educational environments and activities that are well planned may have a major impact on reducing the rate of maladaptive behaviors. These environments also seem to draw a high level of socially skillful behaviors from students. Bates, Renzaglia, and Wehman (1981) described the characteristics of an appropriate education for the severely and profoundly handicapped as including 12 major features. Many of these may be generalized to mildly handicapped educational settings. The relevant characteristics of a well-planned academic environment adapted from their work include functional and age-appropriate objectives, activities, and materials; systematic instructional procedures; frequent review of the educational program; a stable classroom schedule; integrated counseling; interaction with nonhandicapped peers; and family involvement. These will be discussed separately.

Functional and Age-Appropriate Objectives, Activities, and Materials

Handicapped children and adolescents often become bored with academic activities. A disinterest in classroom events results in the student seeking alternative ways to generate satisfaction. Often the alternative responses are disruptive. Gardner (1977) emphasizes that in the absence of skills that allow the student to gain reinforcement for teacher-directed activities, the handicapped engage in *any* behavior capable of producing the limited available reinforcement.

The ability of the educator to plan and implement educational activities that maintain the interest of the student underlies adaptive social responses in the classroom setting. The educator capable of promoting students' attention to task provides little time for students to engage in alternative activities.

This phenomenon is demonstrated by the widely recognized inverse relationship between chemical and physical restraint to program activities in mental health facilities for emotionally disturbed youth. A high rate of restraints and punishment can be expected in units in which there are few activities. Units that have structured leisure, recreational, vocational, academic, and social activities seldom require restraint procedures.

Objectives, activities, and materials should be functional and age appropriate. Functional implies that there is a direct relationship between the skill acquired by the student and the demands of the environment. Learning to ride a public transit system is functional because it is reinforced by the natural environment (assuming that the student may use public transportation in the community). Learning to complete a maze, as in some perceptual motor programs, is nonfunctional as the student will rarely be reinforced for exhibiting this skill in independent living situations. To further emphasize dichotomy, Exhibit 5–1 illustrates several nonfunctional skills along with their functional counterparts.

Clearly, students are more likely to attend to task and avoid disruptions when mastery of the task will facilitate their adjustment to community and vocational settings. Handicapped students are much less likely to be dis-

Exhibit 5–1 A Comparison of Functional and Nonfunctional Activities

Nonfunctional	*Functional*
• Reading from a word list	• Learning vocationally related sight words
• Addition problems on a drill sheet	• Learning to work at a grocery checkout
• Developing fine motor coordination by stringing beads	• Hooking a rug
• Practicing penmanship in a workbook	• Writing a letter to a brother in the navy
• Studying about the invention of the automobile	• Learning to tune a car
• Learning about units of measure through a filmstrip series	• Baking a cake

ruptive in driver education classes or shop classes. Conversely, they may be a frequent source of disruption in the less functional class.

Age-appropriate activities are also more likely to serve as antecedents to prosocial behavior than activities appropriate for younger or older students. Unfortunately, there has been a scarcity of commercially produced curricula materials appropriate for secondary level special education students. This has led many educators to structure lessons around reading and math series for younger, nonhandicapped students. Handicapped students are often left to repeat almost annually the same materials. Under these conditions, students become quite negativistic toward academic activities. Traditional reading and math series readily become antecedents for maladaptive behavior. This phenomenon is not unexpected considering the emotional reaction the students must experience when reminded annually of their intellectual limitations. Very few high school students would readily walk into study hall proudly displaying a fifth-grade reading or math book. In fact, being removed from study hall for disciplinary reasons would seem to be a very acceptable alternative.

This problem can be overcome with a little additional work and planning on the part of the teacher. In a chapter on instructional methods and materials for handicapped adolescents, Miller and Schloss (1982) recommend rewriting texts, alternative high-interest low-vocabulary programs currently marketed by publishers of instructional materials; the use of microcomputers; student-prepared texts; popular press such as newspapers, magazines, comic strips, etc.; language experiences; the completion of a daily school record book; and occupation-centered instruction.

Systematic Instructional Procedures

The relationship between success in academic endeavors, a positive view of self, and socially appropriate behavior has been well documented in the educational literature. Academic success is as much a function of the skills of the educator as the cognitive characteristics of the student (Gardner, 1977). Ineffective teaching strategies invariably result in frustration and failure for the learner. As has been stressed repeatedly, the student is likely to engage in norm-violating behaviors that produce some sense of satisfaction when reinforcement is not available or attainable for academic responses.

Systematic instructional procedures insure success and reinforcement for the handicapped learner by assessing the learner to determine his or her skill level and instructional level; breaking down instructional units into steps that are manageable for the learner; establishing a realistically attainable criterion for success; providing motivating consequences for successful performance; and adopting cue/correction procedures that prompt desirable responses or redirect incorrect responses. Although a detailed analysis of these instructional procedures is beyond the scope of this book, the following section will provide a brief overview of systematic instructional procedures. A more detailed discussion of this topic is available in many fine texts (cf. Gardner, 1977; Payne, Polloway, Smith, & Payne, 1981; Smith & Payne, 1980; Wallace & Kauffman, 1978).

Assessing the Learner

The initial step in systematic instruction is a determination of the student's current level of functioning. Instruction that is initiated at an excessively remedial level is likely to result in disinterest and boredom. Instruction that is beyond the learner's ability may result in frustration and failure. In both cases, the student may be "at risk" to engage in disruptive behavior. Initiating an instructional unit at a level that is challenging yet attainable is more likely to hold the student's attention.

Formative assessment procedures that pinpoint the student's performance levels across a variety of curriculum domains may include:

- criterion-referenced tests
- checklists
- systematic observations
- measures of permanent products
- aptitude tests
- achievement tests
- intelligence tests

It must be emphasized that no single assessment instrument should be used alone to produce an educational decision. Rather, a battery of supportive measures may provide a broader and more precise view of the learner's characteristics. Sabatino and Miller (1979) provide comprehensive views of these techniques.

Establishing Short-Term and Long-Term Objectives

Short-term objectives are brief, instructional units or tasks that collectively comprise the terminal or long-term objective. Short-term objectives may be further divided by the steps in a task analysis. The size or the steps in the task analysis and the magnitude of the short-term objective may change from learner to learner. As a general rule, the more competent the student the larger the instructional steps. Exhibit 5–2 displays the steps in

Exhibit 5–2 Task Analysis and Short-Term Objectives for Students of Different Ability Levels

Student One	Student Two
1. Grasp pencil in right hand.	1. Position pencil and paper for writing.
2. Position pencil between thumb and index finger, resting on middle finger.	2. Write O on the first line one inch from the left margin.
3. Place paper at a slight angle to body.	3. Write L to the right of the O by 1/8″.
4. Hold top corner of paper with left hand.	4. Write an I to the right of the L by 1/8″.
5. Place pencil tip on top of line.	5. Continue until all letters are written.
6. Complete a circular motion with constant pressure on the pencil forming the letter O.	6. Repeat steps 1-5 on the next line down until name is written 10 times.
7. Repeat steps 1–6 on the next line down until the letter O is written 10 times.	
Write first initial of name—*Oliver*.	Write first name—*Oliver*.

a task analysis for a very capable youth in contrast with a task analysis for a more severely handicapped individual. If the task analysis assigned for student one were implemented with student two or vice versa, frustration, failure, boredom, disinterest, or other negative emotional reactions may occur. Thus, the size of the steps in the task analysis as well as the short-term objective must be carefully considered.

As was discussed previously, the long-term objectives should result from a logical sequence of short-term objectives. In the preceding example, the long-term objective for student one may be to write his first name. For student two it may be to address an envelope. The student will be more likely to work through short-term objectives to accomplish some functional and desirable long-term objective. The student should be aware of this sequence and the final skill that will be accomplished.

Establishing a Criterion for Success

To a large extent the teacher dictates the criterion for success through the size of the steps in the task analysis, short-term objective, and long-term objective. Beyond this, however, the teacher has a considerable amount of discretion in evaluating the quality of the resulting performance. A student may successfully write a short story with several misspelled words and frequent tense shifts. The educator should be aware of the level of performance that the child or youth is capable of producing through the instructional unit. The evaluation should reflect the extent to which the student approached this level as opposed to how he or she compared to other students.

The practice of establishing a criterion for success based on the norm is probably defeating not only for the handicapped but also for the more capable learner. The inability of the educator to establish performance expectations based on the student's characteristics not only insures failure for the handicapped but also fails to challenge the more capable learner. Performance problems among the gifted have repeatedly been attributed to a lack of challenge in educational pursuits (Walker, 1978).

Identifying Motivating Consequences

Not all students, and particularly not the handicapped, are intrinsically motivated to learn (Harter & Zigler, 1974). In the absence of intrinsic motivation for academic pursuits, the child or youth is likely to engage in more satisfying activities. Often these activities interfere with the instructional process not only for the handicapped student but also for others in the classroom setting. The educator must be skilled in identifying the motivational characteristics of the learner and adopting motivational strategies that maintain performance.

Motivational strategies fall on a continuum from "intrinsic" (e.g., the task is reinforcing in and of itself) to "highly intrusive" and "primitive" (e.g., task performance results in the delivery of an edible reinforcer). Adopting motivational procedures that are excessively advanced for a student may result in nonperformance. Adopting excessively intrusive procedures may undermine the learner's higher motivational level. Therefore, the educator must be aware of the motivational characteristics of the individual learner, and educational activities should reflect this assessment. Chapter 8 will present a more detailed analysis of assessing and altering students' motivational characteristics.

Cue Procedures

Cueing procedures involve manipulating sensory stimuli in order to prompt desirable responses or correct an undesirable response. A card containing the multiplication tables may be used as a cue for use with workbook assignments. The verbal cue, "it sounds like sheep," may be a cue for an oral reading activity. As with motivational procedures, cue procedures may be placed in a hierarchy based upon intrusiveness. Cues that are established and operated by the learner, including dictionaries, reference books, etc., under many circumstances are minimally intrusive. Cues actively provided by the teacher, such as verbal prompts and physical guidance, are more intrusive.

The educator should be aware of the level of cues required to insure success for the learner. Failure to use necessary cues may produce failure.

An overreliance on unnecessary or excessively intrusive cues will not only produce boredom, but also may undermine the student's ability to benefit from more subtle prompts. The lack of consistency in providing or failing to provide various cues does not allow the youth to anticipate the amount of assistance that will be provided. The student may produce minimal effort under subtle cue conditions because he or she anticipates a more intrusive cue. The later cue may, however, remove the responsibility for reasonable effort from the student.

Ideally, the educator should use the most natural and subtle prompt available that will promote success (80 percent of the time). As success is consistently achieved, the prompt should be faded. Returning haphazardly to more intrusive prompts should be avoided.

Review of Educational Program

The handicapped student is viewed as an active, changing learner. Appropriate educational objectives, activities, and materials adopted one quarter, semester, or year are almost certain to be inappropriate the following quarter, semester, or year. Failure of the educational program to reflect the dynamic nature of the learner may adversely influence the achievement orientation of the student. As has been repeatedly emphasized, disruptive behaviors may replace achievement-related responses.

P.L. 94-142 requires the educational team to meet each time a major program change occurs and at least annually. This schedule should be viewed as a minimum period for formal review. Informal interactions between cooperating educational personnel, the student, and parents should occur more frequently.

In addition, individual service providers should informally evaluate the student's program continually. There is a propensity for teachers to review educational procedures and objectives only when a problem occurs. By that time, the student has already initiated a self-defeating learning cycle. The results of crisis reviews are typically to exclude the student from educational services or remove inappropriate educational demands that promoted disruptive behaviors. While the second outcome is obviously more satisfactory, the student is likely to overgeneralize that disruptions produce the removal of all educational demands. The next time the classroom environment (whether appropriately or inappropriately structured) becomes unpleasant, the student may be likely to engage in similar disruptive behavior.

Frequent evaluation of the educational program enhances the teacher's ability to maintain the 80 percent or better success rate associated with an achievement orientation. Continuous evaluation allows the teacher to manage the educational environment, predicting, to the extent possible, events that will promote positive, social behavior. This approach may be contrasted with a reactive posture in which educational provisions are dictated by nonpupil specific legislation (i.e., once-a-year planning) or by the rate and intensity of isolated, disruptive responses (i.e., crisis planning).

Classroom Schedule

Few, if any, components of the classroom structure can have as dramatic an influence on social competence as the classroom schedule. The classroom schedule is the framework within which all instruction occurs. It translates instructional goals and objectives into actual classroom practice. Further, it serves as an advanced organizer that allows the student, teacher, ancillary personnel, and others involved in the educational program to predict what will occur during the school day. It must be emphasized that the classroom schedule *is not* a piece of paper on which times and activities are planned. Rather, it is the actual time that activities occur. However, there should be a close relationship between the written schedule and actual schedule. Facets of the classroom schedule that directly impact social performance are highlighted by Rotter's (1954) derivation of social learning theory. Rotter equates the probability that a behavior will occur with the expectancy for success and reinforcement. Students who have had a history of well-planned academic activities that frequently resulted in success are likely to approach future academic activities. Conversely, students whose academic activities have frequently been interrupted, altered, or terminated prior to success and reinforcement are less likely to approach future activities (Keogh, Cahill, & MacMillan, 1972; Mercer & Snell, 1977). Task interruption for the handicapped may result from: (1) the occurrence of disruptive behaviors that result in the withdrawal of the scheduled classroom activity; (2) the failure of the learner to persist in the activity until the end of the scheduled period (most often in the case of an undesirable activity); (3) the desire of the learner to continue into the next scheduled period in order to complete the activity (most often in the case of a desirable activity); and (4) spontaneous changes in the classroom routine that result from unplanned events (e.g., fire drill, unexpected visitor, unplanned absence).

Each of these events reduces the extent to which a written schedule and actual classroom events correspond. Further, they allow unplanned and nonbeneficial contingency arrangements to enter the classroom (e.g., "When I forget my pencil, I don't have to do math," or "When I talk out, I avoid oral reading."). It is unrealistic to expect 100 percent correspondence because of uncontrollable events suggested by item four. However, a reasonably high correspondence rate can be readily achieved by controlling events one through three. Guidelines for controlling these events include the following.

- The teacher should work with each student to develop a visible schedule that contains the student's name, the responsibilities of the teacher or ancillary personnel, the educational activity, and the setting. The actual format for the schedule should be age appropriate. Secondary students may use an appointment book; primary students may have a poster on the wall.
- The schedule should be revised on a regular basis. Some events may be entered a week in advance; others may be entered daily. The educator should avoid altering the schedule at other times, especially after disruptive incidents.
- To the extent possible, the child or youth should be involved in developing the schedule. Primary students may simply color their schedules. Secondary youths may plan 80 to 100 percent of the activities for the day or week. This is a very important self-control skill. Also, a recognition that the youth prepared his or her own schedule may be used as a back-up should the student resist participating in an activity.
- The teacher must avoid allowing the student to participate in non-scheduled activities. At the very least, the learner should remain idle in the setting in which the scheduled activity is expected to be pursued.
- The teacher should identify on the schedule pleasant back-up activities that may be conducted upon premature completion of the scheduled activities. (E.g., "When you complete the math problems during this period, you may work crossword puzzles.") This forms a naturally reinforcing consequence for early task completion.
- The teacher must avoid allowing the child or youth to avoid unpleasant scheduled activities when disruptive. Providing a time for the student to make up scheduled work missed while he or she was disruptive will insure that disruptions do not assist the child or youth in avoiding work.
- The teacher should plan scheduled periods so that the student may attain task completion and reinforcement during the scheduled period. Tasks that are not brought to closure during a scheduled period may be viewed as a failure by the handicapped (Keogh, Cahill, & MacMillan, 1972; Mercer & Snell, 1977).
- Pleasant and unpleasant scheduled activities should be alternated. In this manner, completion of an unpleasant event naturally results in the initiation of a pleasant event.

- The schedule should be set up in intervals appropriate to the child or youth's attention span. Young children and severely handicapped learners may benefit from 15-minute schedule intervals. Mildly handicapped adolescents may benefit from scheduling commensurate with actual class periods.
- The teacher should work with the student's parents to encourage the scheduling of evening activities.

Integrated Counseling

Counseling in isolated settings requires the handicapped student to: (1) remember events that led to performance difficulties; (2) associate emotional responses with those events; (3) consider a motive for the resulting behavior; (4) evaluate the efficacy of the behavior; (5) identify potential alternatives for the behavior; (6) evaluate the alternative; (7) form a judgment regarding how to behave in the future; and (8) act on that judgment in future events. This process belies the limited abstract thinking, language, short-term and long-term memory, and other cognitive skills of many handicapped students. Because of these deficiencies, counseling sessions conducted in isolated settings (e.g., a clinical center or counselor's office) are not likely to produce behavior changes that generalize to classroom environments.

An alternative to the practice of conducting isolated counseling sessions is to integrate counseling activities into the classroom setting. This practice addresses a number of the cognitive limitations of the handicapped learner. Integrated counseling encourages the student to process his or her response to environmental events as they occur. In this manner, the dependence on abstract thinking, short-term and long-term memory, and complex language is minimized. Rather than waiting for a weekly counseling session and then attempting to recall social-personal issues, the student is prompted to deal with the issues under immediate and concrete conditions.

Integrated counseling may take a variety of forms depending on the existing classroom structure and available resources. A combination of the following may be ideal:

- The counselor conducts group counseling sessions in the classroom with the teacher present. The teacher then follows up under natural classroom conditions.
- The counselor conducts individual sessions in an isolated setting. The student and counselor jointly prepare a counseling report that is given to the teacher so that the teacher can follow up under natural classroom conditions (Refer to Exhibit 5–3 for an example).

Exhibit 5–3 Counseling Report Prepared Jointly by the Counselor and Student

Student _____	
Counselor _____	
Date _____	
Issue(s) discussed:	Frequent tardiness to English class.
Resolution of issue:	Five tardies will result in a failing grade. If English is failed, it will have to be taken over. It would be inconvenient for me to take English over.
Behavior change expected:	Tardiness to English often results from spending too much time talking to friends in the hallway. It would be better to avoid talking to friends before class in the hall and to talk to them after class. Mrs. (teacher) is encouraged to prompt me to come to class on time.

- The teacher conducts individual counseling sessions and follows up under natural classroom conditions.

Interaction with Nonhandicapped Peers

A substantial body of research has been amassed demonstrating that children and adolescents learn by observing others (Bandura, 1973). Peer interactions form an essential variable in the educational environment of the handicapped. The availability of socially competent peer models provides the opportunity for handicapped learners to benefit from structured interactions. These opportunities may not be available if the student's models are limited to peers with similar handicaps.

This position has been supported by literature indicating that reducing social isolation and stigmatization contributes to the social development of exceptional students (Sabatino, 1972). The ability to manage the amount of time spent by the student with nonhandicapped peers enables the teacher to engineer the gradual return of the student to the mainstream. Creswell (1973) suggests that this approach not only prepares the handicapped learner but also his or her nonhandicapped peers. Budoff and Gottlieb (1974) support this view through their observation that mainstreamed educably mentally retarded students tend to become more internally controlled and reflective in regular class environments. Similarly, Blum (1971) demonstrated that exceptional students who were mainstreamed adapted to the regular classroom setting following initial adjustment problems. The author further demonstrated that the handicapped students could be taught to interact more effectively with their peers.

Family Involvement

There is undeniable evidence that families play a critical role in the social development process of handicapped learners. Conger (1977) summarizes this data arguing that "An increasing body of empirical data indicates that the single most important external influence . . . in the accomplishment of developmental tasks . . . is (the youth's) parents" (p. 221).

Frequent teacher-parent interactions can be positive and mutually beneficial. There is little question that social development objectives addressed in the school setting may be carried out at home. Wehman, Abramson, and Norman (1977) have identified parent implementation of social development programs to be important in promoting the generalization and maintenance of behavior change. The authors argue that parental involvement enhances the possibility that the child or youth will develop social-personal skills that extend beyond the school setting.

Often parents' history of difficulties with school personnel may lead to initial resistance in collaborating with the teacher. This condition emphasizes the need for educators to acquire and use effective interpersonal skills in working with the parents. The educator must be prepared to provide a clear statement and rationale for the objectives identified for the students. Program approaches adopted in school should be delineated clearly and completely. Finally, a modified version of the program that reflects the resources available in the home setting should be mutually negotiated.

The following procedures may be adopted by educators in promoting home-school coordination:

- The teacher should establish an initial meeting with the parents early in the year at a mutually convenient time and place. The teacher should *not* wait for a problem to arise prior to meeting.
- The teacher should identify for the parents the scope, plan, and purpose of the meeting.
- The teacher should review the social development objectives established in the school setting. These should have previously been agreed upon during the multidisciplinary staff conference.
- The teacher should determine whether similar or alternative objectives could be addressed in the home setting.
- The social development procedures that have been adopted in the school setting should be discussed. In addition, the teacher should present any data supporting the efficacy of the approach.
- The teacher should determine whether a modified version of the program could be extended to the home setting.

- The teacher should identify the school's responsibility in assisting the parents in conducting the home-based program.
- The teacher should identify the parents' responsibility in assisting the school in conducting the school-based program.
- An evaluation plan should be established.
- A follow-up should be planned to review progress.

ANTECEDENT CHANGE PROCEDURES

The preceding discussions have centered on planning or engineering a classroom environment to promote the social development of handicapped students. Often, in spite of the best plans, the child or youth reacts adversely to specific events. Seating arrangements, instructional materials, verbal prompts for quiet behavior, and distinct gestures are among the cues intended to signal a particular response from the students. The failure of the desired response to occur consistently indicates that the particular antecedent stimulus does not exert control over the behavior. When this is the case, the educator seeks to develop the strength of the antecedent stimulus controlling the target behavior. The teacher could simply teach the students that when the particular event occurs (e.g., the teacher says, "Be seated!"), they should behave in a specified manner (e.g., sit down).

An antecedent stimulus is an event or object that signals the occurrence or nonoccurrence of a behavior. Reinforcing stimuli increase the probability a behavior will occur while aversive stimuli are associated with a reduced rate of response. For example, a green light is a reinforcing stimulus because it cues the driver to depress the accelerator on his or her car. The presence of the principal in a classroom may be an aversive stimulus resulting in the suppression of disruptive behavior. Antecedent control occurs when a particular event (e.g., receiving a failing grade on a test) consistently affects the likelihood that a response will occur (e.g., depressive-like behavior). Antecedent change involves the systematic attempt to influence behavior by changing the controlling stimuli.

Antecedent change can be used in a planned manner to reduce the occurrence of maladaptive behaviors as well as to promote desirable responses. This may be accomplished in three ways. First, if a naturally occurring event does not cue a desirable response, the educator may develop the discriminative function of the antecedent. For example, a student may be taught to be at her desk when the first period bell is rung, or an appropriate social response to a peer's greeting may be developed. Conversely, if a naturally occurring event cues a maladaptive response, the educator may reduce the discriminative function of the event. If the half-hour period prior to recess cues a reduction in the on-task rate, an educator may teach the student to remain on-task at a consistent rate regardless of the time. Finally, events that cue predictable responses may be manipulated to increase or decrease the frequency of the response. For example, the teacher may separate two talkative students to reduce classroom disruptions.

The use of antecedent change is exemplified by a program developed for Bill, a fourteen-year-old learning-disabled adolescent. During math class Bill frequently looked out the window, around the classroom, or up at the ceiling. This off-task behavior severely limited his ability to perform in class and, subsequently, his achievement level in math was substantially below that of his classmates. In addition to other remedial tactics, his teacher decided to employ a stimulus control procedure in order to increase his on-task rate.

Prior to initiating the program the teacher observed Bill periodically for two weeks. Each time Bill was off-task for an extended period of time, she would record the events that preceded the off-task episode. Similarly, when Bill remained on-task for an extended period of time, she would record the events that occurred during the on-task time. The teacher discovered that the stimuli that were associated with on-task behavior included math work that had a direct vocational application. Stimuli associated with off-task behavior included the immediate presence of his best friend, window shades being open, repetitious problem sets with no direct application, unstructured time, and no stated deadline for work completion.

In order to establish stimuli that would maximize Bill's on-task rate, the teacher made several changes in the class structure. First, Bill was moved from the windows, the shades were closed to block his view, and Bill's friend was seated in the opposite corner of the room. Bill's math time was structured so that he knew in advance the work that was expected, the time in which it was to be completed, and the consequences for completion. Finally, the teacher discontinued using repetitious worksheets in lieu of work that had an obvious vocational function. As Bill's on-task rate improved, the instructional conditions were gradually changed to reflect the preprogram conditions (e.g., the window shades were opened, the seating arrangement made more flexible, etc.).

The importance of observing the learner's behavior in relation to naturally occurring antecedents is highlighted in this example. Antecedent change procedures are based on the careful assessment of events that may be manipulated in order to produce desirable behavior. Randomly or haphazardly changing classroom or work conditions in hopes of changing a student's behavior will produce mixed results at best. Continuous recording, described in Chapter 8, is a critical tool for maximizing the effect of an antecedent change program.

While an antecedent change program may be highly effective, removing a provoking stimulus may not be in the best interest of the student. Such is the case when a student is indefinitely removed from large group activities because of disruptive behavior. The approach may reduce the likelihood that he or she will act out, but it does very little to teach positive ways of behaving under similar stimulus conditions. Thus, while many behaviors may be influenced through antecedent change programs, the educator must consider the importance of developing positive social behaviors in the face of provoking events. As in the previous illustration, an effective strategy may be to limit the provoking stimuli to the extent that the adolescent succeeds. Once the student develops an achievement orientation through success and praise, the provoking stimuli may be gradually reintroduced.

Procedures for educators to follow when designing and implementing an antecedent change program include the following:

- The teacher should conduct continuous recording as described in Chapter 8.
- Stimuli that are associated with the occurrence of adaptive responses should be identified.
- The environment should be arranged so that stimuli that support adaptive behavior are increased while stimuli associated with maladaptive behavior are reduced.
- Once an acceptable rate of the target behavior(s) is established, the teacher should fade unnatural stimuli supporting adaptive behavior and reintroduce stimuli previously associated with maladaptive responses.

CONCLUSIONS

Antecedent control has been described as a procedure whereby events hypothesized to provoke disruptive behaviors are removed while events associated with prosocial responses are intensified. General antecedents for prosocial behavior have been identified and discussed. Sending skills, receiving skills, and directive interactions that may enhance the teacher-student relationship were described as critical foundations for positive social responses in the classroom. Specific classroom structures including functional and age-appropriate objectives, activities, and materials; systematic instructional procedures; frequent review of the educational program; a visible classroom schedule; integrated counseling; interaction with nonhandicapped peers; and family involvement were identified as potential antecedents for prosocial responses when managed properly. When poorly designed, they may be antecedents for disruptive responses. Finally, antecedent change procedures were discussed as an approach to identifying and altering potentially provoking stimuli.

Chapter 6

Related Personal Characteristics

The preceding chapter discussed procedures for altering students' social behavior by controlling antecedent conditions. Antecedent control strategies remove the student from environmental events that provoke disruptive responses, replacing these events with emotionally enhancing conditions. It was emphasized throughout that these procedures *do not* teach the child or youth to behave appropriately when faced with noxious events. In fact, antecedent control procedures used in isolation may restrict the student from learning alternative responses to the provoking events. The example was used in which a child placed on permanent homebound instruction was unable to engage in disruptive classroom behavior. Unfortunately, it is unlikely that this placement will teach the student to interact appropriately in a classroom setting.

A major guideline for using antecedent control procedures that remove the student from common environmental demands was to ensure the gradual return of potentially provoking antecedents commensurate with the student's ability to respond appropriately. The intervention point that promotes the student's ability to adjust to increasingly more demanding environments addresses related personal characteristics. (See Figure 6–1.) The entry point, related personal characteristics, develops skills that mediate between provoking antecedents and disruptive responses. When successfully developed, they permit the student to engage in a desirable response that undermines the need to be disruptive.

Relaxation skills, for example, may permit a youth to take a stress-producing test rather than being truant to avoid the test. Interpersonal skills may allow a student to negotiate a loan with a peer rather than stealing lunch money. In each case, the development of related personal characteristics provided the student with a skill that reduced the likelihood that a maladaptive response would occur.

119

Figure 6–1 Relationship among Related Characteristics and Other Intervention Facets

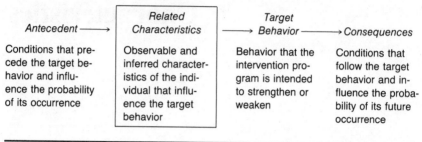

The three major related personal characteristics that will be considered in this chapter are emotional learning, interpersonal skill training, and behavioral self-control training. As with the other social learning approaches, these procedures will be discussed from a classroom application perspective. The integration of these procedures with antecedent and consequent control strategies will be highlighted.

EMOTIONAL LEARNING

Current diagnostic and classification practices emphasize the existence of excessive or deficit emotional characteristics in the identification and classification of behavior disorders. Conduct disorders are defined, in part, by temper disturbances, irritability, and moodiness. Personality disorders are defined by anxiety, fear, tension, timidity, sadness, embarrassment, frustration, and reticence (Quay, 1979). It is apparent that difficulties in emotional expression characterize a substantial number of handicapped children and youths (Gardner, 1977). Therefore, intervention approaches designed to mediate between provoking antecedents and disruptive responses are of critical concern.

The principles and procedures described in this section have been designed to promote positive emotional expression for handicapped children and youths. Prior to recent years, these techniques were reserved for use by psychologists and psychiatrists (Reese, Howard, & Reese, 1978). Present authors emphasize the importance of continuously supporting emotional growth beyond the treatment provided in isolated therapy experiences (Martin & Pear, 1978). There is an increasing demand for "frontline" practitioners to gain expertise in applying emotional learning principles and techniques with the handicapped (Gardner, 1977). To meet this need the present section will: (1) detail the basic social learning principles that promote emotional expression; and (2) describe general and specific procedures that may be applied in educational settings to reduce excessive, negative, emotional reactions and promote positive, emotional expression.

Operant vs. Respondent Learning

The majority of strategies described in this volume are based primarily on an operant conditioning or learning paradigm. The underlying principle of the operant learning model is that behavior is influenced by its consequences. Reinforcing consequences strengthen or maintain behavior, while punishing consequences decrease or extinguish behavior. Observations of children and youths have indicated that not all behavior patterns are controlled through operant principles. This is particularly true of emotional responses. For example, sadness and distress are seldom produced to gain satisfaction, rather they are uncontrollable responses elicited or cued by an event. The individual is not acting on the environment to produce satisfaction, as is the case in operant learning. The environment acts on the individual to produce an uncontrollable emotional response. Learning that results from the environment eliciting an emotional response is referred to as respondent conditioning. (Pavlovian conditioning and classical conditioning are used synonymously with respondent conditioning.) Respondent learning (or emotional learning as it will be referred to here) is contrasted with operant learning in Figure 6–2.

Figure 6–2 Respondent vs. Operant Learning

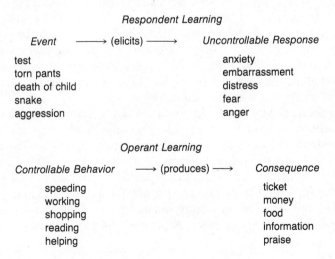

Respondent Learning

Event ⟶ (elicits) ⟶ *Uncontrollable Response*

test	anxiety
torn pants	embarrassment
death of child	distress
snake	fear
aggression	anger

Operant Learning

Controllable Behavior ⟶ (produces) ⟶ *Consequence*

speeding	ticket
working	money
shopping	food
reading	information
helping	praise

While the preceding discussion has highlighted the differences between respondent and operant learning, it must be pointed out that complex behavior patterns often result from both learning paradigms. For example, a depressed youth may cry as the automatic result of social criticism (respondent). His crying results in a reduction of criticism from people concerned for the youth's welfare. Subsequently, the youth cries in a variety of dissimilar situations in order to avoid criticism (operant). In this example, the initial crying response was elicited by the environment as an uncontrollable (respondent) emotional reaction. The consequences of crying resulted in an increase in controllable or operant crying behavior. For the purpose of clarity, the remainder of this section will view emotional or respondent learning as being distinct. Other chapters in this volume will suggest approaches to integrating respondent and operant techniques.

Learned vs. Unlearned Emotional Responses

At birth, events that satisfy basic biological needs automatically produce emotional responses. These are referred to as *unlearned* emotional responses as they occur reflexively or without the benefit of previous experiences. For example, temperature extremes, hunger, thirst, bright lights, etc. automatically elicit distress in an infant. Similarly, warmth, food, water, caressing, removing physical irritants, etc. elicit pleasure. These emotional responses occur automatically and thus are said to be unlearned.

As the infant grows older, a variety of new events begins to produce emotional responses. These events acquire the ability to control the child's emotions as the result of specific learning experiences. Thus, they are referred to as *learned* emotional responses. For example, grades, awards, praise, money, etc. for some individuals produce or elicit feelings of pleasure. In contrast, fines, criticism, failure, etc. for some youths elicit unpleasant feelings. While the set of unlearned emotional responses is the same for all people, learned emotional responses vary across people as the result of individual learning histories.

In general, children and adolescents raised in warm and supportive environments who have had frequent opportunities to engage in satisfying relationships and observe others engage in similar relationships acquire appropriate and enhancing patterns of emotional response. Conversely, children and adolescents who have repeatedly faced uncontrollable, noxious stimuli, whose interactions with adult models are characteristically punitive, and who are frequently isolated from supportive social experiences often develop less desirable, emotional characteristics (Gardner, 1977).

As has been emphasized, both positive and negative emotional responses are learned. An understanding of the principles that influence emotional learning will help the practitioner to: (1) structure learning environments that promote positive emotional development; and (2) structure intensive learning experiences that counter condition or diminish the ability of an event to elicit negative emotionality and increase its ability to promote positive emotional responses. The following section will review and discuss the basic principles that underlie emotional learning.

Rules Governing the Acquisition of Emotional Responses

At birth, very few events elicit an emotional response. As the child grows older, an increasing number of events acquire emotionally arousing properties. The basic rule of emotional learning that explains the ability of a neutral event to acquire emotional control is as follows: A neutral event, paired repeatedly with an emotionally provoking event, will begin to produce the same emotional response when presented alone. The basic rule of emotional learning explains the way in which a mother's voice becomes soothing to a child. The mother's voice, which was neutral to the child at birth, is paired repeatedly with a variety of unlearned emotional events (e.g., food, warmth, removal of irritants, etc.). These pairings occur as the mother talks to the child while changing diapers, feeding, and dressing. Eventually, the mother's voice elicits the same emotional reaction as the unlearned events. Thus, the neutral event (mother's voice) is paired repeatedly with events that produce emotional responses (food, warmth, removal of irritants) and soon the mother's voice alone produces the emotional response.

Events that become pleasing to a child or adolescent through higher order conditioning are referred to as *secondary reinforcing events* when they are effective in strengthening operant behavior. As will be discussed in the next chapter, praise, grades, money, social status, etc. are defined as secondary reinforcing events if they strengthen behavior. Their effectiveness as positive consequences is directly related to the extent to which they have been paired with other learned or unlearned emotional responses. This principle explains why the careful practitioner *always* pairs primary reinforcing events (e.g., candy, pop, ice cream, etc.) with potential secondary reinforcing events (e.g., praise, money, grades, etc.). This practice increases the reinforcer strength of the paired events through the basic rule of emotional learning and the rule of higher order conditioning.

It is not always possible to identify the specific events that have led to the development of an emotional reaction. For example, a child may become fearful in the presence of a lion even though he or she has never been injured by a lion. This process is explained through the rule of vi-carious conditioning, which states that an emotional reaction to a neutral stimulus may result from observing another individual's emotional response to a similar stimulus. Vicarious conditioning, or the acquisition of an emo-tional response through observation, can occur through the media as well as direct observation. Television shows, still pictures, radio announce-ments, and conversations with friends all may result in the development of a learned emotional response. Additionally, an individual's mental image of an event may produce a learned emotional reaction. This process has been referred to as *emotive imagery*.

Another way in which unfamiliar events may cue an emotional reaction is described in the rule of stimulus and semantic generalization. Events that are similar to emotionally provoking events or that are described with the same verbal labels, may begin to produce a similar emotional reaction to the reaction produced by the emotionally provoking event.

This rule includes two factors that may lead to stimulus generalization: (1) the degree to which the new event is physically similar to the emotionally provoking event; and (2) the degree to which two events are described through the same verbal labels (semantics). Objects or events that are very similar on the basis of physical inspection (e.g., 1957 Chevies, school books, threshing machines, elevators, etc.) are susceptible to stimulus generali-zation. A series of fun dates in one 1957 Chevy is likely to result in a positive emotional reaction to all 1957 Chevies. In another example, if an individual is seriously injured by a baseball, he or she is likely to develop a generalized fear of all baseballs. The greater the difference in physical appearance between the two objects or events, the less likely this stimulus generalization will occur. A fear of a 1957 Chevy is less likely to generalize to older cars, and even less likely to generalize to all cars.

Semantic generalization suggests that objects or events with dissimilar physical characteristics but common verbal labels may produce similar emotional responses. For example, a youth may have a generalized dislike for any individual described as *police officer*. The initial dislike for police officers may have resulted from a negative emotional experience with one or two policemen. Subsequent to this, any individual described by the label *police officer* produces a similar emotional response although the individual may differ in appearance (e.g., size, race, sex, clothes, age, facial hair, etc.). Semantic or verbal labels that produce generalized positive or neg-ative emotional reactions for many youths, depending on their experiences, include *principal, teacher, judge, official, coach, reverend, boss, counselor,* and *social worker*.

Rules Governing the Strength and Persistence of Emotional Reactions

The preceding principles have identified environmental influences that promote emotional learning. They suggest that emotional responses, other than primitive or unlearned emotionality present at birth, result from: (1) the pairing of an emotionally provoking event with a neutral event; (2) the observation of another individual's emotional response to a neutral event; and (3) the generalization from one emotionally provoking event to other events that are similar in appearance or carry the same verbal label. It is apparent that the emotional reactions of one individual to different stimuli or for two individuals toward the same stimulus often vary in intensity. Verbal admonishments from an authority figure may produce a highly emotional crying episode for one youth while resulting in a slight frown for another. Similarly, the persistence of an emotional reaction may vary substantially. One child's moodiness may subside in a short period of time while another remains highly emotional through adolescence.

Two closely associated rules account for the strength and persistence of learned emotional responses. The first focuses on the intensity of the emotional response that was paired with the neutral event. As such, it is referred to as the rule of intensity. This rule is stated as follows: The stronger the emotional response produced by the paired event, the stronger the emotional response that will be produced by the previously neutral event.

Events that produce very intense, emotional reactions require few pairings (often only one) to condition negative emotional reactions to neutral events. For example, a tornado may hit a neighborhood destroying a couple's home and injuring their child. Subsequent severe storms, reports of tornado sightings, media weather alerts, etc. may produce fairly strong feelings of fear, anxiety, alarm, and stress. Another couple may experience a severe thunderstorm in which lightning and high winds destroy an oak tree. Given the relatively minor intensity of this emotional event, subsequent storm-related experiences may produce, at most, a mild, emotional response.

The second rule that governs the intensity and persistence of learned emotionality addresses the frequency of pairings between the emotionally provoking event and the neutral event. It is referred to as the rule of frequence of pairings in emotional learning. This rule is stated as follows: The more often a neutral event is paired with an emotionally provoking event, the stronger and more persistent the eventual emotional response will be to the neutral event.

Corporal punishment delivered to a child one or two times through grade school will probably do very little (in and of itself) to condition a negative, emotional response to school. On the other hand, corporal punishment delivered several times a semester will undoubtedly cause the child to develop a strong and persistent negative, emotional response toward school. Similarly, infrequently pairing social praise with edible reinforcers will do very little to develop social praise as a conditioned secondary reinforcing event. The frequent association between food and praise will increase the likelihood that praise will develop reinforcing qualities.

It should be clear that children and adolescents with learning histories characterized by *frequent* associations with *intense* negative, emotionally arousing events (e.g., corporal punishment, physical abuse, loss of cherished items or events, failure, etc.) are likely to develop intense and persistent maladaptive emotional reactions to a range of events (e.g., criticism, school, authority figures, compliance requests, peer taunts, family conflicts, etc.). Knowing the principles by which these disruptive, emotional reactions have formed is useful only in that practitioners can translate them into re-educative strategies. Therefore, a final set of rules will be considered that addresses the modification of existing emotional repertoires.

The Development of Alternative Emotional Responses

It is well known by members of the helping professions that children's and adolescents' emotional characteristics are not static. Once formed, emotional responses are subject to change through new learning experiences. This is exemplified by competent and enthusiastic swimmers who, at an early age, were deathly afraid of water. A less encouraging example is the high school drop-out whose feelings toward school in the primary and preprimary grades were very positive.

Beyond the initial set of rules that described the acquisition of emotional responses, a set of rules can be advanced that considers the ways in which emotions may be changed. The first rule is termed *the rule of counter conditioning* because it describes the process by which a conditioned or learned emotional reaction may be diminished by arranging for the simultaneous occurrence of an incompatible expression. The rule of counter conditioning is if an emotionally provoking event is paired frequently with a more intense incompatible emotional response, the event will lose its ability to elicit the original response and may begin to produce the incompatible response.

Arranging for children to take tests (cue for anxiety) when relaxed and happy (incompatible emotional response) may result in testing situations losing their ability to elicit anxiety. Another example of the rule of counter conditioning practiced for years by barbers involves awarding children lollipops (cue for an incompatible emotional response) during haircuts (cue for agitation).

The rule of counter conditioning emphasizes that the incompatible response must be more intense than the emotionality resulting from provoking events. Applying this rule without considering the relative strength of the two emotional reactions may result in the pleasant event losing its ability to elicit positive emotionality because of the association with a more intense negative emotional reaction. A child who is extremely afraid of haircuts may develop a strong distaste for lollipops rather than becoming less fearful of the barber.

The ill-advised application of this principle may have more severe side effects in other cases. For example, pairing a variety of moderately pleasant events (e.g., riding in the car, being with parents, eating at a restaurant, etc.) with going to school for a school-phobic child may result in each of these events losing its ability to produce positive emotionality. Procedures for counter conditioning extreme emotional reactions that avoid this problem will be discussed later.

The second rule that governs the modification of existing emotional responses is referred to as the rule of extinction. Extinction involves a gradual reduction or elimination of the learned emotional response associated with an event. The rule of extinction states that if an event has acquired the ability to elicit an emotional response through pairings with another emotionally provoking event, repeatedly presenting the original event without the paired event will gradually diminish the effectiveness of the original event in producing the learned emotional response.

For example, having received a number of citations for speeding, an individual may become emotionally aroused at the sound of a police siren. If, over a number of subsequent occasions, the police sirens do not result in a citation (i.e., they produce warnings, are directed to another motorist, etc.), the sirens will gradually lose the ability to elicit an emotional reaction. In another example, if a child has "belly flopped" from a diving board, the child may be afraid to again approach the board. If, through encouragement from his or her parents, the child dives several times from the board without belly flopping, the fear of diving will diminish. Finally, an adolescent who has experienced repeated failure in school may develop a negative emotional reaction toward educational settings. A well-designed, special education program may remove the association of failure with school and gradually diminish the disposition of the school to elicit negative emotionality.

The major factor that influences the rate of extinction is the level of previous learning. As was discussed in previous rules, this is a function of the number of pairings required to produce the emotional reaction and the intensity of the paired event. Emotional learning that has occurred through repeated associations of the previously neutral event with intense emotionally provoking stimuli is highly resistant to extinction. Emotional learning that results from occasional pairings with a mildly provoking event may be extinguished in substantially few trials.

Finally, it is important to note that time and maturation alone will not alter an emotional response. The old axiom "he/she will grow out of it" has little basis in fact. Changes in emotional expression occur only through: (1) new emotional learning; (2) counter conditioning; and (3) extinction. Therefore, practitioners concerned for the emotional development of exceptional children and youth must be prepared to design learning environments that promote change in emotional expression. The following sections will present such strategies.

Emotional Learning Strategies

All behavior is learned through a common set of learning principles. Treatment involves using the learning principles that may have developed maladaptive responses to promote prosocial behavior. Just as operant techniques have resulted from a set of empirical learning principles, the emotional learning strategies are based on rules identified in laboratory and applied settings that have been demonstrated to govern emotional learning and expression. Therefore, the emotional learning strategies presented in this section are closely associated with the rules of emotional learning discussed in the preceding sections.

Developing New Emotional Responses

The objective of many intervention programs for the handicapped is to enhance the range and intensity of emotional expression. The withdrawn youth who is disinterested in activities that elicit positive emotionality in the general population and the aggressive youth who is apathetic toward a variety of potentially emotionally enhancing events benefit equally from strategies that develop their positive emotional responsiveness to social activities, achievement situations, and so on. The basic strategy to promote emotional learning for these youths is enumerated as follows:

1. The event that fails to produce a positive, emotional response must be identified.
2. An event or events that reliably produce the desired emotional response must be specified.

3. Situations must be structured in which the two events occur simultaneously (i.e., are paired) on repeated occasions.

For example, a program objective was established for an adolescent learning-disabled girl that emphasized the development of satisfying emotional responses to interactions with teachers. Anecdotal reports indicated that the young lady thoroughly enjoyed trips to the commissary. This event invariably elicited a pleasant disposition from the youth. A program was designed whereby a specific staff member would walk with her each day to the commissary. It was expected that pairing the neutral event (staff member) with the learned emotional event (going to the commissary) would eventually result in the staff member acquiring the ability to produce the same emotional response.

A related strategy, effective in producing new emotional responses, results from the rule of vicarious conditioning. In general, this strategy relies on evidence that emotional reactions may be acquired through observation as well as direct experience. Vicarious conditioning may be conducted as follows:

1. The event that fails to produce a positive, emotional response must be specified.
2. Situations in which other individuals exhibit positive emotional responses to the same event must be identified.
3. Arrangements should be made for the child or youth to observe the other individuals in these situations.

For example, John was disinterested in sports activities conducted by his school program. His parents were concerned that he enjoyed few events participated in by his peers. The community mental health agency's social worker recommended that the parents arrange for John to attend as many "exciting" competitive sports activities as possible. It was hoped that John would develop pleasant feelings toward sports activities as the result of observing a number of other individuals gaining satisfaction from participation.

Reducing Excessive Emotional Responses

In addition to enhancing a youth's range of emotional responsiveness, emotional learning strategies may also be designed to reduce excessive negative emotional reactions. The basic tool for modifying existing emotional reactions was described in a previous rule as counter conditioning. This procedure involves repeatedly presenting the emotionally provoking event with a more intense incompatible emotional response. This procedure has been demonstrated to reduce excessive emotional responses and sometimes results in the substitution of the incompatible response. The basic guidelines for using counter conditioning are as follows:

1. The event that elicits the excessive emotional response must be identified.
2. An event that elicits a *stronger* incompatible emotional response must be identified.
3. Arrangements must be made for the two events to occur simultaneously (e.g., discuss the death of a family member in a comfortable and relaxed manner).
4. As an alternative, arrangements can be made for the event that produces the incompatible emotional response to precede the provoking event (e.g., conduct relaxation training exercises immediately prior to public speaking class).

The rule of counter conditioning requires that the incompatible response be stronger than the maladaptive response. If this is not the case, the positive response may be extinguished.

For example, a young girl's fear of men may be counter conditioned by arranging for male friends of her parents to take her to a variety of pleasant activities on evenings and weekends. In this case, her fear reaction should not be more intense than the pleasant feelings derived from the activities. If they were, she would become alarmed each time she approached these events, regardless if a male were present.

Counter conditioning may also be combined with vicarious learning to reduce excessive emotional reactions. This procedure involves arranging for the individual to observe other students express positive emotional responses to events that are provoking to the individual. It is expected that the child's or youth's fears will diminish as the result of observing the learned emotional event produce an incompatible positive response in others. This process can be arranged as follows:

1. The event that elicits the excessive emotional reaction must be specified.
2. Situations in which other individuals exhibit incompatible emotional responses to the same event must be identified.
3. Arrangements must be made for the child or youth to observe the other individuals in those situations.

For example, a young man's fear of water may be reduced by arranging a number of outings to public beaches. His observations that water (provoking stimulus) produces delight in others (incompatible emotional response) is expected to gradually reduce the fear response.

A final tactic that has been demonstrated to be effective in reducing extreme emotional reactions is termed *desensitization*. This procedure is principally designed to counter condition emotional reactions for which a sufficiently strong incompatible positive response is not available. Guidelines for implementing desensitization are as follows:

1. The child or youth should be interviewed and/or observed to determine all of the events related to the excessive emotional expression.
2. The educator should confer with the student to rank the events from least anxiety producing to most anxiety producing.
3. An incompatible emotional response should be identified.
4. The program should be initiated by arranging for the simultaneous occurrence (pairing) of the least provoking event with the incompatible emotional response.
5. These pairings should be continued until the emotional response to the event subsides.
6. Arrangements should be made for the simultaneous occurrence of the next most provoking event with the incompatible emotional response.
7. These pairings should be continued until the emotional response to the event subsides.
8. Steps six and seven should be repeated until all of the events in the hierarchy are counter conditioned.

For example, a student experienced an extreme fear of talking in public. She was asked to list all of the events that were associated with the fear. Then she was asked to rank the items from least to most fear producing. The following fear hierarchy was produced:

1. presenting "pleasant" information to one familiar person
2. presenting "pleasant" information to five familiar people at one time
3. presenting "unpleasant" information to one familiar person
4. presenting "unpleasant" information to five familiar people at one time
5. presenting "pleasant" information to one unfamiliar person
6. presenting "pleasant" information to a group of five unfamiliar people at one time
7. presenting "unpleasant" information to one unfamiliar person
8. presenting "unpleasant" information to a group of five unfamiliar people at one time

Having established the fear hierarchy, relaxation was selected as the positive emotional response used in the counter conditioning process. The actual procedure for teaching the youth to induce self-relaxation is described in the following section.

The desensitization sessions were initiated by encouraging the young woman to induce self-relaxation. Then the first event on the fear hierarchy was presented (i.e., she was requested to approach a friend and talk about the school's winning basketball season). This procedure was repeated a number of times over several days until she reported an absence of anxiety through the situation. The same procedure was then followed with the second event on the fear hierarchy (i.e., pairing relaxation with a pleasant discussion with five friends). These pairings continued until the youth reported an absence of anxiety during this event. Then, one at a time, each successive event on the fear hierarchy was paired with relaxation until it failed to produce an anxiety response. In the final step, the young woman was able to present "unpleasant" information to a group of five people without feeling anxious.

The events used in the desensitization process may be real (in vivo), as in the above example, imagined, or observed. Imagery may be used by having the youth close his or her eyes and vividly imagine the event identified on the fear hierarchy. Observation may be used by asking the individual to observe a picture or video tape of events on the hierarchy.

Developing Incompatible Emotional Responses

Excluding extinction, each of the preceding strategies relies on the youth's ability to produce a positive emotional response. In the basic rule of emotional learning, the youth must engage in a positive emotional response that is paired with a neutral event. In counter conditioning and desensitization, disruptive emotional responses are paired with incompatible emotional expressions. It is apparent that the practitioner must be able to encourage youths to produce positive emotionality in order for other systematic forms of emotional learning to occur.

Probably the most frequently cited approach for inducing positive emotional expression is the progressive muscle relaxation technique pioneered by Jacobsen (1938) and discussed more recently by Wolpe (1958) and Bernstein and Borkovec (1973). The progressive relaxation process involves systematically relaxing each of the major muscle groups. As each muscle is relaxed, the individual is asked to focus on the contrast between relaxed and tense muscles. The relaxation technique, in progressive order, is as follows:

1. The individual rests on a mat.
2. The individual is urged to "let go" and be limp.
3. The teacher checks looseness by lifting an arm and letting it fall.
4. The person breathes deeply through the nose, fills the lungs by using the diaphragm and keeping the chest still.
5. Arm relaxation involves the following:
   - The individual clenches the right fist, holds for 6 seconds, and lets go.
   - The person raises the arm, digs the elbow into the floor for six seconds, and lets go.
   - The person compares the right arm to the left arm; one is tense, the other relaxed.
   - The individual follows the same procedure with the left arm.
   - The person focuses on tension, then on the release of tension.
6. The neck and shoulders are relaxed next.
   - The individual pulls both shoulders up to the center of his or her body, holds for six seconds, and releases.
   - The person digs the chin into the chest, holds for six seconds, and releases.
   - The person pulls the head under the body as far as possible, tries to touch the nose to the mat behind, holds for six seconds, and releases.
7. Next, the face is relaxed.
   - The person raises the eyebrows, holds for six seconds, and releases.
   - The individual makes a big smile, shows all of the teeth, holds for six seconds, and releases.
   - The individual closes the eyes, raises the jaw, holds for six seconds, and releases.
   - The person focuses on any remaining tension in the face.
8. Leg relaxation is next.
   - Keeping knees straight, the person stretches the right toes and ankles, holds for six seconds, and releases.
   - The person twists toes toward the center, holds for six seconds, and releases.
   - The individual observes the difference between the right and left leg.
   - The procedure is repeated on the left leg.

9. Guided relaxation is the final step.

• The person concentrates, one after another, on the toes, ankles, calves, thighs, buttocks, abdomen, chest, neck, fingers, wrists, forearms, biceps, shoulders, cheeks, and forehead.

• Any remaining tension is released.

Another less directive approach to producing alternative emotional responses in adolescents is "emotive-imagery." In this process, the youth imagines scenes in which positive emotional responses are exhibited. For example, the youth may imagine being proud after hitting a game-winning homerun, amused after watching a funny movie, or elated after having won a large sum of money. Use of this technique can be highly intense and structured as reported by Reese, Howard, and Reese (1978):

> One 14 year old boy with an intense fear of dogs had a burning ambition to own an Alfa Romeo and race it at the "Indianapolis 500." During the course of therapy he imagined owning the car as the therapist vividly described its beauty and action. Gradually, the anxiety producing stimulus was introduced: ". . . the speedometer is climbing into the 90's; you have a wonderful feeling of being in perfect control; you look at the trees whizzing by and you see a little dog standing next to one of them—if you feel any anxiety, just raise your finger." Eventually, the child imagines that he is showing off his car to a crowd of envious people in a strange town when a dog comes up and sniffs at his heels. (p. 195)

This technique can be used more spontaneously. For example, emotive-imagery may be used to help a youth overcome anxieties that result from an anticipated transfer to a group home and sheltered work setting. When the youth becomes anxious, the practitioner may ask him to imagine earning enough money to buy a car and imagine the pride of taking his friends for a ride.

By this point the utility of emotional learning principles and strategies in special education should be clear. Many antecedents in the school setting arouse intense negative emotional reactions in handicapped students that ultimately result in maladaptive behavior. To illustrate this point, Figure 6–3 suggests common antecedents, emotional reactions as related personal characteristics, and subsequent maladaptive responses. The preceding principles and procedures may be adapted to alter these emotional responses

Figure 6–3 Common Antecedents and Emotional Reactions As Related Personal Characteristics and Resulting Responses

Antecedent		Emotional Reaction/Related Personal Characteristic		Behavior
test	$\longrightarrow$	anxiety	$\longrightarrow$	school avoidance
peer teasing	$\longrightarrow$	anger	$\longrightarrow$	aggression
public speaking	$\longrightarrow$	distress	$\longrightarrow$	refusal to speak
physical education activity	$\longrightarrow$	fear	$\longrightarrow$	avoidance of class
homework assignment	$\longrightarrow$	indifference	$\longrightarrow$	noncompletion
planning of novel activity	$\longrightarrow$	excessive excitement	$\longrightarrow$	off-task

so that more effective behaviors may occur under the antecedent conditions.

INTERPERSONAL SKILLS TRAINING

Interpersonal skills permit individuals to gain satisfaction in conflict situations without resorting to avoidance, aggression, or other maladaptive responses. Spence and Marzillier (1979) highlight this position, arguing that disruptive behavior can be viewed in terms of a failure to learn acceptable means of social interactions. Teaching interpersonal skills is hypothesized to provide an alternative to disruptive behavior, thereby decreasing socially maladaptive responses. An analogy can be drawn between the importance of students acquiring interpersonal skills and nations employing competent diplomats. Nations that do not rely on diplomats are likely to respond to international stress through the build-up of arms and aggression. Conversely, nations with competent diplomats may respond to international stress through negotiation. Aggression here only occurs following the failure of negotiations. It may be assumed that if nations possessed more skillful diplomats and fewer generals (i.e., aggressors), there would be fewer wars.

Interpersonal skill training programs have been demonstrated to be effective in promoting characteristics that mediate between provoking antecedents and potentially disruptive behavior. One such demonstration was reported by Whitehill, Hersen, and Bellack (1980). Socially isolated students aged eight to ten were screened from an elementary school using sociometric questionnaires, peer acceptance situation performance tests, natural observations, and teacher referrals. Four children were selected to receive interpersonal skills training.

Data was collected through classroom observations on three target behaviors: 1) informative statements; 2) open-ended questions; and 3) requests for shared activity. Concurrent data was collected on pauses in speech and total speech duration. The children's overall conversational ability was rated by two judges unfamiliar with the plan or purpose of the study.

Following baseline, the students received three weeks of training with three 20- to 30-minute sessions per week. Training involved the use of modeling and rehearsing interpersonal situations that provided the child with the opportunity to meet someone and to begin and maintain conversation for a period of time. Two adult models were present in each session to guide the behavior rehearsals and serve as models. A multiple baseline across responses experimental design (see Chapter 9) was used to evaluate the program.

The study resulted in an increase in each of the target interpersonal skills. The data revealed that the trained responses were relatively independent as they improved only when training was specifically applied. Only negligible gains occurred in the posttreatment sociometric assessment of peer acceptance. The researchers suggested that this resulted from variables not controlled for in the study.

In another report, Tofte-Tipps, Mendonca, and Peach (1982) evaluated the effectiveness of an interpersonal skills training program on handicapped youths' interactions with adults. The subjects included a 14-year-old mildly retarded girl and an 11-year-old learning-disabled boy. Both had been referred to an outpatient mental health facility for the treatment of social problems in home and school settings. Each student participated in a series of role-played responses to standardized interpersonal situations. Three types of situations were used: (1) training scenes to provide a context for acquiring the skill; (2) generalization scenes to evaluate the transfer of effects to untrained role-play situations; and (3) extemporaneous conversations to evaluate the transfer of effects to natural settings.

Responses targeted for improvement included eye contact, posture, response to questions, minimal reliance on prompts, and opening remarks. Behaviors measured but not taught were speech duration, negative statements, and repetitions. Both of the students demonstrated a marked deficiency in these skills during a baseline assessment.

The results of the investigation suggested that the sequential training of the interpersonal skills produced a substantial improvement in the target responses. The authors also reported a marked increase in interpersonal skills assessed through the generalization scenes. The extemporaneous conversation assessment produced favorable results, though less dramatic.

Turner, Hersen, and Bellack (1978) reported that availability of a structured program is important to training of social skills. Highlights of such a program include (a) an emphasis on teaching of small component behaviors; (b) modeling; (c) a large amount of attention paid to students; (d) a socially reinforcing milieu wherein students receive support and attempt to display prosocial behavior; and (e) many opportunities to practice new responses.

Perry and Cerreto (1977) designed a program in response to the need to prepare institutionalized mentally retarded people for integration into community settings. A prescriptive teaching approach called structured learning therapy, which used modeling, behavior rehearsal, and social reinforcement in a group modality, was used to teach social skills to ten mentally retarded young adults. Ten matched subjects were taught the same social skills in a discussion format, and ten matched control subjects received no treatment. The probabilities of positive change differed significantly between groups in both a mealtime observation and in a structured situation test that measured social interactions. The mealtime behaviors were enhanced by structured learning training while the discussion group showed performance expected by change, and the no treatment group performance appeared to deteriorate.

Bates (1980) investigated the effectiveness of an interpersonal skills training package with 16 moderately and mildly retarded individuals. The package included 12 sessions, including the following four areas of instruction: (1) introduction and small talk; (2) asking for help; (3) differing with others; and (4) handling criticism. Methods of training used were verbal instruction, modeling, behavior rehearsal, feedback, contingent incentives, and homework. Retarded adults acquired new social skills evidenced by performance of a situation role-play assessment. Gains generalized to untrained role-play situations, but did not result in significant group differences when assessed in a natural setting.

Rychtarik and Bornstein (1979) investigated the application of social skills training to interpersonal deficits in the mentally retarded. Three target behaviors were developed: (1) eye contact; (2) conversational questions; and (3) positive conversational feedback. The individually administered behavior training program (incorporating instructions, modeling, coaching, behavior   rehearsal, video-feedback, corrective feedback, and social reinforcement) was assessed during 15 four-minute conversations with unknown, nonretarded adult conversants. For two of the three sub- jects studied, results indicated substantial increases in target behaviors with sequential introduction of the treatment strategy. Overall, conversational ability showed no practical improvement from baseline to final assessment conversations.

Hersen and Ollendick (1979) assigned 27 incarcerated juvenile delin- quents to three different groups: (1) a social skills group; (2) a discussion group; or (3) a control group. Social skills training consisted of instruction, feedback, modeling, behavior rehearsal, social reinforcement, and grad- uated homework assignments. All subjects were assessed before and after treatment on a variety of self-report, role-play, and behavioral measures. Analysis of variance for different scores indicated that the social skills group improved significantly more than the discussion and control groups, which did not differ. Results indicated that appropriate interpersonal skills were achieved; anxiety was reduced; internal locus of control was increased; and significant shifts in adjustment to the institutional program were evi- denced for the social skills group.

The effects of a social skills training program consisting of instructions, modeling, role-playing, videotaped feedback, and social reinforcement were examined by Spence and Marzillier (1979) with five adolescent boys. Train- ing led to specific improvements in certain target behaviors. It was found that whereas improvements in the performance of certain skills (e.g., ap- propriate eye contact) could be brought about relatively quickly, certain listening skills were much more difficult to train. Where training was ef- fective in producing improvements in the performance of a skill, these changes were generally maintained at a two-week follow-up. In a similar study, Edelstein, Elder, and Narick (1979) applied social skill training to modify the aggressive behavior of four adolescents. The training resulted in increased social appropriateness of responses to role-played treated scenes and generalization scenes.

SOCIAL SKILL TRAINING APPROACHES

The preceding reports rely on a series of training components including shaping, modeling, behavior rehearsal, feedback, and homework. Each of these social learning tactics has been demonstrated to be effective in pro- moting new skills. As such, they are a critical part of the process of de- veloping related personal characteristics that may replace maladaptive re- sponses. This section will define, illustrate, and suggest guidelines for applying each strategy.

Shaping

Shaping is used to promote new responses not in the student's repertoire. Antecedent and consequence control procedures cannot develop new skills when used in isolation. These procedures are designed to strengthen behaviors already existing in the student's repertoire. If an individual does not know how to ask for assistance, appropriate behavior will not be emitted and thus, may not be reinforced. Similarly, punishment for failing to ask for assistance will only frustrate the student. When observations of the student reveal that the appropriate behavior is not in his or her repertoire, a shaping procedure may be appropriate to teach the behavior.

Shaping involves the reinforcement of a behavior that approximates the desired response. As this approximation occurs at an acceptable rate, reinforcement is withdrawn and redirected to a closer approximation. Through the course of the program, successive approximations are reinforced as the preceding approximations are extinguished. The shaping program is successfully terminated when the desirable behavior is occurring at an acceptable rate under natural reinforcement conditions.

For example, Jim was a learning-disabled 18-year-old. He seldom shook hands when greeted by an adult. When he did, his grasp was very weak, and he withdrew his hand prematurely. This caused a substantial amount of trouble for Jim as he had great difficulty initiating new interactions with unfamiliar adults. Since Jim wanted to work as a salesman, it was perceived to be a major objective to his future success. Observations of Jim over a period of time and Jim's self-report suggested that he was motivated to shake hands properly but did not know how. Evidence indicating that Jim's problem was the result of primarily a skill deficit included the following: (1) Jim was seldom, if ever, observed to shake hands properly; (2) attempts to correct the problem through the contingent use of praise, a highly motivating event for Jim, were unsuccessful; and (3) Jim expressed the desire to shake hands correctly, but indicated that he wasn't sure what he was doing wrong.

A program was established in which Jim was expected to shake hands with the teacher each morning. He would be socially reinforced initially for any approximation of appropriate handshaking. After approximately two weeks he self-initiated handshaking each morning though his grip was still weak and abrupt. The next step was to socially reinforce Jim only for grasping firmly. If Jim failed to grasp firmly, he would be corrected but not reinforced. Again, Jim's performance met this criterion within a couple of weeks. The next approximation that Jim met was to sustain the handshake until the other person let go. This final step in the shaping process was the terminal objective.

While the preceding example is intended to illustrate the use of a shaping procedure, it is clear that other behavioral tactics were employed. Social reinforcement plays a major role in motivating performance within the established criterion. Also, special verbal antecedents may have been arranged to facilitate success. Shaping procedures are highly compatible with other behavioral intervention techniques.

The major value of shaping procedures lies in their utility in insuring success for the learner. This is particularly critical since a substantial body of literature highlights the impact of failure and punishment on the achievement motivation of handicapped youths (Sabatino & Schloss, 1981). Disinterest in academic pursuits often results because educators establish performance expectations that are beyond the reach of the student. As the student continually strives to meet the teacher's expectations and fails, his or her interest in similar activities diminishes. The shaping process requires the educator to set social performance expectations at a level that will maximize success for the learner. Subtle changes in expectations commensurate with the student's ability to adapt ensure continued success and reinforcement for the student.

Shaping, as with other behavioral tactics, can be done on a formal or informal basis. The following eight guidelines will increase the effectiveness of the procedure:

1. The outcome of the program should be identified in clear and complete terms.
2. Approximations beginning with the student's current behavior and ending with the terminal objective should be established. The distance between each approximation should be based on the adaptability of the student. Less adaptive youths generally require very subtle changes. More adaptive learners may benefit from substantial changes.
3. A positive consequence for successfully meeting each criterion should be identified. The consequence should be as natural to the activity and environment as possible while still being likely to motivate performance.
4. The target objectives, the terminal objective, and the motivational conditions should be described to the students prior to initiation.
5. The actual operation of the program involves the following procedures:
   - The initial behavior should be reinforced each time it occurs.
   - The teacher should move to the next approximation only after the first is mastered.
   - The teacher should not remain at one level too long or move to another level too quickly.

6. Once the terminal objective is achieved, unusual reinforcement conditions should be gradually withdrawn. This will increase the likelihood that the behavior will maintain over time.
7. The individual should be encouraged to practice the new behavior in
a number of other settings.
8. If the program is not effective:
   - The strength of the reinforcer should be tested.
   - The size of the criterion changes should be evaluated. Excessively
     large *or* small changes in the approximations may result in disin-
     terest or frustration.

Modeling

The effectiveness of modeling in developing positive social behavior and
diminishing disruptive behavior has been repeatedly demonstrated in the
behavioral literature. Targets of modeling programs have included pacifier
dependence (Schloss & Johann, 1982); fear of dogs (Bandura, 1967);
aggression (Bandura, 1965); alcohol abuse (Craigie & Ross, 1980); drug
use (Warner & Swisher, 1976); reading related responses (Haskett & Lenfestey, 1974); and bus riding (Sowers, Rusch, & Hudson, 1979). Modeling,
as described in these investigations, involves the arrangement of instructional conditions so that an individual acquires new response patterns through
the observation of another person.

Modeling procedures may be used for three distinct purposes. First,
modeling can be effective in teaching new responses not present in the
individual's repertoire. For example, an adolescent may learn to initiate
conversations by watching a teacher. Second, modeling may increase the
strength or frequency of a previously learned skill. This is exemplified by
an individual who begins jogging after observing a friend lose weight through
an exercise regimen. Finally, modeling may be used to inhibit a response
pattern. An adolescent may discontinue the use of profane language after
observing his employer fire a co-worker for swearing.

Modeling may be a very cost-effective social development strategy. In
the normal course of a school day an educator may take advantage of
numerous opportunities to formally or informally facilitate behavior change
through modeling. Intervention strategies may run the gamut from highly
structured environments in which the opportunities for observational learning are well controlled to brief, unplanned exposures to positive role models.
The structure that an educator imparts on a modeling program may be a
function of the cost of the program weighed against the severity of the
behavior problem.

As with other learning theory principles, modeling can influence the development and persistence of positive as well as negative behavioral and attitudinal characteristics. A student who frequently observes others gain control of situations through the use of violence or physical threats is likely to engage in similar behavior. Conversely, placed in an environment in which the socially skillful behavior of others produces reward, the same student is likely to develop and display positive social behavior. The limited availability of positive peer models in self-contained special education classrooms and residential facilities has been a major factor in promoting mainstream education (Bruininks & Rynders, 1971; Csapo, 1972).

A number of researchers have studied factors that influence the likelihood that behaviors may be learned or strengthened through modeling (Bandura, 1971a; Bandura, 1971b; Kazdin, 1973; Ross, 1970; Stevenson, 1972; Zinzer, 1966). This literature offers five elements that enhance the effectiveness of observational learning as follows: (1) the extent to which the observer has been reinforced for similar behavior under like stimulus conditions; (2) the extent to which the observer views the modeled behavior as common for the situation; (3) the self-esteem of the observer; (4) the degree to which the observer depends on external cues; and (5) the demonstrated competence of the observer in similar situations.

Goldstein, Heller, and Sechrist (1966) and Bandura (1971a) have highlighted characteristics of the model that facilitate observational learning. Strong models have been characterized as being warm, nurturing, powerful, and competent. Also, models of the same sex are likely to exert stronger control over the behavior of the learner. In general, individuals perceived by the learner as having high status are more likely to promote observational learning than low-status models. This is exemplified by the influence that teen-age celebrities have on the behavior, appearance, and attitudes of youths (e.g., consider how the Beatles influenced hairstyles of adolescents in the 1960s).

Bandura (1971a) has enumerated activities in the modeling process that enhance the imitation of the model's behavior as follows: (1) reinforcing the model; (2) enhancing the status of the model through his or her behavior; (3) clearly distinguishing situations in which the modeled behavior is appropriate and likely to be reinforced; and (4) insuring that modeled activities are not excessively difficult for the observer.

In summary, the following six principles should be considered when promoting observational learning:

1. Behaviors that are expected to be influenced through the modeling process should be specified.

2. Situations should be arranged in which the learner may observe high-status models engaged in the behaviors.
3. Reinforcers should be specified and delivered contingent on the behaviors (typically social reinforcement).
4. Behaviors should be verbally labeled as they occur using the person's name (e.g., "You sure have a nice smile today, John!").
5. The learner should be reinforced for engaging in approximations of the desired behaviors.
6. The models and settings should be varied in order to enhance the generalization of the behavior change.

Behavior Rehearsal

Behavior rehearsal is a teaching strategy that goes beyond simply role-playing or playacting adaptive responses. The behavior rehearsal strategy assists the adolescent in identifying environmental conditions in which the behavior is expected to occur as well as the natural consequences of the behavior. In general, behavior rehearsal strategies teach adaptive responses, develop natural cues that are expected to prompt the adaptive response, and assist the student to identify the natural consequences of the adaptive response.

The major advantage of behavior rehearsal tactics is the minimization of dependence on abstract thinking. Rehearsing positive social behavior in the natural environment or closely simulated environments provides a direct link between the desired behavior and the setting in which it is expected to occur. This may not be the case with social skill training approaches that are removed from the natural setting.

Similarly, behavior rehearsal strategies prompt desirable behaviors that previously occurred too seldom to be reinforced. The behavior rehearsal strategy provides a structure in which positive social behaviors occur more frequently than is expected under natural conditions. Since the adaptive behavior is prompted to occur at a higher rate, it can be reinforced more often. This process supports the development of social behavior through the use of positive reinforcement while minimizing the use of punishment for maladaptive behavior.

Behavior rehearsal procedures may involve the use of several behavior management strategies at one time. Social reinforcement may be used as a consequence of the rehearsed behavior. A shaping procedure may be employed to develop approximations of the expected response. Stimulus change may be involved in insuring the individual's success under less demanding environmental conditions. Finally, modeling may be used to develop and prompt the rehearsed behavior. For example, an 18-year-old moderately retarded student frequently coaxed a friend to obtain her lunch from the cafeteria line. It was agreed at her multidisciplinary staff conference that independence in obtaining food from a cafeteria line would be critical to her adjustment to a vocational placement.

The student's teacher designed a behavior rehearsal strategy to teach and reinforce independence in the lunch line. The program involved conducting practice sessions prior to lunch in the cafeteria setting. Approximately 15 minutes prior to the time the other students arrived for lunch, the cafeteria line was set up, tables were in place, and the cashier was in position. At that time, the student and her instructor went to the lunchroom so that she could rehearse obtaining lunch independently.

Every attempt was made to make the practice session as close to the real event as possible. Upon completion of each trial, her instructor would label the specific behaviors she performed (e.g., "You did a fine job of picking up your sandwich, drink, and salad. You also paid for the food. You didn't even drop anything."). Also, the instructor helped the young lady to identify the consequences of her behavior (e.g., "You went through the line and obtained your food like everyone else. You are acting as an independent student when you do that."). Following three consecutive days with no mishaps, the student was encouraged to obtain lunch on her own during the regular cafeteria time. Once this was accomplished successfully, the structured rehearsal sequences were discontinued, and the instructor simply socially reinforced the youth for being an independent student.

This example emphasizes that behavior rehearsal situations should be structured as closely as possible to the natural events expected to cue and reinforce the rehearsed behavior. To meet this objective the actual events should be used, if possible. For example, if an individual frequently runs down the hall, structured practice may occur each time the student is to go to another classroom. Exhibit 6–1, for example, describes a format that educators may follow using behavior rehearsals in the natural environment. Sometimes, however, it is preferable to practice the behavior without others present, as was the case in the preceding example. In this event, every effort was made to simulate the actual environmental conditions associated with the behavior.

In designing a simulated environment for behavior rehearsals, special attention should be given to establishing comparable antecedents and consequences of the rehearsed behavior. If behavior rehearsals are to focus on a student's social greetings toward fellow students, then the students should be involved in the behavior rehearsals, if possible. Similarly, if social praise is the natural consequence of a polite greeting, then social praise should occur following the rehearsed greeting.

Exhibit 6–1 A Suggested Behavior Rehearsal Sequence

1. The teacher should identify the reason for rehearsing the behavior.
2. The student should be encouraged to identify events that may provoke an inappropriate response.
3. The teacher should assist the student in evaluating his or her response in reference to the following outcomes: (1) its effectiveness in reducing agitating behavior of others; (2) its influence on personal goals; and (3) its influence on the work behavior of others.
4. The teacher should assist the student in identifying alternate behaviors that are socially skillful (i.e., facilitate the acquisition of rewards from the environment).
5. The teacher should role-play a potentially provoking situation with the student exhibiting socially skillful behavior.
6. The adolescent should be assisted in evaluating the appropriate response in terms of the following outcomes: (1) its effectiveness in reducing agitating behavior of others; (2) its influence on personal goals; and (3) its influence on the work behavior of others.
7. The teacher should guide the student in rehearsing the socially skillful behavior under varying conditions and encourage the individual to verbally label the positive features of the newly acquired behavior. The student should be socially reinforced for demonstrating adaptive responses.
8. The teacher should elicit a statement from the adolescent that indicates his or her intent to use socially skillful behaviors in response to provocations in the school setting.

Finally, the instructor should frequently label the rehearsed behavior, the antecedents to the behavior, and the consequences of the behavior. For example, the instructor may say, "Jack, when the bell went off (antecedent), you got up from your desk quietly (rehearsed behavior), so you can now go to your locker (consequence)." When behaviors are rehearsed in structured situations outside of the natural setting, these verbal labels may provide a channel that increases the likelihood that the behavior will generalize back into the natural setting.

In summary, the following seven procedures should be used in conducting behavior rehearsals:

1. The behavior that is to be developed should be specified.
2. The natural antecedents to the behavior should be identified.
3. The natural consequences of the behavior should be identified.
4. Times should be determined in which the desired behavior is to be practiced around the natural antecedents and consequences.
5. A plan for rehearsing the desired behavior should be developed and initiated.
6. The desired response should be frequently labeled in relation to the antecedents and consequences of the response.
7. When necessary, behavior rehearsal procedures should be combined with other behavior management strategies.

Feedback

Feedback is defined as the process of providing evaluative information to a student for the purpose of maintaining or improving future performance. Feedback may be arranged through one or more of a variety of media. It may be delivered by peers, the teacher, parents, or an audio- or videotape. The latter two options permit the student to use direct feedback to evaluate his or her own performance.

Feedback should be clear and complete. Well-delivered feedback leaves little doubt in the student's mind as to the quality of his or her performance in relationship to the expected performance. For many handicapped students the clarity of feedback may be enhanced through a number of tactics, including using short sentences, using multiple concrete examples, avoiding symbolic or abstract terms, and using feedback in combination with other social learning procedures (e.g., behavior rehearsal, modeling, social reinforcement, shaping, etc.).

Feedback statements should be limited to present expectations (i.e., short-term objectives) for performance. The performance standard should be consistent, increasing only when the current short-term objective is achieved. Arbitrary variations in expectations do not allow the student to gauge his or her progress in relation to a stable benchmark. The inability of a student to gradually approach and achieve an objective prior to establishing a new objective may be viewed by the student as failure. The facets of the student's performance subjected to feedback should be restricted. Handicapped children and youths are not as likely to benefit from feedback delivered simultaneously on affect, gestures, voice inflection, content, volume, etc., as they are to benefit from volume and inflection. Items not targeted for providing feedback may be added later as the current objectives are achieved.

Feedback statements should be discrete and repetitive. The same, or at least a similar, feedback statement should be used for each performance deficit. This guideline accommodates the limited language capabilities of many handicapped students. The student is more likely to learn the relationship between "standard" statements and his or her performance. Variability in the feedback statements may be erroneously interpreted by the student as resulting from variability in his or her performance. For example, in commenting about the way a student has combed his hair, the teacher may say, "Your hair is very well combed," or "Your hair is messy." Interjecting alternative statements may create "confusion." Once the student responds appropriately to the initial feedback statement, additional ones may be added.

Not all feedback must be corrective. Consistent with the 80 percent success rule discussed previously, eight of ten feedback statements should identify positive features of the individual. This approach will make the student more responsive to the corrective feedback statement made 20 percent of the time. Continuous negative feedback is likely to cause the student to avoid the teacher.

Whenever possible, audio- or videotape feedback should be built into social development programs. These media are exceptionally well suited for the handicapped as they do not rely on complex language. Rather, they present the student with a direct and concrete image of his or her performance. In this manner, the student is able to evaluate his or her own behavior as a somewhat detached observer. Upon viewing or listening to a tape, the student can formulate and act on his or her own corrective statements. This process reduces the likelihood that the student will develop defensive reactions to corrective information.

Finally, peers may be highly effective agents for delivering feedback. Peer feedback may not only influence the performance of the student receiving information but may also improve the behavior of the sender. Providing accurate feedback requires students to be aware of the standards for acceptable performance. Further, it requires them to publicly affirm a desire for others to meet these standards. A logical consequence is that students will attempt to meet these standards themselves.

Many students, particularly adolescents, are more likely to respond favorably to information provided by their peer group. Peer pressure has been described as a major influence on the behavior of secondary students (Jones, 1980). The educator must be cautious, however, in structuring peer feedback because of the potential for negative effects. The result of unstructured peer pressure is likely to be an increased rate of aggression or withdrawal. Students should be impressed with the guidelines previously discussed for providing feedback, including the 80 percent rule, careful selection of language, well-defined expectations, and consistency.

Homework

The initial principles identified in the first chapter of this volume emphasize that the most powerful social learning strategies are conducted in natural environments. The interpersonal skill training programs reviewed in a preceding section were conducted in a clinical or artificial classroom setting. These locations were used for the sake of expedience. Many of the programs did, however, include a homework component to transfer training into the natural environment. Homework, in this case, is defined as interpersonal skills that the student is expected to practice under natural conditions. For example, following a session in which participants learned to ask for directions, the students may be asked to go to a gas station and ask for directions to a store. Exhibit 6–2 illustrates a number of other homework activities.

The purpose of homework is to increase the likelihood that responses acquired during interpersonal skills training sessions will generalize to natural environments. Assisting a student to exchange social amenities during a group session does not ensure that the appropriate response will occur when expected in the natural environment. Different cue conditions and motivational factors may account for this inconsistent performance. For example, when practicing amenities in class, the student's attention is focused by the teacher, a relatively stable and familiar set of people is involved, often external prompts are supplied by the teacher or other peers, and the student has a high expectancy for social reinforcement following successful performance. Most of these conditions do not exist in the natural environment. Often, the student must identify when to initiate the interaction, unfamiliar people may be involved, there is no one available to supply prompts, and the student has a limited expectancy for social reinforcement.

The homework assignment, therefore, requires the student to overcome these obstacles. The student is expected to go out into natural environments and practice skills acquired in artificial settings. Specific guidelines for conducting homework include the following:

- The teacher should assign homework when skills are acquired under artificial conditions.
- The teacher should work with the student to determine an equitable and effective homework assignment.

Exhibit 6–2 Sample Homework Activities

- Go to a restaurant and order from the menu.
- Return a duplicate gift to a store.
- Ask a stranger for the time.
- Provide constructive feedback to a fellow student.
- Exchange amenities with a salesclerk.
- Ask a friend for assistance in working a math problem.
- Introduce yourself to a new teacher.
- Apply for a job.
- Answer the telephone properly.
- Apologize to a friend for being late.

- The teacher should provide the student with a clearly written description of the assignment. The paper should include an evaluation section that allows the individual to record the quality of the performance. (See Exhibit 6–3.)
- Following the completion of the assignment, the teacher should review the evaluation statement with the student as soon as possible. If follow-up is required, an additional assignment may be established.

BEHAVIORAL SELF-CONTROL TACTICS

Thoresen and Mahoney (1974) have proposed a model of self-control that is founded on learning theory principles. The authors emphasize the departure of the behavioral self-control orientation from the traditional construct of "willpower." The authors suggest the notion of willpower is limited by a circularity of logic in which an inner psychic force or trait is explained by the behavior from which it was defined (e.g., Ralph has willpower. How do you know? Because he was able to quit smoking. How was he able to give up smoking? Because of his willpower). This logic does little to provide educators tools for developing willpower. Further, traditional willpower constructs often propose an all or nothing view of behavior control. This is exemplified by the fatalistic attitude of an individual who gorges himself when eating because he does not have willpower.

The behavioral view suggests that an individual's control of his or her actions results from a knowledge and control over environmental events that influence behavior. Self-control skills result from the adolescent's ability to manipulate the antecedents and consequences of behavior so that desirable behavior is more likely to occur. For example, the husband who

---

Exhibit 6–3 Homework Recording Form

Assignment: _____

_____

_____

_____

Self-Evaluation: _____

_____

_____

_____

_____

attempts to lose weight by avoiding occasions in which cocktails and hors d'oeuvres are served, removing sweets from the house, and avoiding Girl Scout cookie sales in the fall is practicing self-control by avoiding the antecedents for eating. Similarly, setting a goal for weight loss that will result in a special activity (e.g., I'll buy new clothes when my weight reaches 180 pounds) is an example of self-imposed consequences.

Thoresen and Mahoney (1974) have proposed three essential processes that are involved in self-control. These are: (1) the self-identification of behaviors to be influenced; (2) the self-identification of antecedents and consequences associated with the target behavior; and (3) the initiation of a plan that alters the antecedents and consequences of the target behavior.

A wide range of tactics that involves the student in the planning and implementation of the behavior change program can be identified by the creative teacher. The major consideration in establishing the self-control program is the extent to which the child or youth can be expected to fulfill the requirements of the program without externally imposed contingencies.

Two major advantages are evident in self-control procedures. First, they place the control and responsibility of behavior change in the hands of the adolescent. This is especially critical since one of the major objectives of education is to provide students with skills that sustain their development into adult life. Self-control procedures can be developed and implemented by young adults without the direct support or supervision of others. Thus, the youth's ability to exhibit self-control skills enhances his or her adjustment in adult life. The second advantage of self-control procedures is that they can be highly cost efficient. Since the youth is primarily responsible for program analysis and implementation, the educator can assume the role of a consultant. As such, the educator is free to arrange and monitor a larger number of intensive social, vocational, and academic development programs.

Probably the major limitation of the self-control approach is that it relies on the student's motivation to participate in the self-control process. A self-control program may not be a viable option for a youth who is not willing or able to: (1) identify a behavior change goal; (2) complete a valid analysis of antecedent and consequent events; (3) establish a restructured environment; or (4) consistently abide by the requirements of the restructured environment. When one or all of these deficiencies occurs, the educator is left to impose program conditions on the adolescent. In any case, to the extent possible, self-control components that will not reduce the effectiveness of the program should be used. It is likely that once the student succeeds under externally imposed contingencies, more self-control components may be added. Potential components of self-control programs described in the literature include self-recording (McKenzie & Rushall,

1974); environmental planning (Goldiamond, 1965); self-management of consequences (Frederiksen & Frederiksen, 1975); and various combinations (Anderson, Fodor, & Alpert, 1976; Epstein & Gross, 1978; Glynn, Thomas, & Shee, 1973).

Self-Recording

Self-recording involves the student systematically obtaining data reporting his or her own actions. The process of self-recording is expected to assist the child or youth in making decisions about behavior change. Additionally, numerous psychological theories emphasize self-awareness as the cornerstone of behavior change. For example, rational, emotive therapy (Ellis, 1973) emphasizes an awareness of irrational thoughts; client-centered therapy (Rogers, 1965) emphasizes the self-exploration of feelings and their relationship to current events; and psychotherapy (Gendlin, 1969) involves working through disruptive feelings by becoming aware of their origins.

Three major steps involved in self-recording include: (1) selecting target behaviors; (2) designing and initiating a recording procedure; and (3) graphing the recorded behaviors. Collectively, these procedures provide the self-observer with a reliable display of his or her behavior. They also allow the individual to associate various rates of the recorded behaviors with naturally occurring events.

Selecting target behaviors is the first step in a behavioral self-control program. Identifying target behaviors, as in other behavior change procedures, involves prioritizing all of the potential targets for self-monitoring. The student should be encouraged to select *only* one to three most important targets. Limiting the number of responses to be self-observed increases the likelihood of success. Target behaviors not included in the initial program may be added later.

The educator should assist the student in defining the target behaviors. The resulting definitions should be clear and complete. Vague or incomplete definitions will reduce the extent to which the student will be able to produce reliable data. Some potential targets may be very difficult to define and monitor. It is unlikely, for example, that a student will be able to reliably monitor "happiness," "on-task," or "enthusiasm" as trained researchers have extreme difficulty in quantifying these responses. Therefore, the teacher may encourage the student to monitor more discrete behaviors that reflect these responses. Number of problems completed may be substituted for on-task; positive statements may replace happy, and so on.

The second step involves designing and initiating a recording procedure. Once the student has identified the behavior(s) to be self-observed, he or she must establish a recording procedure. The procedure selected should be as pragmatic and unobtrusive as possible. Highly complex or elaborate systems are more likely to fail because of the difficulty the handicapped student may have in recording the data. Even if the student is able to record fairly reliably, he or she will be less able to interpret the data. For these reasons a simple frequency recording may be most desirable.

Small children may benefit from a beaded bracelet arrangement reported by Holman and Baer (1979) in modifying off-task and disruptive behaviors of preschoolers. Each child was provided a bracelet that contained a wire strand. Red and white movable beads were laced onto the strand. The red beads and one white criterion bead represented the number of pages expected to be completed that day. The number of red beads prior to the criterion bead was determined by the child's rate of page completion in baseline production rate. The child was told to attempt to move all of the beads up to the white bead. Finally, there were also a number of red beads on the strand after the white bead, allowing for achievement beyond the criterion.

Adolescents may use an appointment book to self-record. For example, each time a youth eats between meals, the type and amount of food are written in the corresponding time slot. This procedure not only establishes the frequency of between meal snacks but also identifies the type of food and the time of day.

Numerous variations of the recording procedures discussed in Chapter 8 may be used by the creative teacher and student. The ultimate test for any recording procedure is the rate of agreement for independent observers. This reliability test involves the teacher (or another student) and the self-observer monitoring the target behavior simultaneously. At the end of a specified period of time, the two frequency counts may be compared. A reliability coefficient of .80 or better, determined by dividing the smaller number of observations by the larger, is generally considered acceptable. A lower reliability coefficient should prompt a revision of the definition and/or recording procedure.

The final step, graphing, involves translating the recorded data to a summary chart. This chart should provide a clear representation of the rate of the student's behavior over time. As with recording, graphing should be a simple and direct representation of the data as possible. In the preschool example, the graph may consist of pasting paper beads onto a chart as in Figure 6–4. The adolescent may benefit from a more traditional line graph as discussed in Chapter 8.

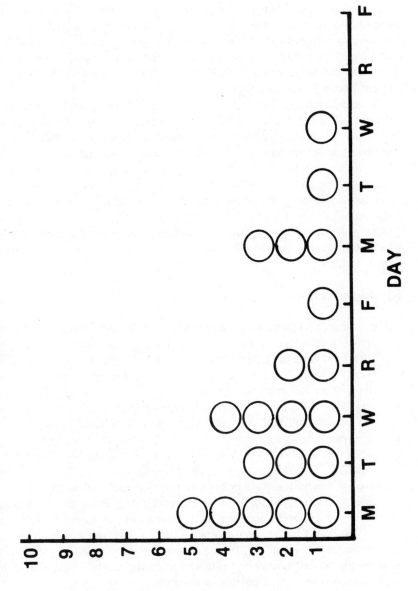

Figure 6-4 Preschooler's Self-Recorded Data Graph

Environmental Planning

A preceding section detailed the use of antecedent change as a social development tactic. The procedure involved: (1) identifying events that increase the likelihood that disruptive behaviors will occur; (2) arranging for the provoking events to be present less often; (3) identifying events that trigger or prompt prosocial behavior; and (4) arranging for these cues to be present more often. These procedures may be conducted by the student in a self-control program.

The initial step is assisting the student to specify from one to three target behaviors. The criteria for identifying these responses have been discussed previously. In short, they should be observable, measurable, stated in clear and complete terms, and reasonably amenable to treatment. The second step is to identify the associated antecedents. This may be accomplished by encouraging the student to identify events that precede the occurrence of target behaviors. The form presented in Exhibit 6–4 may serve this purpose.

A plan should be developed by the student to avoid the provoking events. Alternative events associated with more acceptable responses should be substituted.

Self-Reinforcement

Just as students can be taught to monitor their own behavior and arrange supportive antecedent conditions, they may also be taught to reinforce their own behavior. In self-reinforcement, the students present themselves with pleasant items or events contingent on specific performances.

As with other self-control techniques, the initial step in program development is for the student to clearly define the target behavior or behaviors. Once this is accomplished, reinforcers for desirable behaviors and punishers for undesirable behaviors may be identified. A logical test for the use of a reinforcer in a self-control program has been proposed by Watson and Tharp (1977). They suggest asking the students if they really believe that engaging in the undesirable behaviors will decrease and engaging in the desirable behaviors will increase as the result of gaining the reinforcers. The selected reinforcers need not be elaborate and should be readily available. Natural and logical contingencies should be favored over contrived consequences. For example, taking 15 minutes to play video games after cleaning the bedroom may be preferred to eating candy. Hard work often produces free time under natural conditions.

Premack's (1965) discussion of reinforcement selection and effect has major implications for self-reinforcement programs. He argued that rein-

Exhibit 6–4 Environmental Planning Self-Recording Form

| | | | Name: _____ |
| | | | Date: _____ |

Time	Place	Events that occurred before the behavior	Specific description of the behavior

forcers are effective because they are activities or events preferred to other events. Any response already available in a student's repertoire that would be displayed when given a choice may become an effective reinforcer for less pleasant (low frequency) behaviors. For example, most older adolescents would rather drive than wash their parents' car. Driving could therefore be used to motivate washing. A youth's self-reinforcement program may arrange a high probability behavior to occur only as a consequence of a low probability behavior. Various examples are illustrated in Exhibit 6–5.

The final step involves stipulating the contingency arrangement between the target behavior and consequences. Contingency contracts and token systems, described in the next chapter, may be used to formalize these arrangements. For example, Exhibit 6–6 displays the target behaviors, operational definition, points achieved, and back-up reinforcers established by a youth for a self-control program.

It should be clear that self-monitoring, environmental planning, and self-reinforcement are highly compatible procedures. Although they are discussed separately, most self-control applications involve some combination of the three. For example, a youth may be asked to self-monitor, identifying the frequency and antecedents of swearing episodes. The antecedent data may be used to initiate environmental planning (e.g., avoiding events associated with swearing). In addition, the student may establish certain privileges that result from days in which swearing did not occur.

Exhibit 6–5 The Arrangement of High-Probability Behaviors As Consequences for Low-Probability Responses

Low-Probability Behaviors	Contingent High-Probability Behaviors
• Clean room.	• Play in the room.
• Wash face and hands.	• Eat a Popsicle.
• Eat dinner.	• Eat dessert.
• Play with sibling.	• Play with friends.
• Do homework.	• Watch television.
• Complete paper route.	• Go to show.
• Purchase clothes.	• Purchase a video game cartridge.
• Mow the lawn.	• Play ball.
• Read a chapter in a text.	• Read a popular magazine.

Exhibit 6–6 Contingency Arrangement for a Youth's Self-Reinforcement Program

Target Behavior	Operational Definition	Points
Math homework	Turning in assigned work to the teacher on time	10
English homework	Completion of reading assignments	10
History homework	Studying for tests	10
Science homework		10
Daily house duties	Make bed, pick up clothes, clean kitchen, wash dishes, take garbage out	20
Weekly house duties	Wash floors, dust furniture, clean bathroom, vacuum carpets	50
Mow lawn		30
Wash car		20
Laundry	Wash, iron, and fold clothes	30
Backup Reinforcers		*Cost*
Skating		20
Fishing (3 hours)		20
Movie		30
Pizza		30
Six-pack soda		30
Football game		30
Television (1 hour)		10
Stereo (1 hour)		10
Candy bar		5

In summary, the following six-step procedure should be considered in designing and implementing a self-control program:

1. The child or adolescent should be assisted in clarifying and defining the target behavior(s) of the intervention program.
2. The child or youth should be taught to conduct continuous recording.
3. The student should be assisted in using a recording procedure to identify environmental events associated with the target behavior.
4. The educator should work with the child or adolescent in designing a program that restructures environmental events to promote prosocial behavior.
5. The student should be assisted in developing a continuous monitoring procedure that may be used to determine the effectiveness of the intervention program.

6. The educator should assist the student in implementing and monitoring the program and should provide social reinforcement and corrective feedback as required.

CONCLUSION

This chapter has described a range of procedures to develop responses that mediate between provoking events and potentially disruptive behaviors. The goal of each of these approaches is to promote the child's or youth's ability to behave acceptably in situations that previously led to disruptions. The entry points are not to be used in isolation. For example, teaching social skills in the related personal characteristic entry point will have little effect if reinforcing consequences for newly acquired social skills are not present. The next chapter will discuss the final entry point—consequence control.

Chapter 7

Consequence Control

Consequence control procedures involve the presentation or removal of events following a behavior in order to increase or decrease the likelihood that the behavior will reoccur. (See Figure 7–1.) Specifically, consequence control emphasizes the careful use of the principles of reinforcement and punishment. These principles state that an event that follows a behavior may increase or decrease the likelihood of the future occurrence of the behavior. A behavior that is followed by a pleasant consequence and subsequently increases in strength is said to have been positively reinforced. Homework completion, for example, is often positively reinforced by good grades and praise. Behaviors that are followed by the avoidance or removal of an unpleasant consequence and subsequently increase in strength are said to have been negatively reinforced. For example, a student arrives in class on time because he or she is motivated to avoid after school detention. Finally, behaviors that are followed by unpleasant or aversive consequences and subsequently decrease in strength are said to have been punished. Foul

Figure 7–1 Relationship among Consequences and Other Intervention Facets

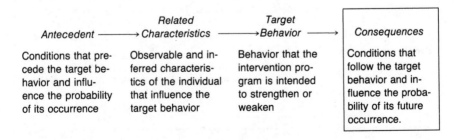

language is punished when it occurs less frequently as the result of verbal reprimands.

It is important to emphasize that these principles refer to relationships between specific behaviors and consequences that can be observed and evaluated. An event qualifies as a reinforcer for a child or youth's behavior *only* if its contingent presentation results in an increase in the target behavior for that child. Likewise, a contingent aversive event must produce a reduction in the strength of the target behavior in order to meet the technical criteria for a punishment procedure. A negatively reinforcing event is identified only when the removal of an aversive event does, in fact, result in an increase in the target behavior. Exhibit 7–1 illustrates the principles of positive reinforcement, negative reinforcement, and punishment.

Exhibit 7–1 The Principles of Positive Reinforcement, Negative Reinforcement, and Punishment

Principle	Definition	Example
Positive reinforcement	A response that is followed by a satisfying consequence increases in strength. The response is defined as having been positively reinforced. The consequence is defined as a positive reinforcer.	Staying within the lines while coloring is followed by the teacher awarding a Smiley Face. Subsequently, coloring within the lines occurs more often. Staying within the lines has been positively reinforced. Receiving a Smiley Face was a positive reinforcer.
Negative reinforcement	A response that is followed by the avoidance or removal of an unpleasant event increases in strength. The response is defined as having been negatively reinforced. The consequence is defined as a negative reinforcer.	Completing work on time results in the youth avoiding a detention, and subsequently, work is completed on time more often. Completing work on time has been negatively reinforced. Detention was the negative reinforcer.
Punishment	A response that is followed by an aversive consequence decreases in strength.	Lying results in a child being grounded, and subsequently, lying occurs less often. Lying has been punished. Being grounded was the punisher.

Reinforcement and punishment relationships are specific to each individual. Events that are reinforcing to one student may or may not be reinforcing to another. Similarly, events that are punishing to one student may not be punishing to another. A systematic analysis of the student's behavior during a baseline period (i.e., prior to the implementation of the reinforcement or punishment procedure) and while the procedure is in effect, is used to determine whether or not reinforcement, punishment, or neutral relationships exist between the behavior and consequence.

Beyond being specific to the student, reinforcement and punishment relationships are specific to responses in the individual's repertoire. Contingent free time may be sufficiently strong to positively reinforce a student's silent reading behavior yet fail to reinforce oral reading. Once again, reinforcement and punishment relationships can only be described in connection with specific behaviors of specific individuals. Confidence in describing a relationship between a response and consequence can only be achieved through systematic observation. Observation and evaluation procedures are described in the following chapters.

Relationship between Other Entry Points

The preceding chapter reviewed approaches that have been demonstrated to be effective in teaching alternative social behaviors to the handicapped. The underlying assumption was that a handicapped child or youth may not have the *skill* to exhibit the expected social behavior. By providing conditions through which the responses are acquired, the student may be in a more tenable position to display prosocial as opposed to disruptive responses. In short, the entry point of related personal characteristics emphasized skill training approaches. The limitation of this entry point when used in isolation is that the acquisition of a skill does not ensure that the skill will be used.

Combining skill training procedures with reinforcement procedures not only provides the skill, but also establishes motivational conditions that promote the student's use of the skill. For example, a student may learn assertive statements that may be effective in gaining extra dessert after meals. In spite of this training, if the child or youth is more likely to gain extra dessert by being aggressive as opposed to being assertive, he or she will probably still be aggressive. If, on the other hand, assertiveness training is accompanied by procedures that reinforce the new skills (e.g., provide dessert *only* when assertive responses are used) and/or punish the existing aggressive responses (e.g., withdraw dessert and remove the child or youth to an isolated setting when aggressive), the child or youth will be more likely to exhibit the prosocial response.

Consequence control procedures are also closely connected to the antecedent control strategies presented in Chapter 5. Antecedents acquire their ability to influence behavior as the result of the child's or youth's expectation for reinforcement or punishment under the antecedent conditions. Antecedents that signal the occasion for reinforcement are likely to promote behavior. Being handed the ball at the free throw line in basketball cues a player to shoot with the expectation for reinforcement once the shot is made. A teacher walking into the room cues the students to be quiet because of the expectation for praise for good behavior. Altering the consequences also alters the control that the antecedent has over the behavior. If a rule change were to occur and basketball players were no longer awarded points for shooting free throws, standing at the free throw line would no longer cue a player to shoot with the expectation of reinforcement. Free throw shooting might be expected to cease. If a teacher no longer praised his or her class for being quiet, the teacher's walking into the room would no longer cue quiet behavior. The antecedent of the teacher's walking into the room would no longer signal the occasion for praise as a reinforcer. Therefore, the teacher's walking into the room would no longer be an antecedent for quiet behavior.

The empirical literature has described a number of social learning strategies based on the principles of reinforcement and punishment. A review of applied behavioral interventions with the handicapped suggests that various consequence control procedures are often involved in the treatment of more severe behavioral reactions. The following sections will review prevalent consequence control strategies including social reinforcement, contingency contracting, differential reinforcement of low rates of behavior (DRL), differential reinforcement of other behavior (DRO), extinction, response cost, overcorrection, and token reinforcement.

Social Reinforcement

Interpersonal interactions that increase or decrease the likelihood of a behavior occurring are defined as social reinforcers. These may be positive (e.g., a smile, pat on the back, hug, wink, enthusiastic statement, or favorable acknowledgment) or negative (e.g., a frown, criticism, dejected expression, or verbal admonishment). As emphasized in the principles of reinforcement, an event cannot be labeled as a social reinforcer until the relationship between the events and the frequency with which the behavior occurs are demonstrated. Praise, in and of itself, cannot be said to be a reinforcing event for students. Only after it is demonstrated that praise strengthens a behavior can praise be labeled a reinforcer. Even then, praise can only be said to be a social reinforcer for the specific behavior to be influenced.

Events not intended to motivate behavior may also acquire socially reinforcing qualities. This is evidenced in a number of disruptive behaviors that are socially reinforced by attention. Talking out in class often produces laughter from peers that reinforces future talking out. Verbal aggression frequently results in praise from classmates, increasing the likelihood that verbal aggression will reoccur. Hasazi and Hasazi (1972) have reported a study that demonstrated that a behavior characteristic of the learning disabled may be inadvertently socially reinforced by teachers' interactions. The subject of the investigation, an eight-year-old boy, frequently reversed the order of digits when adding numbers yielding a two-digit sum. The child and his classmates were given 20 addition problems a day throughout the study. During a baseline period the teacher recorded reversed digits as incorrect and provided one-to-one attention until the problems were corrected. This approach had been used by the subject's teachers for the past year. The experimental approach involved: (1) marking the sums as correct whether or not reversed; (2) discontinuing one-to-one attention following reversals; and (3) providing a pat on the back and brief comment for each nonreversed answer. Baseline and treatment phases were alternated through an A-B-A-B design. (See Chapter 9.) The resulting data demonstrated a rate of reversals of approximately 18 of 20 under the baseline condition and 3 of 20 under the treatment condition.

Hasazi and Hasazi (1972) emphasize the unexpected negative effect that misdirected social reinforcement had on academic performance as follows:

> . . . It is a typical teaching practice to give a student individual attention when learning problems develop, and hence, the possibility of (social) reinforcement of inappropriate academic behaviors exists. The teacher should remain aware of this possibility and attempt to determine which student behaviors are discriminative for his attending behavior. (p. 160)

Numerous other studies have demonstrated the impact of manipulating teachers' attention and praise in altering the behavior of students (Becker, Madsen, Arnold, & Thomas, 1967; Broden, Bruce, Mitchell, Carter, & Hall, 1970; Kazdin, 1973; Kazdin & Klock, 1973; Thomas, Becker, & Armstrong, 1968; Thomas, Nielsen, Kuypers, & Becker, 1968). In a highly unique investigation Truax and Mitchell (1971) studied the selective use of empathy, nonpossessive warmth, and directiveness in Carl Rogers' interactions with a schizophrenic patient. An analysis of taped therapy sessions resulted in the conclusion that Rogers responded selectively toward five classes of client behaviors with higher levels of empathy, warmth, and directiveness. These client behaviors were reported to have changed significantly with one exception; four additional classes of behaviors that Rogers did not respond to selectively failed to show significant changes.

It has been emphasized that social reinforcement is defined by the influence that the interaction has on the specific behavior. If saying "good work" results in *no* change in performance, then the interaction was *not* socially reinforcing. Social reinforcement, however, may be an effective procedure for motivating a range of behaviors with handicapped youths. It is particularly useful in that: (1) no special apparatus or commodities are required; (2) it can be administered with very little time and effort; (3) social reinforcement is natural to almost all educational settings; (4) the effects are likely to generalize to other students through vicarious reinforcement; and (5) social reinforcement can easily be combined with other educational procedures.

The research literature suggests that the following eight guidelines be followed when using social reinforcement:

1. The teacher should label both process (e.g., "working fast") and product behaviors (e.g., "completed a workbook page").
2. The teacher should use the individual's name frequently (e.g., "I really like it when you work that fast, John. You surely have completed a lot of math work").
3. The teacher should tell the individual the behaviors that are likely to result in social reinforcement (e.g., "I like to talk to you when you work fast").
4. The teacher should demonstrate that social reinforcement is effective in motivating the desired behavior.
5. If it is not, a more intrusive procedure should be used. The more intrusive procedure should always be paired with social reinforcement.
6. The teacher should encourage a number of people, including parents, peers, and other teachers, to socially reinforce the target behaviors. This will increase the likelihood that the behavior change will generalize to other settings.
7. When working with severely handicapped youths, the teacher should restrict the range of socially reinforcing statements to one or two. More adaptive and verbal adolescents may benefit from a range of statements.
8. Once the target behavior(s) reach an acceptable level, the number of socially reinforcing interactions should be gradually reduced. This

will increase the likelihood that the behavior change will be maintained in the absence of high rates of social reinforcement.

Contingency Contracting

Contingency contracts include: (1) concise descriptions of behaviors expected to be performed by the adolescent in order to gain the designated consequences; (2) a clear statement regarding the positive consequences that will result from performing the behavior to the specified criterion; (3) a clear statement regarding aversive consequences, if any, that will result from failing to perform the behavior to criterion; (4) a delineation of the teacher's responsibilities in facilitating success for the adolescent; and (5) a statement indicating how maintenance of the desired behavior will be reinforced. Contingency contracts result from mutual negotiation between the educator and the student. This ensures the individual's involvement in the planning, implementation, and evaluation of the behavior change strategy. As such, the student involved in developing the contingency contract becomes a co-engineer of his or her educational program. It is generally recognized that children and adolescents who participate in the formation of their educational program are more likely to adhere to the stipulations of the program (Gardner, 1977).

Homme, Csanyi, Gonzales, and Rechs (1969) emphasize the application of the Premack Principle in developing contingency contracts. The Premack Principle (Premack, 1965) states that a student's low-probability behavior may occur more often by providing him or her the opportunity to participate in a high-probability behavior (e.g., "When you finish your reading workbook, you can go to recess."). The authors state that a contingency contract is used to formalize the arrangement between high-probability behaviors (i.e., reinforcers) and low-probability behaviors (i.e., the target behavior).

Contingency contracts can include reinforcement and punishment principles. A positively reinforcing element states a pleasant event that will result from the performance of a behavior (e.g., "If you complete your work, then you can watch television."). A negatively reinforcing element states how performance of a behavior will result in the removal or avoidance of an unpleasant event (e.g., "If you keep your desk clean during class, then you will not have to spend your recess time washing it."). A punishing element states an aversive event that will result from the performance of a behavior (e.g., "If you talk out in class, then you will write lines from the dictionary.").

Reinforcement and punishment elements may be used separately or in combination, depending on the objectives of the program. Contracts designed to decrease the performance of a behavior will probably include punishing elements. Those designed to increase responses will include rein-forcing elements. Whenever a punishing element is included, a reinforcing element should be added to promote a behavior that may replace the response being eliminated. For example, if verbal aggression produces a loss of free time, an element of the contract may award special privileges for assertiveness skills. In this way, assertiveness may be developed through the contract to replace aggression.

Clear and complete terms should be included in the contract. Behaviors, responsibilities, and consequences addressed by the contract should be delineated so that all individuals involved in the program are aware of the scope and plan of the contract. Attention given to the details of the contract in the planning stage will avoid possible controversies that may result from poorly worded or vague agreements. The process by which the contract is developed is just as important as the final written product. Contingency contracts should result from mutual negotiation between two or more par-ties. This process may assist in maintaining the student's interest in the behavior change program. Negotiation sessions are also excellent oppor-tunities for the teacher to assist the student to clarify personal goals, under-stand the teacher's expectations, explore potential behavior change strat-egies, and examine the consequences of current and future behavior patterns.

The use of an objective observational and recording system is an addi-tional concern in developing a contingency contract. The observational system is essential to evaluating the effectiveness of the program as well as providing feedback to individuals involved. The student may be re-sponsible for recording progress toward the goal with the teacher or another individual conducting reliability checks. This is consistent with the under-lying theme of placing as much control over the behavior change process in the hands of the student as possible.

The following six procedures should be considered in developing and implementing a contingency contract:

1. The expectations to be made of the student should be stated in clear and complete terms.
2. The responsibilities of others involved in the contract should be stated clearly and completely.
3. The pleasant events available to the student through fulfilling the stipulations of the contract should be described.
4. The unpleasant events, if any, that will result from failure to fulfill the requirements of the contract should be stated.
5. An objective observational and recording system should be used to monitor progress under the contingency contract. Information pre-sented in Chapter 8 may help in meeting this guideline.
6. A maintenance goal should be included in the contingency contract.

The following four points should be kept in mind:

1. To the extent possible, the contract should be developed through interactions between all concerned persons.
2. The objectives of the program and its consequences should be equitable.
3. The contract should emphasize what the students may gain through compliance with the contract.
4. All concerned individuals should fulfill their responsibilities under the contract.

Exhibit 7–2 displays a sample contract.

Differential Reinforcement of Low Rates of Behavior (DRL)

The preceding consequence control procedures have been demonstrated to be effective in promoting behaviors. DRL and the other consequence control procedures that follow have been designed to reduce excessive responses. DRL achieves this goal through the reinforcement of behavior at successively lower rates. For example, the administration of reinforcement for talking out in class only twice a day when compared to a baseline period of five times a day would constitute the differential reinforcement of a lower rate of talking out. The concept of a DRL is somewhat paradoxical in that a reinforcement procedure is used to reduce behavior. Of course, the reinforcement procedure strengthens a lower rate of the excessive behavior. DRL procedures may involve successive changes in the expected performance. For example, once the youth's talking out behaviors occur at a consistent rate of twice a day, the criterion for reinforcement may be changed to once a day. As this objective is achieved, the expected rate may be changed to no occurrences a day.

It should be apparent that DRL is a highly positive approach to reducing undesirable behaviors. The educator who reinforces an adolescent for working at a slower rate on a shop project, thereby increasing the quality of the project, is using a DRL procedure. This may be contrasted with the aversive approach of criticizing the youth for sloppy work habits. The DRL procedure reinforces slower rates of performance while the aversive approach punishes excessively fast performance.

This approach has several advantages over potentially effective aversive procedures. Foremost, DRL has a positive orientation that promotes behavior change through the student's seeking to acquire positive consequences. This may be contrasted with aversive procedures that promote behavior change through the adolescent's avoidance of unpleasant con-

Exhibit 7–2 Contract between Bob J. and Mrs. Smyth

I, Bob J., agrees to adhere to the following rules as of July 2, 1983:

1. Arrive in my homeroom class every morning prior to the first bell (8:30 a.m.).
2. Complete all of my in-class assignments prior to the time they are due.
3. Provide my parents with all of my daily work once it has been graded.
4. Remain in eighth hour study hall until all of my homework is completed or until the period ends.
5. Complete at home all homework not finished during study hall.

The teacher agrees to:

1. Check with Bob every day at the start of study hall to be sure he knows how to complete his assignments.
2. Provide tutorial assistance, if necessary.
3. Award Bob a passing grade, thereby assuring his eligibility for football, if he complies with his responsibilities under this contract. Three or more truancies in the grading period and/or six or more incomplete assignments will result in a failing grade.
4. Release Bob from study hall permitting him to work out in the gym once all of his assignments are completed.

Bob's football coach agrees to:

1. Supervise Bob in the gym once his study hall work is complete.
2. Monitor and provide support in assisting Bob to fulfill his responsibilities under this agreement.

Bob's parents agree to:

1. Monitor the completion of evening assignments.
2. Provide Bob with the opportunity to use the family car when evening assignments are completed.
3. Provide Bob with the use of the family car and five dollars each week that he complies with the stipulations of this contract.

Maintenance bonus:

Bob will be given tickets and transportation for two to a professional football game if he is not truant more than three times in the grading period, and fails to complete less than 6 assignments.

Date: _____   _____
                                     Bob J.

_____   _____
Mrs. J.   Coach Jackson

_____   _____
Mr. J.   Mrs. Smyth, Teacher

sequences. The development of a success and reward orientation is consistent with the social development viewpoints underlying this book. A related advantage of the DRL approach is that it promotes adaptation at a level that is easily attainable by the adolescent. DRL does not require an abolishment of the target behavior. Rather, the goal of the procedure is to promote the performance of the target behavior in moderation.

Finally, DRL can easily be applied as a shaping procedure designed to reinforce successively lower rates of behavior until the terminal target rate of the behavior is achieved. For example, Deitz and Repp (1973) have demonstrated the effective reduction of misbehavior in a secondary classroom by reinforcing progressively lower rates of disruptive behavior. Their procedure was applied to 15 girls in a high school business class. The girls were reported to change the topic of class discussion to less relevant interests. A baseline rate (frequency per minute) of "subject changes" was established over a six-day period from .10 to .16 subject changes per minute. An initial criterion for subject changes was set at .10. If the students changed the topic lower than that rate for the first four days of the week, they were awarded free time on Friday. Following the first week when this criterion was achieved, a new, more rigorous criterion was set. Following four successively lower rates for reinforcement, the rate of topic changes stabilized at zero for a four-day period.

In a similar demonstration, Deitz, Flack, Schwarzmueller, Wilander, Weatherly, and Hilliard (1978) reduced inapproprate school behaviors of a seven-year-old learning-disabled child. Target behaviors included running in the room, pushing, shoving, hitting other students or teachers, rolling on the floor, sliding under the desk, pounding on the desk, pencil tapping, throwing objects, dropping objects, destroying objects, sliding furniture, standing or jumping from furniture, and yelling. Tokens that could be exchanged for free time on the playground were used to reinforce successively lower rates of the disruptive behaviors over longer time periods. The report demonstrated that the DRL brought the rate of inappropriate behavior substantially below the baseline rate. The reduction in response rate corresponded with the level expected through the DRL procedure.

Three potential disadvantages of DRL procedures must be considered prior to implementing a program. First, it may require more time to achieve control over the maladaptive behavior than through aversive procedures. The selection of a DRL procedure for reducing aggressive behavior, for example, may be inappropriate as the procedure would ensure a gradual reduction in behaviors that should cease relatively quickly. Second, there are instances when engaging in the disruptive behavior is more rewarding than the positive consequences available. This is especially the case for some handicapped youths who find few reinforcing events in the school setting. Finally, the DRL procedure focuses the educator's attention on undesirable behavior. This may have an undesirable influence on adolescents who observe the educator deliver reinforcement for the inappropriate behavior.

Differential Reinforcement of Other Behavior (DRO)

DRO is defined as the reinforcement of any behavior other than the maladaptive behavior. As such, it also involves reducing the strength of excessive behaviors through positive means. DRO procedure is designed to increase the strength of behaviors that will replace the maladaptive behavior. For example, an educator may wish to reduce the frequency with which a child leaves her desk. Rather than (or in addition to) punishing the student, the educator may frequently reinforce the youth for any behavior emitted while in the seat.

Aside from being a positive approach, the DRO procedure produces more immediate results than extinction or noncontingent reinforcement approaches (Goetz, Holmberg, & LeBlanc, 1975). By design, the DRO procedure increases the strength of behaviors that may replace the maladaptive response. Given that these behaviors are functional, once the DRO procedure is withdrawn, the alternate behaviors would likely be practiced in the place of the deviant behavior. The likelihood of this happening may be increased by specifying the behavior or behaviors to be differentially reinforced. For example, a teacher may differentially reinforce positive social interactions between a child and her classmates. This may increase the probability that the child will engage in positive verbal interactions with her peers and decrease the probability that she will engage in inappropriate conversations. As the child's social skills improve, it may become apparent that prosocial behavior produces more favorable consequences than disruptive verbal behaviors. Thus, the prosocial behavior will be practiced consistently even after the intervention is withdrawn.

Thompson, Iwata, and Poynter (1979) demonstrated the use of a DRO procedure in reducing tongue thrusts of a ten-year-old boy with cerebral palsy. The intervention approach involved presenting food to the child only when his tongue was inside his mouth. The rate of tongue thrusts dropped from a baseline (preintervention) level of 94.7% to a rate of 27.2% during the final treatment condition. In this example, "tongue in mouth" was reinforced through the presentation of food. As "tongue in mouth" occurred more often, the child was less available to thrust his tongue out of his mouth. Thus, reinforcement of "tongue in mouth" reduced tongue thrust responses.

The use of DRO procedures could be limited in that the alternate behavior may be less rewarding than the disruptive behavior. This may result because others in the environment reinforce disruptive behaviors that the DRO procedure is expected to replace. Potential solutions may include identifying and removing competing reinforcing events (e.g., if a student leaves his seat to talk to a friend in the hall, reduce occasions in which his friend is in the hall), and/or using the DRO procedure in combination with other reductive procedures (e.g., reinforce the student for work done while in his seat while providing a response cost for getting out of his seat).

Extinction

Extinction is defined as the identification and removal of positive consequences that maintain a behavior. The inability of the behavior to produce previously reinforcing consequences is expected to diminish its strength. Ignoring an argumentative student exemplifies an extinction procedure. Arguing previously produced attention and possibly a change in the teacher's requests. When the teacher ignores the student these reinforcers are no longer available. Therefore, arguing loses its function in producing satisfying consequences. The rate of arguing can be expected to decrease. Another example frequently used by elementary school teachers involves not including substandard work in bulletin board displays. In this case, reinforcement in the form of the visible display of work is not given for poorly completed work. The educator expects that the frequency of substandard work will decrease if the child's performance is not reinforced.

Extinction procedures have been demonstrated to be effective in reducing a wide range of classroom behaviors (Hall, Lund, & Jackson, 1968; Solomon & Wahler, 1973; Wilson & Hopkins, 1973; Zimmerman & Zimmerman, 1962). Factors that have been demonstrated to increase the effectiveness of extinction procedures include the following:

- All sources of reinforcement must be eliminated from the target behavior. Simply removing a portion of the reinforcement may have the detrimental effect of developing a more persistent response pattern as the result of a thinner schedule of reinforcement.
- The exact setting must be specified in which the extinction procedure is to be conducted.
- The procedure must be continued for a sufficient amount of time to avoid the reinforcement of a higher rate of response that typically occurs at the start of an extinction program (extinction curve).

- The use of extinction in combination with DRO or DRL procedures generally will produce more favorable results.

Several disadvantages are associated with extinction procedures. As was discussed previously, there often is an increase in the strength of the target behavior immediately following the removal of reinforcement (the extinction curve). If reinforcement inadvertently occurs at the higher rate, a stronger maladaptive response may be developed. For example, a teacher may choose to ignore students who seek attention by waving their hands back and forth. Since this is not reinforced, the students may begin hopping up and down and calling the teacher's name. At some point, if the teacher does not call on the students, the disruptive handwaving will cease. However, if the teacher "gives in" and calls on students after the behavior has accelerated, the teacher may inadvertently increase the likelihood that the higher rate of the behavior will occur.

The potential inability of the teacher to control events that reinforce the response may be an additional disadvantage. It is often difficult to identify all consequences of disruptive behavior, especially if the behavior is maintained by infrequent positive consequences. Even when identified it is often difficult to control all consequences. As was previously discussed, the failure to remove all of the positive consequences may have the deleterious effect of increasing the persistence of the disruptive behavior. For example, a student's disruptive behavior in class may be motivated by attention received from others. The teacher may ask others to stop attending to that student. If all of the students do not comply all of the time, the continuous schedule of reinforcement that developed the behavior may diminish to a variable schedule of reinforcement. Over time, the behavior may be maintained under successively less reinforcement from peers. This is the same process used by the educator in planful fashion to develop the persistence of positive behavior.

Because of these limitations, extinction procedures should be used with great caution. Planning that precedes the implementation of the behavior change strategy should consider: (1) Can all the reinforcers that support the behavior be identified? (2) Can they be removed? and (3) Is it possible to ignore the behavior for a sufficiently long period of time to produce the desired effect? If these questions cannot be answered in the affirmative, then an alternative reductive strategy should be considered.

Response Cost

Response cost is defined as the removal of a specified amount of a reinforcer following the occurrence of a behavior. A library fine for failing to return a book is an example of a response cost familiar to most college students (and instructors). The failure to return the book results in the removal of a specific amount of money. This procedure is intended to reduce the likelihood that books will be returned late. Another familiar example of a response cost procedure is a traffic citation (the withdrawal of money) delivered for the purpose of reducing future occurrences of improper driving behavior.

Response cost procedures are fairly easy to administer in school settings. The loss of privileges is often a natural consequence in educational settings. The procedures have the advantage of being highly effective in reducing inappropriate behavior over a relatively short period of time. Because response cost programs can be designed in educational settings analogous to response cost procedures in the community, they can be expected to have a lasting effect on social performance. For example, if a student learns that tardiness to a class results in a loss of free time, it is likely that punctuality developed through the response cost procedure would transfer to a work situation in which tardiness produced the loss of money.

Unfortunately, response cost procedures have been demonstrated to result in negative emotional reactions and aggressive behavior (Boren & Colman, 1970; Doty, Mcinnis, & Paul, 1974). Anyone receiving a parking ticket, library fine, speeding citation, or dockage of pay can attest to these findings. This, in and of itself, may not be bad since the negative emotionality may do as much to deter future occurrences as the actual loss of reinforcement. However, the educator must be careful not to reinstate the reinforcer as a result of the emotional outburst. Doing so may have the undesirable effect of strengthening maladaptive emotional behaviors (e.g., threats of aggression, somatic complaints, excessive crying, swearing, etc.).

A major element in the effective use of response cost procedures involves balancing the amount of the reinforcement to be withdrawn for a given response with the supply of the reinforcer. Withdrawing too much of the reinforcer may deplete the supply to the point that the reinforcers are no longer available. This is exemplified by the merchant who attempted to sue an impoverished woman for failing to pay her bill. Withdrawing too little reinforcement may not be effective in suppressing the excessive behavior. Such is the case when the Internal Revenue Service fines a multimillionaire industrialist several hundred thousand dollars for tax evasion. The response cost can be expected to have little effect on future tax evasion behavior.

Overcorrection

Overcorrection has two major components. The first involves *restitution* in which environmental damage resulting from disruptive behavior is corrected. The second is the repeated *positive practice* of a behavior that is more acceptable than the disruptive behavior (Foxx & Azrin, 1972). An overcorrection procedure applied to a student yelling at another student may involve an apology (restitution) and the repetitious practice of a polite statement that serves the same function as yelling (positive practice). The overcorrection of throwing food in the lunchroom may include a thorough cleaning of the lunchroom (restitution) and the repeated practice of holding and using eating utensils in an appropriate manner (positive practice).

Overcorrection procedures, in contrast with response cost or extinction, engage the student in a learning experience centered around the events that provoke inappropriate behavior. Because the student is forced to practice prosocial behaviors that may replace the inappropriate behavior, a more rapid and durable behavior change can be expected (Foxx & Azrin, 1973). A related issue is that since the adolescent is practicing appropriate behavior, the likelihood of another maladaptive behavior replacing the reduced behavior is diminished.

Overcorrection, as other strategies, should be applied consistently and immediately following the target behavior. Overcorrection applied immediately following the target behavior has the benefit of removing the function of the disruptive behavior. For example, John may shred his worksheet in order to avoid completing it. The overcorrection procedure effectively replaces the worksheet. Future occurrences of this behavior are diminished as John learns that tearing up a worksheet does not result in its removal. If, however, this is not enforced consistently, the procedure may simply reduce the likelihood that the behavior will be reinforced. Inadvertently thinning the schedule of reinforcement may have the effect of producing a more durable and persistent disruptive behavior.

A final consideration in using overcorrection involves the selection of restitution and positive practice activities. In both cases, the activity used should be relevant to the maladaptive behavior. An activity relevant to destructive behavior, for example, is the repair of damage to the environment. Apologies in written or verbal form may be relevant restitution approaches for disruptive verbal interactions. The positive practice procedure should develop a behavior that may function in place of the disruptive or maladaptive behavior. For example, assertiveness skills may be practiced following verbal aggression and walking in the halls may be practiced following a running incident.

Token Reinforcement

Token reinforcement involves the delivery of a token immediately following the occurrence of a target behavior. The tokens may then be exchanged for a reinforcing object or event at a later time. There are many natural parallels to token systems in society. Probably the most obvious token program is our economic system. Money (as a token) is received following a period of work. The money may be exchanged for backup reinforcers such as food, entertainment, housing, commodities, and so on. There have been numerous applications of token programs in the literature (Barkley, Hastings, Tousel, & Tousel, 1976; Frederiksen & Frederiksen, 1975; Hobbs & Holt, 1976; Thomas, Sulzer-Azaroff, Lukeris, & Palmer, 1977).

Russo and Kuegel (1977) demonstrated the use of a token system in integrating an autistic five-year-old girl into a normal, public school class-room. The girl received a poker chip each time a positive social behavior occurred (e.g., any response involving direct interaction with another person). Social reinforcement was paired with the delivery of the token. This procedure was intended to strengthen the reinforcing qualities of social praise. During each one-hour session the girl accumulated tokens in a cellophane bag attached to her clothes. Following the session she was permitted to exchange her tokens for backup reinforcers at a "store," described as a corner of the classroom that contained a variety of food items. At later points in the program a response cost phase was initiated. In this phase a token was removed from the bag each time the girl initiated a self-stimulatory behavior. Finally, a phase was initiated in which the girl received tokens for verbal responses to commands. The program resulted in a substantial increase in social behavior and responses to commands and a decrease in self-stimulatory behavior.

A number of principles should be adhered to in designing and implementing a token economy. First, as with all reinforcers, tokens should be delivered immediately following the occurrence of the target behavior. The duration of time between receiving and being permitted to exchange the tokens should be based on the characteristics of the learner. Excessively long delays may result in a weakening of the reinforcement strength of the token. Excessively short delays do not encourage the child or youth to develop an ability to delay gratification. Second, the number of tokens exchanged for an item must be carefully considered. Expecting too few tokens to be exchanged for the backup reinforcer may satiate the child or youth. Expecting too many may frustrate the student. The individual will not be likely to work for an item or event that he or she has little expectation of acquiring.

Third, tokens must be delivered consistently. There should be little doubt to either the student or teacher as to the level of performance that will be reinforced. Fourth, as with all behavior management procedures, the procedures that will be followed in implementing the token system should be described in detail to the student. For more severely handicapped students the procedures may be rehearsed prior to the implementation of the program. Prompts may be used to ensure the student's knowledge of the operation of the program. These may include a poster or card indicating the behaviors to be reinforced or response cost and the amount of tokens to be awarded or deducted; a reinforcement menu describing backup reinforcers and their cost; and a rack or tray for holding tokens in such a way that progress toward achieving the backup is graphically displayed. Fifth, the reinforcement strength of the backups should be evaluated. Students are not likely to work for tokens that can only be exchanged for disinteresting backup reinforcers. The quality of the backup reinforcers can be maximized by providing a range of items from which the students may select. This procedure (referred to as a token store or reinforcement menu) reduces the likelihood that a child or youth will become tired of (satiated with) any one reinforcer. It is also a good way to evaluate the strength of various reinforcers. Items selected most often by the student are those most reinforcing. Also, the strength of existing reinforcers can be maximized by limiting their availability outside the token program. Students are not likely to work to gain candy in class, for example, if they have free access to candy at lunch and after school.

Finally, token programs are fairly intrusive. They require a reasonable amount of time and expense to operate. Also, in some cases they may be difficult to fade from the student's educational program. Therefore, care should be taken not to adopt a token program when more subtle approaches may be equally effective. When using a token program, token delivery should always be paired with social reinforcement. This procedure may facilitate the strength of praise as a reinforcer and eventually result in the fading of the token program.

Appendix 7–A illustrates a token economy developed by the author for a vocational program serving mildly and moderately mentally retarded adolescents and young adults.

CONCLUSION

A number of procedures have been reviewed that have been demonstrated to be effective in altering the social responses of handicapped children and youths. Specifically, this chapter has considered consequence control procedures that increase or decrease the likelihood of a behavior's occurrence. The strengths and limitations of the procedures reviewed in this chapter have been highlighted. Beyond these guidelines, a word of caution is in order for the selection of reductive procedures. No other set of social development strategies has as strong a potential for misuse and harm to the learner.

Gardner (1977), in a comprehensive review of the punishment literature, has developed a series of guidelines for the use of reduction procedures. Adherence to these considerations is critical to insuring the success of reductive programs while minimizing the influence of negative side effects.

Gardner's guidelines include:

1. Use punishment infrequently and only in combination with positive procedures.
2. Prior to punishment, define precisely the inappropriate behavior, the conditions under which it occurs, and its strength.
3. Define precisely the punishment procedure to be used before initiating it.
4. Define explicitly the circumstances in which punishment will be used.
5. Specify alternative behaviors which will replace the punished ones along with the reinforcement procedure for strengthening these.
6. Time out or response cost are favored over procedures involving the presentation of aversive events.
7. Inform the child in a clear and precise manner about those behaviors resulting in positive consequences and those producing negative consequences.
8. Implement rules regarding punishment consistently and immediately.
9. Provide alternative behavioral possibilities.
10. Present maximum intensity of the aversive event from the beginning.
11. When using a punishment procedure, exercise care to insure that consequences are in fact unpleasant to the child.
12. Insure that the unpleasantness of aversive consequences is stronger than the positive consequences associated with the undesirable behavior.
13. After the child is informed of the punishment rule, routine use of a threat or warning about further undesirable behavior producing unpleasant consequences is to be discouraged.
14. When reprimand is used as a punishment procedure, present it so that it does not attract the attention of other children.

15. If punishment effects are not evident rather immediately, it is probably best to discontinue the procedure.
16. In using mild punishment to suppress behavior which occurs in numerous settings, it will typically be necessary to implement the punishment contingency in each setting.
17. Punishment procedures should be phased out of an educational program as quickly as possible.
18. To reemphasize, when punishment is used, label the contingencies for the child. (pp. 371–376)

Token Economy for Mildly and Moderately Mentally Retarded Adolescents

Tokens (Currency)

Target behaviors will be reinforced with United States currency. Students will possess a purse or wallet that enables them to carry money at all times.

Store

A store will be housed in the school area. Five types of transactions may be conducted at the store: (1) exchange of money for low-cost, immediately consumable items; (2) exchange of money for high-cost, substantial items; (3) exchange of money for trip tickets; (4) exchange of money for special privileges within the residential or work settings; (5) exchange of money for a certificate of deposit that allows the individual to save for items one through four without carrying large amounts of money in his or her wallet or purse.

Charges and Reinforcers

A schedule of charges will be prepared that indicates the cost of each item, trip, or special privilege available at the store (Exhibit 7A–1). Also, a schedule of reinforcers (Exhibit 7A–2) will be made available to each participant. The schedule will include behaviors that are reinforced and the amount of money provided as a consequence of the behavior.

Fines

A schedule of fines (Exhibit 7A–3) will be made available when a program includes a response cost component. Fines will be assessed from the individuals' pocket money and savings in that order. Under no conditions

179

Exhibit 7A–1 Schedule of Charges

Item	Cost	Item	Cost
Consumables		Trips	
1.		1.	
2.		2.	
3.		3.	
4.		4.	
5.		5.	
Long-Term Items		Privileges	
1.		1.	
2.		2.	
3.		3.	
4.		4.	
5.		5.	

Exhibit 7A–2 Schedule of Reinforcers

Name _____	Date _____
Behavior	Money Earned
1.	1.
2.	2.
3.	3.
4.	4.
5.	5.
6.	6
7.	7.
8.	8.

will staff members deduct money from savings in order to settle a debt. Rather, the staff must issue the students debt slips that must be "paid off" by the individuals before another purchase is made from the store. Debt slips (Exhibit 7A–4) can be paid off by the individuals withdrawing money from their accounts.

Pocket Money

The participants will be permitted to carry a reasonable amount of money in their wallets or purses. This money can be used in a variety of ways (see currency). An individual program may specify the time at which some or all of the money must be exchanged and a maximum amount of money that can be carried.

Exhibit 7A–3 Schedule of Fines

Name _____   Date _____

Behavior   Fine

1. _____   1. _____

2. _____   2. _____

3. _____   3. _____

4. _____   4. _____

5. _____   5. _____

6. _____   6. _____

7. _____   7. _____

8. _____   8. _____

Exhibit 7A–4 Debt Slip

Name: _____   Date: _____

Behavior: _____   Amount owed: _____

This debt must be canceled before a purchase can be made.

Savings Account

Currency may be exchanged for a certificate of deposit. This will indicate the amount of money placed in savings and the total amount in the savings account (Exhibit 7A–5). When useful to the student, this may be graphically displayed. Money can be withdrawn from the savings account at any time. Savings must be withdrawn by an individual to "pay off" a fine before they can be withdrawn to purchase an item. Miscellaneous tickets and records are shown in Exhibits 7A–6–7A–10.

Exhibit 7A–5 Savings Record

Date	Deposit	Withdrawal	Outstanding Fine	Balance

Name: _____

Exhibit 7A–6 Reward Record

Name:	Date:
Amount of money earned: Behavior:	
Amount of money earned: Behavior:	
Amount of money earned: Behavior:	

Exhibit 7A–7 Fine Record

Name:	Date:
Amount of money fined: Behavior:	
Amount of money fined: Behavior:	
Amount of money fined: Behavior:	

Exhibit 7A–8 Trip Ticket

Congratulations _____!

You have earned a trip to _____

with _____.

You will leave at _____

and return _____.

Exhibit 7A–9 Special Privilege Ticket

Congratulations _____

You have earned the special privilege of _____

_____

This privilege will begin _____

and end _____

Exhibit 7A–10 Individual Token Economy Plan

Name: _____ Date: _____

Target Behaviors	Schedule	Rewards
1. _____	_____	_____
2. _____	_____	_____
3. _____	_____	_____
4. _____	_____	_____
5. _____	_____	_____

Fines

1. _____	_____	_____
2. _____	_____	_____
3. _____	_____	_____
4. _____	_____	_____
5. _____	_____	_____

Savings: Frozen   ☐

            Open   ☐

Maximum pocket money: _____

Schedule for exchange: _____

_____

_____

Special aids (e.g., graphic displays, penny boards, etc.)

_____

_____

_____

Exhibit 7A–10 continued

Available Purchases

Consumable   Long-term

1. _____   _____

2. _____   _____

3. _____   _____

4. _____   _____

5. _____   _____

6. _____   _____

7. _____   _____

8. _____   _____

9. _____   _____

10. _____   _____

Trips   Privileges

1. _____   _____

2. _____   _____

3. _____   _____

4. _____   _____

5. _____   _____

Chapter 8

Program Planning

The preceding chapters have identified three major entry points through which interventions may occur. Each of the entry points is described through its temporal relationship with the target behavior. Antecedent conditions were described as events that precede the target behavior and influence the likelihood of its occurrence. Related personal characteristics were described as observable or inferred features of the learner that mediate between provoking antecedents and the target behavior and influence the probability of the target behavior's occurrence. Finally, consequent conditions were described as events that follow the target behavior and influence the probability of its future occurrence.

Social development strategies subsumed under each of the entry points have been described in detail. Antecedent control procedures included establishing a positive student-teacher relationship, classroom structure, and specific antecedent change procedures. The related personal characteristics entry point included emotional learning, interpersonal skill training, and social skill training. Finally, the consequence control entry point considered social reinforcement, contingency contracting, the differential reinforcement of low rates of behavior (DRL), the differential reinforcement of other behavior (DRO), extinction, response cost, overcorrection, and token reinforcement.

A substantial body of literature has evolved supporting the effectiveness of these strategies. Unfortunately, a brief review of this literature may lead the reader to believe that social development procedures are selected indiscriminately. Contrary to this view, an underlying assumption presented in Chapter 1 is that the selection of intervention approaches results from a careful study of the student's behavioral characteristics in association with influencing environmental events. The present chapter will discuss procedures that facilitate the selection of social learning strategies based on learner and setting characteristics.

ETHICAL ISSUES

The social learning orientation is based on the tenet that one individual (i.e., the teacher) can influence or control the behavior of another individual (i.e., the student). Further, an assumption is made that procedures that are more reliable in controlling students' behavior are superior to those that leave the outcome of intervention open to a large degree of chance. This view is contrary to the firmly entrenched doctrine of free will characteristic of Western culture. Free will implies that people's actions, to a large extent, result from inner motives or drives. While hereditary endowment or environmental impact may be interesting in considering a person's actions, the individual has ultimate control over his or her choice of friends, courses of study, extracurricular activities, health habits, etc. Contrary to this notion, the task mandated to educators is to use the most effective strategies available to alter a learner's performance commensurate with predetermined objectives.

P.L. 94-142 specifies that an individualized education plan (IEP) will be developed for all handicapped children and youths (aged 3 to 21). The IEP must contain the student's current level of performance, annual goals and short-term objectives, the services to be provided, projected date of initiation, projected date of completion, evaluation procedures, and schedule for revising the program. These procedures require a directive approach to academic and social development. The multidisciplinary team must agree on objectives and approaches for the year. Further, behavior change must be evaluated. If behavior does not change or change occurs at an excessively slow rate, the program must be modified. In short, whether the educator adopts a psychoeducational, humanistic, or behavioral orientation the task remains to change the student's behavior until it is congruous with the preestablished objectives.

Another issue associated with the social learning orientation involves the methods by which educators who employ behavioral principles attempt to change behavior. There is an unfortunate view in the field that behavioral strategies are limited to token reinforcement, time out and other contingency management procedures (Gambrill, 1977). Contrary to this, there is a wide range of behavioral intervention strategies many of which closely parallel procedures employed by nonbehavioral practitioners. The preceding chapters, for example, include over a dozen intervention options that may be used independently or as part of a more comprehensive educational program. As discussed earlier, these tactics are designed not only to punish or reinforce behavior, but also to control the stimulus conditions that cue behavior. Other approaches are designated to systematically teach appropriate responses. The list of intervention tactics in these chapters is limited to procedures most applicable to primary and secondary education settings.

A related issue is that misguided interventions have led to an overgeneralized criticism of behavioral technology. There has been an unprecedented rate of media attention to unethical treatment approaches suggesting that the application of some behavioral principles is inherently unethical. For example, a recently criticized use of token economy involves establishing items necessary for the support of life (e.g., meals, clothing, water, warmth, etc.) as backup reinforcers. This caused undue hardship and a potential for injury to the recipients. Criticizing the preceding program is highly justified. However, relevant criticism would not be toward token economies as a social learning procedure but toward the denial of life-supporting items and events. To argue on the basis of the preceding example that token economies should be banned is tantamount to arguing that client-centered therapy should be banned because, in the process of establishing an open relationship, some therapists become intimately involved with their clients.

Behavioral principles are valid descriptions of relationships that exist in nature (e.g., a behavior that produces satisfying consequences is likely to recur as will behavior that leads to the avoidance of unpleasant conditions). While the principles, as stated, can be ignored, the relationships that they describe will continue. Using behavioral strategies simply allows the practitioner to enhance student change through systematic and planned procedures that reflect the practitioner's understanding of learners and their environment. Because of the strong influence that an educator may have in controlling a student's behavior, the need to protect an individual's rights is extremely important. A number of authors have advanced detailed discussions of ethical issues in the design and application of behavior change programs.

One of the more concise statements of ethical practice is presented in *Law and Behavior* (1976). Exhibit 8–1 presents a summary of the guidelines. An adjoining column demonstrates how the IEP process can be used to facilitate these safeguards.

A final concern is the selection of social development approaches that are maximally effective yet minimally intrusive. Intrusiveness is defined as the extent to which the procedure removes the student from the mainstream of educational activities; is unpleasant to the child or youth; consumes educational resources in the form of, for instance, staff time, materials, and money; is unusual to the educational environment; and is potentially dangerous to the student or other individuals in the setting. Establishing an a priori ranking of behavior change strategies on the basis of intrusiveness is a difficult, if not impossible, task. Differences in the setting in which

Exhibit 8–1 Ethical Standards and the IEP Process

Ethical Standard	IEP Mechanism
1. Prior to establishing the behavior change program, a specific description of the student's behavioral characteristics and needs should be prepared.	Psychological and behavioral data supporting the need for the behavior change program should be obtained prior to intervention.
2. The objectives of the plan should be stated in behavioral terms. Anticipated short-term outcomes should be clearly defined and a timetable for their attainment provided.	The IEP should include the goals of the behavior change procedure, short-term objectives, and expected date of completion.
3. The relationship between the program objectives and procedures should be described to the learner.	The parents and student should be aware of the goals of the educational program as well as the procedures adopted to meet the goals.
4. People from the student's natural environment involved in the program should be identified. Their responsibilities should be clearly articulated.	The IEP is developed and implemented cooperatively by teacher, parents, ancillary personnel, and the student, when appropriate.
5. All persons involved in the intervention procedures should be identified.	Implementors for each goal statement are identified in the IEP.
6. The progam should be reviewed and revised monthly.	Annual multidisciplinary staff meetings are conducted for the purpose of developing the full service program. Beyond this, periodic review is necessary whenever a major program change is anticipated.

intervention is conducted and the characteristics of the learner quickly invalidate such ranking. For example, it may be argued that a response cost procedure is more intrusive than the differential reinforcement of other behaviors. However, for a specific individual, a response cost administered consistently may reduce the excessive behavior to an acceptable rate in a week or two. The DRO procedure, on the other hand, may require several months. In the meantime, the student is less able to benefit from academic instruction for an extended period of time under the DRO condition. In this example, it could be argued that a response cost procedure is less intrusive than the use of DRO because it is less likely to be a detriment to the student's academic development.

The following ranking may be valid assuming that:

- skill development procedures are likely to be supported by the natural environment
- procedures involve the systematic use of natural consequences, such as contingent free time and planned ignoring
- programs alter the stimulus environment, such as separating antagonistic students and providing cues to prompt performance
- procedures involve unnatural positive contingency arrangements, including token systems and contingent delivery of edible reinforcers and
- procedures involve unnatural aversive consequences such as timeout, overcorrection, and corporal punishment.

To summarize, intervention strategy selection is a function of the careful analysis of the learner and his or her environment. It is the responsibility of the educator to select the least intrusive of available approaches expected to be effective. The following sections will present a detailed analysis of procedures used to match an intervention program to the characteristics of the learner.

PLANNING FOR CHANGE

A review of the principles that underlie this text emphasizes that children's and adolescents' social responses are influenced by interactions with the environment. The principles of reinforcement and punishment have been advanced to describe the relationship between the student's responses and historical or contemporary events. A learner's social characteristics are shaped through these principles regardless of parents', teachers', or peers' recognition of their existence. Children and adolescents raised in a nurturing, supportive environment characterized by liberal positive reinforcement for prosocial behaviors and neutral unpleasant consequences for disruptive behaviors generally develop acceptable social-personal attributes.

Exceptional learning characteristics, as described in Chapter 1 and Chapter 2, result in the general environment being less responsive to the handicapped individual. The criterion for success and reinforcement, established for the general population, is often unattainable. In the absence of reinforcement for prosocial behavior, the handicapped learner may exhibit alternative responses to gain satisfaction. Reinforcement relationships may include truancy or tardiness to avoid unpleasant aspects of the academic environment, dishonesty to avoid aversive aspects of academic failure, excessive disruptive responses to gain peer attention, etc. Over time, these responses may become a stable part of the student's social characteristics.

In some cases, these responses become resistant to common antecedent and consequence control procedures (e.g., changing seats, changing assignments, verbal reprimands, etc.). Further, these attempts to bring disruptive behaviors under control result in more severe behavior problems as is the case of a student becoming aggressive to avoid detention. On these occasions, educators must adopt procedures that: (1) are better matched to the characteristics of the student and setting; (2) can be more consistently applied; (3) minimize the likelihood of negative side effects, such as higher rates of the behavior or greater persistence; (4) include more influential consequences; (5) expect more modest performance expectations; (6) account for and remove natural consequences that interfere with the goals of the program; and (7) include components that monitor and substantiate even subtle changes in the behavior.

Individual social development programs, therefore, result from the careful study of the student and the setting. This study must be translated into program planning activities. Planning activities to be described in the balance of this chapter include determining that a problem exists, prioritizing problem behaviors, defining problem behaviors, establishing the setting of the intervention program, establishing a criterion for performance, identifying influencing events, identifying potential reinforcers, formalizing the intervention program, and establishing procedures for fading the program. Strategies for evaluating the intervention program will be discussed in the following chapter.

Determining That a Problem Exists

The logical first step of program development is to decide that a problem of sufficient magnitude exists that warrants intervention beyond the scope of general program procedures. This decision is reached by: (1) identifying the expectations of the student and significant people in the environment; (2) determining the current strength of the student's behavior; and (3) determining the discrepancy between the student's present behavior and expectations of self and others for future behavior.

The goals of the program may include: (1) increasing the consistency with which the student performs existing skills, such as completing assignments prior to the end of study hall; (2) developing new skills, such as learning sight words from the Dolch list; (3) refining existing skills, such as improving voice tone when responding to a teacher's criticism; and (4) reducing excessive disruptive responses, such as eliminating the use of swear words when talking to peers. The precise targets of the intervention program must be considered prior to the development of specific strategies.

Social development objectives may be based on data from a variety of sources. Teachers, parents, siblings, peers, and employment supervisors, as well as the individual student, may all contribute information that assists in determining expected program outcomes. The multidisciplinary staffing, during which the student's IEP is developed, may be an ideal time to discuss intervention priorities. Sulzer-Azaroff and Mayer (1977) have proposed the following questions to be raised in evaluating the appropriateness of social development goals:

1. Is the goal:
   a. Constructive?
   b. Likely to be supported in various settings?
   c. Likely to be maintained in the natural environment?
2. What is the likelihood of success in achieving the goal?
3. Does the behavior analyst (teacher) have sufficient:
   a. Knowledge of procedures?
   b. Competence to implement procedures?
   c. Interest to achieve the goal?
4. Can existing programs achieve the goal more efficiently?
5. Does the goal permit placing more and more responsibility on the client (student)?
6. Is the goal accessible to direct measurement?
7. Does the goal fit appropriately into a task analysis sequence?
   (p. 43)

Assessment data that support the identification of program targets may include criterion-referenced and norm-referenced tests, anecdotal reports of direct observations, situational performance tests, and measures of permanent products. Collectively, these data should provide a general idea of the frequency or intensity of potential intervention targets across relevant settings. Vague descriptions such as inhibited, lazy, unhappy, flighty, uncooperative, and so on, are of little use in deciding the program focus. Specific behavior descriptions, such as "fails to participate in oral reading" or "completes fewer than 50 percent of homework assignments," describe the behavioral deficiency with greater precision.

As Sulzer-Azaroff and Mayer (1977) emphasize in their criteria for goal selection it is important to know what significant people in those environments view as being the optimal level of social functioning for the student. Parents, peers, supervisors, and others should provide information that allows the designer of the program to determine the expected level of the target behavior following intervention. This level will become the terminal objective of the intervention program. For the purpose of program development, a handicapped adolescent's exceptionality will be defined by the discrepancy between others' expectations and what he or she does across a number of important settings. This view is consistent with the principles outlined in the functional classification chapter (see Chapter 3).

Prioritizing Target Behaviors

Any number of exceptional characteristics may be identified for an individual through the preceding procedures. In order to maximize the probability of success and minimize the initial demand on the learner, priority behaviors should be selected. The number of behaviors targeted by the behavior management program should be limited by the degree to which the student may be expected to respond favorably. It is generally understood that excessive demands result in frustration and failure for handicapped youths. Programs that induce high rates of failure violate the basic assumptions of a social learning theory view by confirming the student's expectancy for failure and punishment in social situations (Gardner, 1966). The goal of behavior management programs is to promote a positive association between prosocial behavior and pleasant social outcomes. Therefore, an intervention program should focus only on the range of high-priority behaviors that can be developed or reduced without establishing excessively frustrating conditions for the student. Behaviors that are excluded from the initial intervention program may be identified as the targets of future programs.

As a general rule, programs designed to reduce the likelihood that an adolescent will exhibit a certain behavior should have a very narrow focus. At most one or two behaviors should be associated with the punishing consequence. Targeting one or two well-defined behaviors will maximize the effectiveness of the punishment procedure while minimizing emotional side effects resulting from potential unpleasant consequences (Johnston, 1972). Programs that seek to increase the occurrence of positive consequences may have a broader focus. Reinforcement programs may associate up to five behaviors with potentially pleasant consequences. The program should be designed so that the student is continually striving for positive consequences by exhibiting prosocial behavior. A fortunate side effect of a well-designed program may be that a number of related behaviors may change beyond those specifically targeted (Twardosz & Sajwaj, 1972).

For example, Schloss, Sachs, Miller, and Schloss (1982) recently reported a study that involved the reduction of stereotypic behaviors and increase in positive social behaviors of a 20-year-old woman in a workshop setting. While production rate was not directly addressed by the intervention procedure, an increase from 20 percent of the production norms to 80 percent of the production norms was reported to be a collateral benefit of the behavior management program.

Defining the Target Behaviors

Clear and complete response definitions serve three major purposes: (1) they increase the likelihood that contingencies are delivered consistently; (2) they assist the learner in identifying exact behaviors that will produce reinforcement or punishment; and (3) they facilitate the reliable measurement of program effects.

General descriptions of a student's characteristics, such as insensitive, unfriendly, lazy, uncooperative, etc., will invariably produce confusion for the student as well as unreliable assessment data. Such data are of little use in implementing, monitoring, or evaluating intervention programs. Laziness, for example, may refer to deficits in academic performance, refusal to participate in physical education exercises, excessive sleeping during the day, excessive television watching after school, and/or frequent daydreaming at work. Any one or all of the specific behaviors may be characteristics of the individual. The general description *lazy* does not specify precise behavioral excesses or deficits. Also, *lazy* does not describe important conditions that may be relevant to measurement. For example, is the individual lazy all of the time, only at school, only in math class, etc.?

The adequacy of response definitions is traditionally evaluated by determining the extent to which two independent observers agree on the occurrence or nonoccurrence of the behavior. This test of a response definition is called interobserver reliability. The actual procedure for determining the reliability of a response definition will be presented in the following chapter.

Examples of clear, objective, and complete response definitions include:

- worksheet completion—the ratio of worksheets completed each week to worksheets assigned
- tardiness—the discrepancy between the time the class period begins and the time the student arrives in class
- answering questions—the frequency with which the student responds when called upon
- swearing—emitting the following words sufficiently loud to be heard by another individual . . .

- screaming at others—directing voice sounds toward another individual with sufficient intensity to be heard at a distance of 80 feet (Any voice sound that does not include words is also recorded as screaming at others regardless of the intensity.)

Establishing the Setting for Intervention

Social development programs for handicapped students have the greatest impact when conducted in the setting in which change is expected to occur. A number of studies have demonstrated that behavior changes do not automatically transfer from one setting to another (Bates, 1980; Koegel & Rincover, 1974; Schloss, Sachs, Miller, & Schloss, 1982). Recent literature emphasizes the importance of teaching exceptional students in natural settings (Kazdin, 1980). For example, social skill training would best be implemented during activities in which social greetings are appropriate, including school parties, sport events, free time in class, walking down the school halls, on entering a new room, etc. Each of these areas would best be included within the scope of a social skill development program. A highly ineffective approach would be to limit social greeting training to the classroom or a counseling setting and expect that social greeting skills would generalize.

Additionally, conditions that may influence the student's performance within each setting should also be identified. If a program is to focus on improving the independent work rate of an adolescent in study hall, it is important to know the conditions under which the student is expected to work. The program may focus on teaching and motivating the student to work quickly when sitting at an isolated part of the room or when seated in a large group. A program designed to reduce verbal aggression should specify important conditions under which the student will not be verbally aggressive, such as when confronted by a fellow student, when criticized by a teacher, or when frustrated by a difficult assignment. As with setting specifications, the most effective way to influence the student's behavior is to teach and motivate with reference to specific conditions (Risley & Wolf, 1967).

As a final concern, the implementors of the program should be identified prior to the formalization of the plan. Professionals, paraprofessionals, work supervisors, relatives, peers, and others may all be responsible for implementing parts of the program. The teacher must ensure that all program participants are aware of their responsibilities as detailed in the intervention plan. If the objective of a program is to develop positive self-statements while the student is at school and home, the student's teachers, siblings, and parents may be asked to frequently label the student's positive social and academic behavior and encourage him or her to do the same. In this example, the success of the intervention plan will rely on the teacher communicating the program approach to a variety of other people.

Determining Short-Term and Terminal Objectives

The importance of success experiences in motivating positive motivational characteristics cannot be understated (Cromwell, 1963; White, 1960; Zigler, 1973). Social development procedures that radically alter the learning environment or impose a substantially higher performance expectation may result in frustration or failure for the handicapped student. The careful selection of short-term and terminal objectives allows the educator to progress gradually toward the goal of the program. Short-term objectives are small, easily attainable behavior changes that progress in a logical sequence toward the long-term objective, or the major objective of the social development program. The identification of short-term objectives results from the teacher's understanding of the individual student's: (1) entry skills; (2) learning rate; and (3) competing behavioral characteristics.

Short-term objectives should identify the criterion level considered to represent acceptable performance. Once the student performs at criterion consistently, the intervention may be redirected to a subsequent objective. Once mastery is achieved on all of the sequential short-term objectives, the terminal objective will be completed. Figure 8–1 illustrates the flow of sequential short-term objectives that comprise a terminal objective.

The process described above is illustrated in a program designed to develop positive student-teacher interactions. The terminal objective is that Bob will be able to respond appropriately when addressed by his teacher at school. Four sequential short-term objectives were identified that comprised the terminal objective as follows:

1. For short-term objective 1, Bob will be able to respond with an appropriate statement indicating compliance following a request by the teacher.
2. For short-term objective 2, Bob will be able to respond with an appropriate statement indicating compliance following a request by the teacher.
3. For short-term objective 3, Bob will be able to verbally acknowledge error and indicate future corrective action when criticized by his teacher.
4. For short-term objective 4, Bob will be able to exchange an appropriate amenity when greeted by his teacher.

The scope of each short-term objective should reflect the learning characteristics of the student. Students expected to benefit very quickly from

Figure 8–1 Short-Term and Terminal Objective Sequence

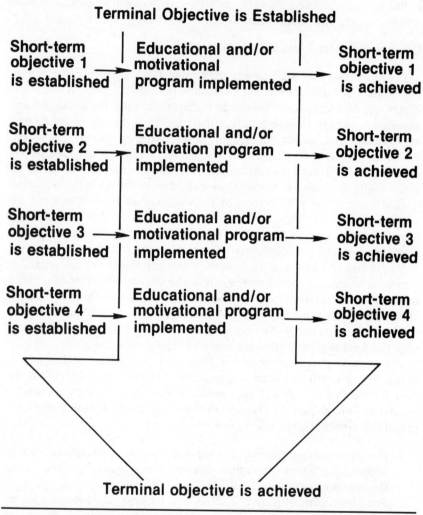

new instruction will have large performance expectations within each short-term objective. Smaller expectations may be appropriate for students less able to benefit from instruction. This is exemplified by the following sequence:

1. For short-term objective 1, Jill will be able to say "thank you" following the teacher's compliment.

2. For short-term objective 2, Jill will be able to say "thank you" and make a general statement as to how she enjoys doing good work.
3. For short-term objective 3, Jill will be able to say "thank you," make a general statement about pleasant aspects of her job and identify a specific part of her work activity that is particularly satisfying.

Identifying Antecedents and Consequences

Chapters 5, 6, and 7 have emphasized the importance of observing the student in relevant environments prior to developing an intervention program. The stated purpose of these observations was to identify events that may be associated with the problem behavior. These target events may be identified as being antecedent conditions that influence the likelihood that a behavior will occur and as consequence conditions that either reinforce or punish the target response. The environmental target areas and related personal characteristics, which will be addressed in the next section, will become the focus of an intervention program. Antecedents and consequences that are believed to maintain or strengthen disruptive behaviors will be identified and removed, while antecedents and consequences that support positive social behaviors will be intensified.

Antecedent conditions discussed in Chapter 5 can either: (1) cue a desirable response; (2) cue an undesirable response; (3) fail to cue a desirable response; or (4) fail to cue an undesirable response. Once it is known that a specific event cues disruptive behavior, the cue can be altered, thereby reducing the frequency of disruptive behaviors. For example, being teased by a peer may be an antecedent to a verbal outburst. Intervention in this case may focus on antecedents by removing the children from situations in which teasing is likely to occur. Once the students learn to respond appropriately in other less demanding conditions, they may gradually be reintegrated to the problem settings. Similarly, if it is observed that a naturally occurring event that should cue a positive social behavior does not, the cue control of the event can be developed, thereby increasing the strength of the positive social behavior. For example, observation may reveal that an adolescent, working in the school cafeteria, seldom says "thank you" as students pay for their food. Intervention may develop the receipt of money as an antecedent for saying "thank you."

Similarly, consequent conditions, described in Chapter 7, can either increase, decrease, or maintain the strength of behavior. Observing the student may help to generate hunches as to the function of specific consequences. If it is known that a specific consequence increases the likelihood that an undesirable behavior will occur, the reinforcing consequence may be removed. If it is known that there are few positive consequences associated with a desired social behavior, favorable consequences may be established.

As previously discussed, consequences are described as being positively reinforcing, negatively reinforcing, or punishing. Positive reinforcers are events that follow a behavior and increase the probability that the behavior will recur. Positive reinforcers are generally pleasant to the individual. However, as emphasized in Chapter 7, consequences perceived by the teacher to be unpleasant may be positive reinforcers. Negative reinforcement involves the removal of unpleasant events following a behavior, thereby increasing the probability of the behavior's occurrence. Finally, punishment is defined as a reduction in the strength of a behavior resulting from the presentation of an unpleasant consequence. The contingency relationships previously described occur over time as a part of the adolescent's natural learning environment. Continuous recording is used to identify contemporary events that reinforce or punish target behaviors in a specific setting. The data are then translated directly into an environmentally based intervention program.

Exhibit 8–2 illustrates a form that may be used when conducting continuous observations. The student's name, the time when observations were conducted, the observer's name, and the setting in which observations were made are reported at the top of the form. Specific target behavior(s) is identified in the middle column. Antecedents and consequences are described in relationship to the target behavior(s).

Data for continuous recordings are acquired by observing a student throughout the time in which the program will be conducted. For some students, observations may be conducted for one specific instructional period (e.g., a mainstreamed math class). For others, observations may include the entire day and weekends. Observations may be conducted by one or more individuals. The individual designing the program may take responsibility for instructing others in the continuous observation procedure. It may be especially useful to involve the student's parents in continuous observation in home and community settings when the ultimate program is expected to be conducted in these environments. Finally, more adaptive students may be taught to continuously record their own behavior. This is a particularly effective self-control strategy as it encourages the students to study the conditions under which their problem behaviors occur. The students may subsequently avoid these conditions.

The continuous recording form should be completed during or immediately following observations. Waiting extended periods of time (e.g., until the end of the day or week) will invariably reduce the comprehensiveness and accuracy of the information. Continuous recording should be integrated with other classroom activities. Forms may be placed at con-

Exhibit 8–2 Continuous Observation Recording Form

| | Student's Name _____ |
| Teacher's Name _____ |
| Setting _____ |

Time	Antecedent Conditions	Target Behavior	Consequent Conditions

venient locations in the classroom so that classroom instruction is not disrupted during the recording process.

Continuous recording involves three major steps. First, the teacher stipulates the target behaviors to be observed. Each time the student engages in one of the target behaviors, a precise description of the response is entered into the Target Behavior section. These descriptions may later be used to formalize the response definition. Second, the teacher records the events that immediately preceded the occurrence of the target behavior in the Antecedent Conditions section. Finally, events that immediately followed the occurrence of the target behavior are recorded in the Consequent Conditions section.

Related personal characteristics, described in Chapter 6, may also become the target of an intervention program. Related characteristics include inferred or observed features of the student that are hypothesized to mediate between antecedent or cue conditions and target responses. For example, specific social skills were discussed as potential related personal characteristics that, if developed, would reduce aggressive outbursts for the handicapped adolescent. Continuous recording may demonstrate that verbal confrontations by peers are antecedents to aggressive behavior, and informal observations may suggest that the individual lacks assertiveness skills. It may be speculated that the student is not able to exhibit assertive behavior that would allow him or her to avoid verbal confrontations with peers.

Determining the Student's Reinforcement Hierarchy

Continuous recording often reveals that consequences that normally occur in school are not effective in motivating performance for some students. For example, the average student is generally motivated by personal pride in the product, praise from the teacher, peer popularity, good grades, etc. These are generally considered to be the consequences of diligent school work. Because of cognitive deficits, a deficient learning history, excessive failure experiences, and so on, the same events may not motivate the handicapped student. While a prevalent position may be to label the student "lazy," "disinterested," or "immature," it is the responsibility of the educator to alter the motivational characteristics of the student. Central to the analysis of motivational deficits is the instructor's knowledge of events that occur as consequences of performance that are satisfying or aversive to the individual. Two general recommendations can be made when a motivational deficit is attributed to the inability of consequent conditions to maintain consistent performance. First, natural consequences should be presented more frequently or immediately. Second, alternate consequences that may be expected to motivate the student should be structured into the environment. In either case, the teacher must be skilled in identifying viable reinforcers, prioritizing potential alternate reinforcers, and assessing the reinforcement hierarchy of the student.

Consequences may be either primary or secondary reinforcing events. Primary reinforcers are those events that satisfy basic biological needs and are important to sustain life. These events do not depend on previous learning or conditioning for the development of their reinforcing properties. Primary reinforcers are used more frequently with primary aged children and the severely developmentally disabled. Secondary reinforcers, on the other hand, are used more frequently in intervention programs for the mildly and moderately handicapped adolescent. Secondary reinforcers include events that have acquired reinforcement status through frequent association with a primary reinforcer. For example, money acquires its power as a reinforcer through its association with the acquisition of food, water, shelter, and other primary reinforcers. Secondary reinforcers frequently available in the school setting include grades, praise, approval, privileges, and activities. Secondary reinforcers associated with independent living and vocational settings include money, work evaluation reports, production data, and special privileges based on rank.

Primary and secondary reinforcers can be prioritized from least to most effective in motivating a behavior and least to most likely to occur naturally in the educational or vocational environment. Prioritization on the basis of reinforcer strength is critical to establishing incentives that are sufficiently powerful to motivate the target behavior. Once a range of reinforcers is identified that is likely to be effective, potential reinforcers natural to the setting can be selected. For example, a teacher may suspect that candy, money, and free time will reinforce school work completion. Food items and money are seldom natural incentives in the school setting while free time is a natural and logical result of early completion of work. Free time would be an appropriate incentive for work completion because it is hypothesized to be sufficiently powerful, and it is a natural and logical consequence of work completion.

Several procedures may be used to assess the strength of potential reinforcers. The most simple is to ask the individual what she or he enjoys. In addition to an informal discussion, the self-report data can be developed through a number of interesting and enjoyable social activities. Small groups can be structured that focus on identifying and clarifying pleasant events in the school environment. One approach may be for the instructor to ask the students to write independently 20 things that they really enjoy about school. Next, the teacher may ask the pupils to rank the items from most to least enjoyable. The class members may then discuss their top five selections and write them on the board. Finally, the class may be asked to reach consensus on the rank order of items placed on the board. Information provided by students should be substantiated through other assessment approaches. It is generally understood that an individual's verbal behavior (what a person says he or she will do) is not always the same as the person's overt behavior (what he or she actually does).

Observing what the student does during free time or unstructured activities may be used to augment self-report data. It can be expected that the student will engage in preferred activities when free to do so. If a student frequently plays basketball during an unstructured recreation or recess period, basketball is an enjoyable and potentially reinforcing activity. Another method of identifying potential reinforcers is to observe what a student does with his or her spending money. If a student often purchases record albums, it is likely that listening to records is a rewarding activity, and "stereo time" and record albums are potential reinforcers. Parents, siblings, and peers may be valuable resources in identifying potential reinforcers. They are often in a position to observe what a student does during free time as well as how the student spends money.

Reinforcer sampling is another effective approach to identifying and developing incentives. Reinforcer sampling involves exposing the student to a potentially enjoyable activity. Once the student has been exposed to the activity, the teacher may make the activity contingent on a desirable behavior. For example, a teacher may initiate a special break period in which all of the students are encouraged to participate in board games. After several sessions, the teacher may say that students will be allowed to play only if they have completed their homework. This procedure is particularly useful when exposing students to unfamiliar or novel incentives. Students may not have worked for break time initially. However, once they have a chance to experience the new card sessions, the reinforcement value may increase.

FORMALIZING THE PROGRAM

The preceding sections have addressed the major questions that may be raised prior to formalizing and implementing a social development program. As has been discussed, program analysis involves three major activities. First, the teacher raises specific questions that are related to the student's performance problems. Second, the teacher identifies sources of information that may answer these questions, thereby providing a better understanding of the performance problems. Finally, the teacher uses the resulting information to develop a social development program that reflects the needs of the students, the expectations of significant people in their environment, and the resources available to the teacher and students.

Exhibit 8–3 presents a program summary sheet that may facilitate the design, implementation, and evaluation of an intervention program. The format of the program summary sheet is consistent with the methods discussed throughout this chapter. The intervention target(s) section requires

Exhibit 8–3 Program Summary Sheet

Student _____

Date _____

Teacher _____

Intervention Target(s)

Behavior _____

Definition _____

_____

Criteria for success _____

Behavior _____

Definition _____

_____

Criteria for success _____

Behavior _____

Definition _____

_____

Criteria for success _____

Settings

Location(s) _____

_____

Important conditions _____

_____

Implementors _____

_____

Potential Reinforcers

Tangible _____   Social _____

_____   _____

_____   _____

_____   _____

_____   _____

Activity _____

_____

_____

_____

_____

Exhibit 8–3 continued

Evaluation Procedure _____

Program Approach

Antecedent components _____

Related personal characteristics components _____

Consequence components _____

Fading procedure _____

the teacher to specify the focus of program, define the target behavior, and establish a criterion for success. The setting section requires the identification of the setting or settings, important conditions and change agents that are expected to be associated with the program. The potential reinforcer section provides a summary of items and events that may be used to motivate the student. The evaluation procedure section requires the teacher to identify a procedure for measuring, recording, and displaying the strength of the target behavior. (These procedures are discussed in the following chapter.) The program approach section provides a summary of procedures for altering antecedent and consequent conditions, as well as related personal characteristics.

Finally, the fading procedure section stipulates strategies that may be followed to dismantle the program once acceptable responses are attained.

This section is particularly important as the rapid removal of program procedures may result in a deterioration of performance gains. The following section will review procedures for minimizing the likelihood of regression once the program is withdrawn.

FADING PROCEDURES

Unnatural or intrusive elements of an intervention program should be gradually and systematically withdrawn once the target responses stabilize at an acceptable rate. As was stated, the abrupt removal of program procedures will most probably result in a regression of the target behaviors. This effect may be due to: (1) the program not being in effect long enough for natural consequences to develop reinforcing properties; (2) the immediate loss of high rates of reinforcement; (3) the immediate return of antecedents that have a long history of cuing unacceptable behavior; (4) the immediate loss of antecedents for acceptable behavior; (5) the student's failure to acquire self-control skills. Intervention approaches should include strategies that increase the likelihood that the student will exhibit positive social behavior once the program is withdrawn (Baer, Wolfe, & Risley, 1968).

Program Duration

The first consideration in fading intervention is to leave the program in place sufficiently long to develop a positive association between naturally occurring consequences and stronger contrived incentives. Potential reinforcers develop their strength by being paired continually with better established primary or secondary reinforcing events. Over time this association develops the strength of the weaker, more natural reinforcer. Once the naturally occurring event has acquired stronger reinforcing properties, the continued reinforcer may be gradually withdrawn. The performance gains achieved through the program are expected to be maintained because of the increased strength of the natural reinforcer.

Forming Complex Responses

Once a number of discrete positive social responses are developed, they may be combined to promote more complex social competencies. Early in the program each of the discrete behaviors may have been reinforced separately. In forming complex responses, the teacher may provide reinforcement only at the conclusion of a series of previously separate responses. For example, a student may be reinforced separately for sitting in his seat on time, completing assignments, and complying with the teacher's requests. In fading the program, the teacher may begin to reinforce the entire sequence of "appropriate classroom behaviors." Under this condition, reinforcement is delivered if the student exhibits *all* of the responses rather than individual behaviors.

Thinning the Reinforcement Schedule

A similar consideration involves thinning the reinforcement schedule. Most intensive interventions require continuous reinforcement (e.g., reinforcing each occurrence of the behavior) to establish the desired response. While this is the most powerful approach to developing a new or low-probability behavior, behavior maintained by continuous reinforcement is highly susceptible to deterioration following the withdrawal of reinforcement. Therefore, once a behavior is established through a schedule of continuous reinforcement, an intermittent schedule of reinforcement should be introduced. Reinforcement may be thinned through a fixed or variable schedule of reinforcement.

A fixed schedule involves reinforcing the student every two, three, four, or more times the behavior occurs. With the fixed schedule, the student and teacher are aware of when the reinforcement will be delivered. For example, the student may be reinforced following every four assignments completed or for every three days of good behavior.

Variable schedules are different in that the student is not aware of when reinforcement will occur. With the variable schedule, the student may be reinforced on the average of every third day. In either case, the student does not know exactly when reinforcement will be delivered.

When possible, reinforcement programs should be faded through the use of variable schedules of reinforcement. It has been demonstrated that fixed schedules produce a highly variable rate of behavior as the student predicts when reinforcement will occur and increases performance prior to delivery. Following reinforcement the student may be inclined to reduce performance. Variable schedules, on the other hand, produce stable response rates that are highly resistant to deterioration following the withdrawal of reinforcement.

Reintroduction of Natural Antecedents

Another important consideration in promoting maintenance is the gradual reintroduction of the natural antecedents that, prior to the program, cued inappropriate behavior. For example, if failure generally preceded aggression for a learning-disabled student, once aggression control was established under failure-free conditions, reasonable amounts of failure may be reintroduced. This process challenges the student to exhibit control over his or her behavior under conditions that, prior to intervention, resulted in descriptive behavior. The termination of intervention prior to reintroduction of provoking cue conditions does not permit the student to practice and be reinforced for positive social behaviors under adverse conditions.

CONCLUSIONS

The social development program planning activities described offer a comprehensive approach to teaching and motivating prosocial behavior. The procedures emphasize the study and modification of antecedents, related personal characteristics, and consequences associated with precise behavioral objectives. Additional emphasis is placed on teaching and reinforcing prosocial competency behaviors that may replace disruptive behaviors. Fundamental to the behavior management system described is the careful assessment of learner characteristics and ecological influences. While the preceding chapters have described a number of isolated intervention approaches, the careful educator may use these planning activities to select several strategies for use at one time. The practice of developing a treatment package can often produce a more comprehensive and powerful behavior change program. For example, the differential reinforcement of other behaviors should always accompany reductive strategies. This is to develop and strengthen prosocial behaviors that can function in the absence of disruptive behaviors. Self-control strategies (e.g., individually selected consequences, self-monitoring of the target behavior, etc.) may accompany teacher-directed approaches.

A final important consideration in the development of effective social development procedures involves the evaluation of intervention procedures.

The confidence that the teacher has that the prescribed consequences will motivate or punish the desired behavior is important to intervention. The evaluation procedures described in the following chapter provide a level of confidence in the efficacy of the social development program. The measurement of behavior strength prior to and during intervention provides the teacher with information on the student's performance while the program is in effect. More sophisticated evaluation designs that will be discussed provide even stronger evidence of the effect of intervention procedures on the student's social development.

Program Evaluation

The principles that underlie this text highlight the importance of program evaluation endeavors. There is a repeated emphasis in these chapters on the adoption of procedures that substantiate the impact of intervention on the learner's performance. Unfortunately, teachers' apprehension toward program evaluation activities has been widely documented (Krathwohl, 1977). This is in spite of the fact that teachers are in a key position to implement program evaluation efforts (DeVault, 1965). Kerlinger (1977) has emphasized the demand by teachers for a practical and relevant data base from which to select, evaluate, and modify educational interventions. The position advanced in this chapter is that educators should be the primary agents for generating this data base.

SYSTEMATIC OBSERVATION

Systematic observation procedures are especially appropriate for this purpose. Six major features highlight their utility. First, systematic observation procedures rely on the educator's assessment of the individual learning and behavioral characteristics of the handicapped student. Second, alternative educational procedures may be prescribed on the basis of the learner's characteristics. Third, systematic observation procedures are highly adaptable to systematic instructional approaches. Fourth, they are sufficiently flexible to allow the modification of social development strategies as indicated by the pupil's performance. Fifth, they do not require the comparison of separate individuals but emphasize the progress of one individual under various program conditions. Finally, systematic observation procedures allow the practitioner to validly and reliably assess the effectiveness of a given social development procedure.

Systematic observation procedures may be developed along a seven-step plan as follows:

1. selecting a measure of behavior strength;
2. establishing the reliability of the measure of behavior strength;
3. selecting an evaluation design (e.g., case study, reversal design, multiple-baseline design, or changing criterion design);
4. initiating the evaluation design;
5. charting results;
6. modifying treatment, if necessary, based on the charted data; and
7. communicating findings to those concerned with the social development of the student.

These steps will be discussed in the following sections of this chapter.

Selecting a Measure of Behavior Strength

The evaluation of a social development program requires the continuous monitoring of the target behavior(s) prior to and during the implementation of treatment. The continuous monitoring of performance is particularly useful for teachers in special education classrooms as it facilitates the on-going evaluation of intervention plans. An ineffective program can be quickly identified and modified. Subsequent data can test the efficacy of the modified approach. This may be contrasted with a pre-post evaluation design in which evaluative data are generated only after the program is completed.

The validity of program evaluation decisions is closely associated with the accuracy of the observational data. The most elegant and sophisticated evaluation procedure cannot produce important results from inaccurate data. Sulzer-Azaroff and Mayer (1977) offer the following three major criteria for precise behavioral measurement: 1) observations must be objective in that personal interpretations and feelings do not influence the data; 2) observations must be valid, measuring the behavior they intend to influence directly; and 3) observations must be reliable. The reliability of data is judged by the extent to which a measurement procedure will produce similar results when used by independent observers. In most cases, direct naturalistic observations using a well-defined target behavior meet these criteria (Jones, Reid, & Patterson, 1975). The direct measurement of behavior can be conducted through a number of techniques.

Event Recording

Event recording is often the most useful and least time consuming of all measures of behavior strength. The strength of a behavior is determined by counting each episode of the behavior over a specified period of time. The selection of frequency recording is appropriate when the observed behavior has a distinct start and stop such as chairs stacked, papers torn, or greetings acknowledged and when the response lasts a relatively constant amount of time (Kazdin, 1980). Event recording is inappropriate when the target behaviors are not discrete or of constant duration. For example, a social development procedure may reduce the duration of tantrums from two hours in length to ten minutes, but not alter the frequency of the tantrums. Therefore, event recording would not be sensitive to the behavior change.

Simple frequency data from day to day are often not directly comparable because of varying times available for observation. A student may be in the lunchroom for 20 minutes one day and 60 minutes on the next. On the first day, there were two aggressive outbursts, while there were three on the second. It cannot be concluded that the child was more aggressive on the second day because the amount of time observed influenced the measurement. When the observational time is variable, frequency of response should be transformed to a rate of response giving comparable data across observation periods. The rate of response is computed by dividing the number of occurrences (frequency) by the duration of the observation. In the previous example, there were two aggressive outbursts in 20 minutes on the first day, yielding a rate of .1 aggressive outbursts per minute,

$$\text{Rate} = \frac{\text{Frequency}}{\text{Time}} = \frac{2}{20} = .1$$

while there were three aggressive outbursts in 60 minutes on the second day, producing a .05 rate of aggressive outbursts per minute (i.e., $\frac{3}{60}$ = .05).

A number of devices have been suggested to reduce the amount of time involved in event recording. For example, Mahoney (1974) used an abacus watchband and Lindsley (1968) used a golf counter. Mechanical counting tools are especially useful in school settings because they require only one hand to make a tally, are portable, and can be operated without disrupting other classroom activities. Beyond the instrument used to tally the information during the day, a recording sheet that stores data from day to day is essential. Exhibit 9–1 illustrates a commonly used data sheet for observations of varying length.

Permanent Product

The measurement of permanent product is very similar to event recording. This measure may be selected over event recording when the target response results in some quantifiable product. Products may include units

Exhibit 9–1 Recording Sheet for Rate Data

Student _____   Setting(s) _____
Target Behavior _____
Definition _____   Teacher(s) _____
_____   _____
_____   _____

| Date | Time | | | Frequency | Rate |
	Start	Stop	Total		

of work completed, items collected, area cleaned, objects broken, and so on.

The measurement of permanent products is exemplified in a study reported by Trap, Milner-Davis, Shirley, and Cooper (1978). The authors developed an elaborate scoring procedure to determine the correctness of cursive letters. The percentage of correctly trained letter strokes was used to evaluate the influence of feedback, rewriting, and reinforcement on cursive letter formation. When using permanent product as a measure of performance, the educator must insure that the task demands are relatively stable throughout the program. This ensures that the individual's performance level is not obscured by tasks that vary in difficulty from session to session. Also, when an individual is expected to do a different number of tasks from day to day, permanent product data should be expressed as the percentage of correct responses over the number of opportunities to respond. Exhibit 9–2 illustrates a recording form that may be used to obtain and summarize permanent product data. The word task used in the form may include problems completed, sentences written, pages read, etc.

Interval Recording

This measure of behavior strength is often used to monitor behaviors that do not have discrete start or stop times and/or that vary in length (e.g., singing, talking, running, sitting, etc.). Interval data are collected by dividing the school day into several (e.g., from two to five) shorter time periods (e.g., 10 to 30 minutes). These shorter time periods are then divided into from ten-second to one-minute intervals. The behavior then is scored as occurring or not occurring at any time during the shorter time interval (partial interval), through the entire interval (whole interval), or only at the moment the interval started (momentary interval). The resulting measure of behavior strength reflects the percentage of intervals in which the behavior occurred. Because this is a time-sampling method, these data should represent the strength of the behavior through the entire day.

For example, from a six-hour instructional day three *random* 15-minute time periods may be selected for observation. Each of the 15-minute time periods may then be subdivided into 60 intervals of 15 seconds each. For a partial interval technique, the measure of behavior strength would result from recording whether or not the behavior occurred in each of the 15-second intervals. The duration of the response would be important only when the episode lasted for more than one interval. The resulting data then would be the number of intervals in which the response occurred, not the actual duration. It is expected that the resulting rate of intervals in

Exhibit 9–2 Recording Form for Permanent Products

Student _____   Setting(s) _____
Product _____
Quality Standard(s) _____   Teacher(s) _____
_____   _____
_____   _____

| Date | Task | Time | | | # Tasks Completed | Rate |
		Start	Stop	Total		

which the behavior occurred would represent the rate at which the behavior occurred throughout the entire day.

Another example of an interval recording procedure is offered by Marholin and Steinman (1977). The authors assessed on-task behavior of adolescents with academic and behavioral problems. They divided five-minute observation periods into 20 intervals of ten seconds each with five seconds for recording (i.e., ten-second observation followed by five-second recording, repeat). An observation interval was scored as on-task if the child was engaged in an assigned task for at least nine seconds of the ten-second interval.

Three types of time-sampling data have been described in the literature. A *whole interval* time sampling method requires that the response be sustained through the total interval for that interval to be scored. A *partial interval* time sampling method requires that the response occur any time during the interval. Finally, a *momentary interval* time sampling method involves recording only when the response occurs at the end of an interval.

Kazdin (1980) described an interval procedure useful in observing a number of children during the same period of time. The first child was observed in the first interval, the second child in the second interval, and so on, until all children were observed. Then the recorder returned to the initial child and repeated the sequence until all of the children were observed for a number of intervals. Another variation of the interval time sampling method involves observing the child through an interval and then taking a short period of time to record the response before beginning the second interval. Observation intervals may be 15 seconds in length, while scoring intervals are 5 seconds in length.

Exhibit 9–3 represents a common scoring sheet used with interval recording. The numbers over each square denote the time of the interval. A + or a − is used to indicate the occurrence or nonoccurrence of the behavior. The interval data are transformed to the percentage of intervals in which the behavior occurred by dividing the number of occurrences by the number of intervals.

Duration Recording

Duration recording is useful when the intervention approach is expected to increase or decrease the amount of time an individual engages in an activity. An investigator may seek to increase the amount of time an individual spends working on homework or decrease the amount of time an adolescent spends in the halls between classes. In these cases, the dependent measure would be duration. Whitman, Mercurio, and Coponigri (1970) utilized duration data in a study designed to evaluate the effectiveness of a social interaction training procedure. The researchers measured the number of minutes spent in social interaction by program participants. Exhibit 9–4 illustrates a standard form for recording duration data.

Response latency is a variation of duration data used when the dependent measure is the amount of time from some event to a specific response. Phillips (1968) used latency data to assess the effectiveness of a strategy designed to reduce tardiness of predelinquent youth.

Exhibit 9–3 Interval Data Recording Form

Student _____	Setting _____
Target Behavior _____	Recorder(s) _____
Definition _____	_____

Interval
Length _____

− = nonoccurrence
+ = occurrence

	1	2	3	4	5	6	7	8	9	10	% scored +	Time Period
Date _____											_____	_____
Average											_____	_____

	1	2	3	4	5	6	7	8	9	10		
Date _____											_____	_____
Average											_____	_____

	1	2	3	4	5	6	7	8	9	10		
Date _____											_____	_____
Average											_____	_____

	1	2	3	4	5	6	7	8	9	10		
Date _____											_____	_____
Average											_____	_____

Interobserver Reliability

The most elaborate observational system is of little use if it fails to provide a reliable estimate of the student's performance. Generating program recommendations from observations conducted with an unreliable system is analogous to building a house with an elastic tape measure. In either case, the decisions that result from the data are likely to be incorrect. The accuracy of an observational procedure is defined as interobserver reliability. Interobserver reliability is determined by assessing the degree to which independent observers agree on the occurrence/nonoccurrence or duration of the target behavior. In general, reliability indicates the consistency with which the target behavior is observed and scored (Kazdin, 1980). High reliability allows the teacher to attribute variability in the data to the treatment procedure rather than observer error. Low interobserver

Exhibit 9–4 Duration Data Recording Form

Student _____	Setting _____
Target Behavior _____	Recorder(s) _____
Definition _____	_____
_____	Observation Time _____

Date	Time		Duration
	Start	Stop	

reliability is often the result of an inadequate response definition or observational procedure. For example, it is unlikely that independent observers would agree on the occurrence of "depressive episodes" using a frequency measure (e.g., number of hyperactive episodes). On the other hand, if the response definition were changed to number of times the individual made negative self-statements, two observers would probably agree fairly consistently.

Interobserver reliability for event recording is determined by two individuals observing the student for the same period of time. The lowest frequency of occurrences is then divided by the highest frequency of occurrences to produce the reliability coefficient (i.e., percent of agreement between two observers). For example, two teachers record the number of negative self-statements uttered by a child for a two-hour period. One teacher records ten, while the other records nine. The resulting reliability coefficient would be computed by dividing the smaller number of observations (nine) by the larger (ten), producing 90 percent agreement as shown below:

$$\frac{\text{smaller frequency}}{\text{larger frequency}} = \frac{9}{10} = .90$$

Reliability in duration recording is computed by dividing the shorter duration recorded by the longer duration recorded by two independent observers as shown:

$$\frac{\text{shorter duration}}{\text{longer duration}} = \frac{75}{90} = .83$$

The reliability coefficient in interval recording is determined by dividing the number of intervals in which both observers scored an occurrence by the number of agreements and disagreements. Intervals in which both observers did not score an occurrence are excluded from the computation. The formula is:

$$\frac{\text{\# agreements}}{\substack{\text{\# agreements \& disagreements} \\ \text{excluding nonoccurrences}}} = \frac{12}{16} = .75$$

Interobserver reliability should be evaluated prior to the initiation of baseline, during baseline, and every few weeks throughout the program. Baseline refers to the period of data collection prior to intervention. Reliability should be tested at a level of .75 or better prior to the initiation of baseline. Consistently high reliability (e.g., .98) requires fewer checks. As was previously mentioned, low reliability prior to baseline may indicate the inadequacy of the response definition or observation procedure. Before continuing with data collection, the teacher should redefine the target behavior and/or modify the observation procedure until reliability exceeds .80.

Kent, O'Leary, Dretz, and Diament (1979) have demonstrated that observers obtain higher rates of agreement when they are aware that a reliability check is being made as compared to the level of agreement obtained when they are not aware. Therefore, to obtain a more conservative estimate of reliability, the primary observer should not be aware of times in which reliability checks are conducted. Unfortunately, practical limitations often make this practice difficult, if not impossible. In lieu of blind reliability checks, researchers increase the frequency of reliability checks throughout the study (Taplin & Reid, 1973). In general, if the data-keeping system, response definition, and method for collecting reliability data are structured by the classroom teacher to reduce or eliminate subjective judgment and bias, the reliability of obtained data will be defensible and, more importantly, usable for decision-making purposes within the classroom.

COLLECTING BASELINE DATA

Systematic observation procedures use the continuous measurement of the target behavior through a baseline (A) phase and treatment (B) phase. The baseline provides a measure of behavior strength under "natural" conditions, against which subsequent treatment effects may be compared. In order for comparisons to be valid, the baseline must be representative of the true behavior strength under normal program conditions. A valid representation of behavior strength is achieved by collecting reliable baseline data through four or more days in which there is neither an ascending trend, when a reductive intervention is planned, nor a descending trend, when an accelerative intervention is planned. Also, there should be some degree of stability in the data.

An ascending trend indicates that the target behavior is increasing in strength. A descending trend indicates that the target behavior is decreasing in strength. If the examiner shifts to the B phase while an ascending or descending trend is present in the expected direction of treatment, comparisons between phases cannot be made with any degree of confidence. Figure 9–1 exemplifies a descending baseline trend and a subsequent downward trend in treatment data. The effect of treatment on the target behavior is not clear because the trend following treatment is the same as prior to treatment. It is questionable whether the treatment had an effect. Similarly, when an ascending baseline precedes a treatment designed to strengthen a target behavior, the influence of treatment on the behavior is not clear. In order to overcome this problem, the baseline condition should be continued until a plateau is reached or until the behavior attains acceptable levels through natural program conditions.

Another baseline pattern involves an ascending baseline preceding a deceleration program or a descending baseline preceding an acceleration

Figure 9–1 Improperly Descending Baseline Trend

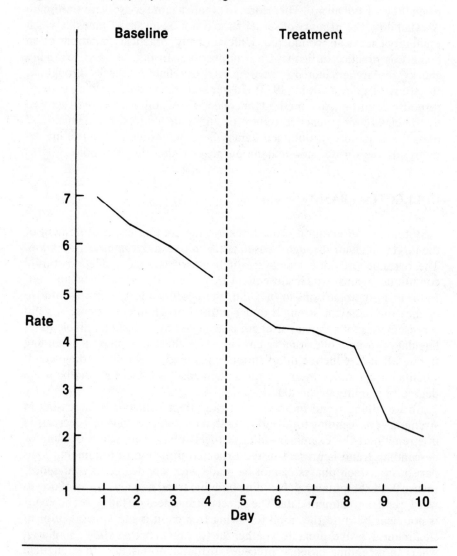

program. In these cases, the trend in the baseline data indicates a deterioration in the behavior that treatment is designed to improve. These patterns present less of a concern to applied researchers than the previous pattern as treatment effects can be ascertained from a redirection of the dependent variable.

The final baseline pattern of concern is the unstable baseline. Wide variations in baseline data collected over short periods of time reduce the teacher's ability to ascertain the strength the target behavior had if treatment was not applied. An unstable baseline can often be corrected by delaying the introduction of the B phase until some degree of stability is obtained or until sufficient baseline data are accumulated to demonstrate that the data are neither ascending nor descending under natural conditions.

The influence of the observer on behavior strength or reactivity is the final consideration in establishing valid baseline observations. The presence of observers may influence the occurrence or nonoccurrence of the target behavior (White, 1977). While several researchers have presented contradictory findings (Mercatoris & Craighead, 1974; Nelson, Kapist, & Dorsey, 1978), there is general agreement in the literature that investigators should guard against reactivity as a contaminating influence on behavioral data (Kazdin, 1980). Reactivity can be minimized by taking extended baseline data (thereby reducing the novel effect of data keeping and allowing the student to acclimate to the observation procedure), by using individuals frequently present in the setting as data takers, or by arranging for observers to be hidden from view (e.g., behind a one-way mirror, with a counter hidden in the teacher's pocket or desk, etc.).

Data Display

Recorded data are often difficult to read and interpret. Subtle trends indicative of improvement are not easily identified when data appear in tabular form. The relationship between data trends and the initiation of an intervention program is more easily understood when presented in graphic form. The traditional format for charting behavioral data involves three major components: (1) a vertical axis that clearly reports the measure of behavior strength; (2) a horizontal axis that reports the day or session number associated with each data point; and (3) broken vertical lines that indicate the initiation of the intervention program or subsequent changes in the program. Figure 9–2 illustrates these components. Notice that the vertical and horizontal axes are clearly labeled and that missing data points due to absence are connected with a broken line.

SINGLE SUBJECT EVALUATION DESIGNS

The preceding discussion emphasized the use of a baseline-treatment or A-B design for evaluating treatment effects. This approach, also referred

Figure 9–2 Display of Recorded Data

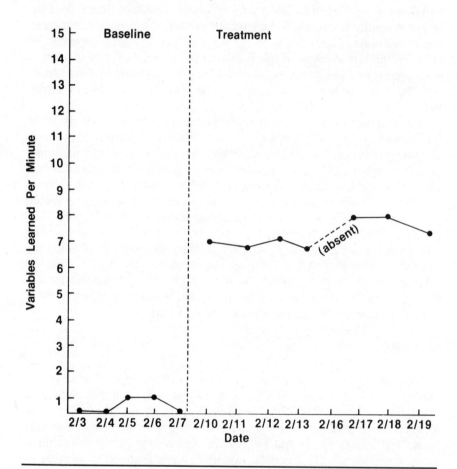

to as a case study technique (Hersen & Barlow, 1976) has a major limitation. Although the design is sensitive to improvement in the student's behavior following intervention, the educator cannot confidently attribute change solely to the social development procedure. A wide range of alternative explanations may be advanced to explain the change other than the specific program.

Cook and Campbell (1979) suggest a number of threats to the confidence in demonstrations of program effectiveness. Two are especially germane to the use of an A-B design. The first involves the influence of *history* in producing a behavior change. Kazdin (1980b) defines history as "any event occurring outside of the experiment (other than the treatment approach) that may account for the results" (p. 34). He suggests that unplanned events such as a power failure, medical emergency, fire drill, change in classroom, or other events may alter performance and be mistaken for effects resulting from the treatment. History, in this case, does *not* refer to the individual's experience prior to participation in the treatment.

The second unexpected influence is referred to by Cook and Campbell (1979) as maturation. Christensen (1980) defines maturation as "changes in the internal conditions of the individual as a function of the passage of time . . . including both biological and psychological processes such as age, learning, fatigue, boredom, and hunger, which are not related to specific external events but reside within the individual" (p. 97). Growing older, stronger, more tolerant, smarter, more interested, less distractible as a function of time exemplify maturation. Kazdin (1980b) emphasizes that history and maturation often occur together as rival explanations of the potential treatment effect.

Single case experimental designs, also referred to as single subject research, have been developed to rule out alternative explanations for a treatment effect (Kazdin, 1982). Single case designs replicate the treatment effect within a subject to support the internal validity of the approach (i.e., extent to which behavior change can be attributed to the social development procedure). The major advantage of using single case experimental designs is that they allow the educator to make precise and valid statements regarding the effectiveness of specific procedures with specific students. This information may be transferred to other professionals and parents working with the student. For many classroom situations, the use of single case experimental designs requires little more time and effort than using a case study technique (Schloss, Sachs, Miller, & Schloss, 1982; Schloss, Sedlak, Elliot & Smothers, 1982).

Reversal Designs

The reversal design involves the systematic application and removal of the social development procedure to demonstrate control of the target behavior by treatment. A convincing A-B-A pattern involves a stable low (or high) rate of behavior in the first baseline (A) phase, followed by a high (or low) rate of behavior in the treatment (B) phase, followed by a return to the initial baseline pattern in the second baseline (A) phase. Confident statements of the impact of treatment on the behavior can be the result of the behavior improving during treatment and reversing to its original baseline level once treatment is withdrawn.

The A-B-A design has been used to demonstrate a functional relationship between teacher attention and thumbsucking of a preschool child (McLaughlin and Malaby, 1975). A study of the data in Figure 9–3 reveals a high and somewhat variable rate of thumbsucking behaviors under baseline (A) conditions. Thumbsucking reduced dramatically under treatment (B). The thumbsucking behavior began to return to its original baseline rate when the teacher returned to the baseline (A) condition.

Figure 9–3 A-B-A Design Illustrating the Relationship between Teacher Attention and Thumbsucking

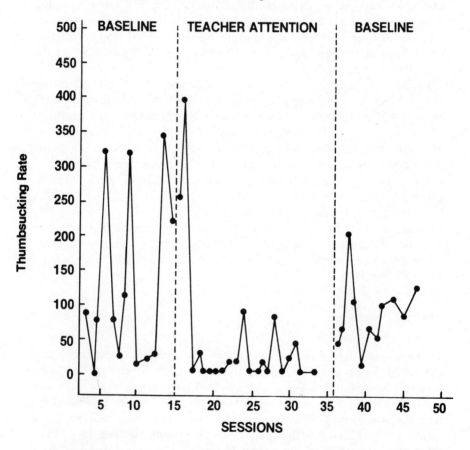

Source: Adapted with permission from McLaughlin, T.F., & Malaby, J.E. Elementary school children as behavioral engineers. In E. Ramp & G. Semb (Eds.), *Behavior analysis: Areas of research and application.* Englewood Cliffs, N.J.: Prentice-Hall, © 1975.

The preceding study does not include a return to the treatment procedure that the teacher sought to validate. Consequently, the experiment concluded under natural program conditions, which were demonstrated to be inferior to the treatment condition. The A-B-A-B design, a second variation of the reversal design, addresses this criticism.

Another frequently used reversal design is designated the A-B-A-B design. This approach differs from the A-B-A design in that treatment phase is reinstated following the second baseline phase. Aside from providing for the reinstatement of an effective treatment, the A-B-A-B design provides a more convincing demonstration of the program's effectiveness because the return to treatment allows for two comparisons to be made between treatment and baseline conditions. The first A-B-A compares baseline to the initial treatment phase, while the second B compares the subsequent treatment to the preceding baseline phase. Thus, the behavior change can be expected to coincide with the introduction of treatment on two occasions.

Miller and Feallock (1975) used the A-B-A-B design to demonstrate the effectiveness of a token economy system in reducing the number of interruptive behaviors of an adolescent special education student. Data presented in Figure 9–4 show a high rate of interruptive behavior in the first baseline phase. The initial treatment phase dramatically reduced the number of interruptions from an average of ten to four. The subsequent return to baseline resulted in an increase in the target behavior to a mean of 5.8. This was reduced to a mean of .6 in the final treatment phase. It is important to note that the behavior did not return to the original baseline level in the second baseline phase. To some extent, this reduces the amount of confidence in the influence of treatment on the target behavior.

The B-A-B design is another variation of the reversal design useful in evaluating the effectiveness of an educational procedure. The first phase (B) usually includes the previously implemented social development procedure, the second phase (A) involves the discontinuation of the procedure, and the final phase (B) includes the reinstatement of the procedure. To exemplify the B-A-B design the author was asked to determine if a study carrel being used with a moderately retarded adolescent in a vocational training program was effective in improving her speed of production. The author took production rate data for one week with the carrel in place. The carrel was then removed for a ten-day baseline period. Finally, the carrel was reinstated. Data in both treatment phases were stable at an average of .3 units per minute. The baseline phase produced unstable production rate data averaging .1 unit per minute. The author concluded that the removal of the carrel was functionally related to an erratic and

Figure 9–4 A-B-A-B Design Illustrating the Effectiveness of a Token Economy in Reducing Interruptive Behaviors

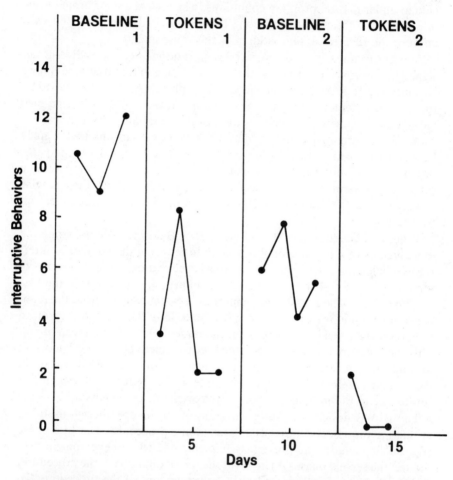

Source: Adapted with permission from Miller, L.K., & Feallock, R. A behavioral system for group living. In E. Ramp & G. Semb (Eds.), *Behavior analysis: Areas of research and application.* Englewood Cliffs, N.J.: Prentice-Hall, © 1975.

low production rate for this adolescent. The educators decided to continue the use of the carrel.

Concerns in the Selection of Reversal Designs

Reversal designs rely on removing treatment and documenting a deterioration in the target behavior. This limits the reversal design's usefulness in educational settings as it is difficult and sometimes unethical to withdraw an effective teaching strategy. For example, the author was asked to design a program to reduce the frequency and strength of aggressive episodes displayed by a 14-year-old boy. The teacher reported four to seven hitting episodes per day through a five-day baseline period. (It should be noted that "natural conditions" associated with baseline imply that the teacher followed his general approach of isolating and reprimanding the child.) The experimental approach was introduced, and the number of aggressive episodes was reduced to one a week. Returning to baseline to demonstrate the control of treatment over aggressive episodes could not be considered because the potential (and predicted) increase in disruptive behaviors would threaten the safety of other students.

Another limitation of the reversal design is that it may not be effective in evaluating programs that produce changes not expected to return to baseline. For example, a self-control program may be designed to teach an adolescent to employ stimulus control procedures to increase homework completion. Withdrawal of the training procedure would not be expected to result in the reduction of homework performance since the stimulus control procedures are expected to remain a part of the individual's repertoire regardless of external intervention. Failure of the behavior to return to baseline rates following training would reduce confidence in the validity of the treatment approach. Fortunately, other designs can be used that do not require the withdrawal of the intervention procedure to make confident causal statements. These will be presented in the following sections.

Multiple Baseline Designs

The multiple baseline design may be a more ethical and useful alternative to the reversal design. Three general types of multiple baseline designs are described in the literature: the multiple baseline across behaviors, across settings, and across individuals. The treatment approach remains the same in each variation while the target of the intervention differs (Kazdin, 1980a; 1982).

The multiple baseline across behaviors design involves collecting (baseline) data for three or more behaviors of a given individual. Once stability exists in each baseline, the intervention procedure is initiated for the first behavior alone. After the rate of the first behavior becomes stable at a more favorable rate, intervention is introduced to the second behavior. Finally, when the second behavior is stable, the intervention procedure is applied to the final behavior. While the present discussion includes only three behaviors, a stronger statement of the treatment effect can be made by introducing treatment to a larger number of responses.

Furman, Geller, Simon, and Kelly (1979) exemplify the use of a multiple baseline across behaviors design in the validation of a job interview training program for psychiatric patients. As can be seen by a representation of the authors' data in Figure 9–5, the examiners collected baseline data on three behaviors: (1) positive information; (2) questions to the interviewer; and (3) expressions of enthusiasm. Once stability was achieved in the positive information baseline, a behavior rehearsal procedure designed to teach the client to offer positive information about employment and ed-

Figure 9–5 Validation of a Job Interview Training Program with a Multiple Baseline across Behaviors Design

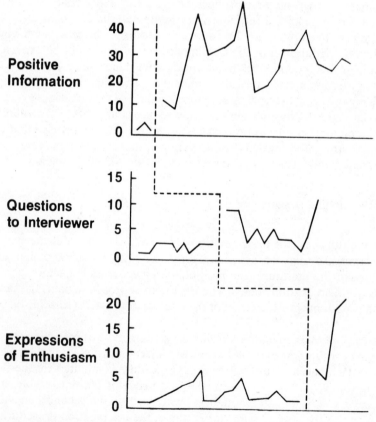

Source: Adapted with permission from Furman, W., Geller, M., Simon, S.J., & Kelly, J.A. The use of a behavioral rehearsal procedure for teaching job interview skills to psychiatric patients. *Behavior Therapy,* © 1979, *10,* 157–167.

ucational history was introduced. After the rate of positive information stabilized, behavior rehearsals focused on increasing appropriate questions asked of the interviewer. Following a stabilization in the higher rate of appropriate questions, the behavior rehearsals focused on the third target behavior—expressions of enthusiasm. These data demonstrate that the behavior rehearsal procedure was effective in improving the three target behaviors.

The multiple baseline across settings design involves collecting baseline data on the same behavior in three distinct settings. Once a stable rate of the behavior is represented in each baseline, the intervention procedure is applied in the first setting. As the behavior stabilizes in the first setting, the intervention is applied in the second setting, and so on. Control of the target behavior by the intervention procedure is established by replicating the procedures effect on the behavior in each setting. Schloss, Sachs, Miller, and Schloss (1982) have demonstrated the use of a multiple baseline across settings design in evaluating the effectiveness of a positive practice procedure on irrational verbalization of an emotionally disturbed adolescent in a vocational training setting. As can be seen in Figure 9–6, baseline data were collected in the workshop, music classroom, and physical education classroom. Each time the intervention procedure was implemented in a different setting, there was a substantial change in the frequency of irrational verbalizations. The association of the intervention procedure with a reduction in irrational verbalizations across each setting demonstrates that the positive practice procedure was effective in reducing irrational verbalizations.

A final variation is the multiple baseline across individuals. This design involves collecting baseline data across the same behavior of three or more students. Once stability exists in the three baselines, the intervention procedure is applied with the first child or youth. As the behavior of the first individual becomes stable, the intervention procedure is applied with the second student. Once the behavior stabilizes, the intervention procedure is applied with the third. Control of the dependent variable by the intervention is established as the strength of the target behavior for each individual change.

Schumaker, Havell, and Sherman (1977) used a multiple baseline across individuals design to evaluate the effectiveness of a daily report card system in modifying the school conduct of junior high school students. The report card system was systematically applied to each of three students, and there was a substantial increase in the percentage of class rules followed. The systematic introduction of the report card system and concurrent change in rate of the target behavior for each of three subjects demonstrate the validity of the intervention approach.

Figure 9–6 A Multiple Baseline Design across Behaviors Design Used to Validate a Positive Practice Procedure

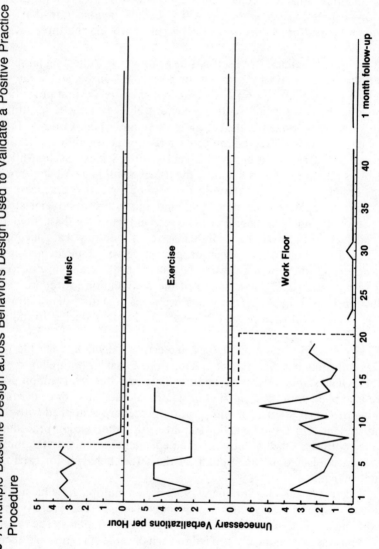

Source: Adapted with permission by Schloss, P.J., Sachs, J.J., Miller, S.R., & Schloss, C.N. Increasing work production of a mentally retarded student through the systematic analysis of continuous data. Journal of Industrial Teacher Education, © 1982, 19, 20–26.

Concerns in the Selection of Multiple Baseline Designs

Multiple baseline designs involve introducing treatment to several behaviors, individuals, or settings without interrupting treatment. This design provides a systematic framework in which to conduct intervention. For example, the author was asked to develop a program to develop social skills with severely withdrawn adolescents. Following a careful behavior analysis, it was determined that: (1) the behaviors may not be in the individual's repertoire; (2) the classroom conditions do not motivate the use of socially skillful behavior; and (3) it was unlikely that the students would acquire and demonstrate a large number of skills in a short period of time.

The resulting program involved teaching and motivating one behavior (saying "hello" to people entering the room) until the specified criterion was reached, then teaching and motivating a second behavior (saying "goodbye" to people leaving the room), and so on, until four behaviors were learned and used in the natural environment. The multiple baseline across behaviors design not only validated the training procedure, but provided a positive and systematic approach to teaching social skills. New concepts were introduced only as previous skills were mastered. The expectations for the adolescents on any given day were clearly specified by the design. Finally, at no time did the number of demands placed on the adolescents exceed their abilities to respond successfully.

The multiple baseline design is limited in that a strong demonstration of treatment effect is made only if the target behavior changes when treatment is applied. If the behavior begins to improve prior to treatment, a clear statement supporting the effectiveness of treatment cannot be made. The likelihood of this confounding influence has been addressed by several studies. For example, Kazdin (1973a) demonstrated that a treatment applied to one behavior may improve other behaviors. The improvement in one individual's behavior may result in the improvement of another's (Kazdin, 1979), and the application of an intervention procedure in one setting may generalize to another (Kazdin, 1973b). While the unexpected improvement in untreated behaviors may be a welcomed problem, it significantly reduces the confidence the educator may have in the validity of the treatment procedure. When a spontaneous generalization of treatment effects across people, settings, or behaviors can be anticipated, an alternate design should be employed.

Changing Criterion Design

Another design that does not rely on a reversal or multiple baseline to demonstrate experimental control is the changing criterion. The individual's behavior continually exceeding a specified criterion for reinforcement provides evidence for the effect of treatment on the behavior. Baseline data are collected on the target behavior. Once stability is achieved, a criterion for reinforcement slightly higher than the baseline level is established. When the behavior is equal to or greater than the first criterion for a number of sessions, the criterion is elevated. As the behavior consistently exceeds the second criterion, a third, more stringent, criterion is imposed, and so on until the behavior reaches a level specified by the program objective. As the target behavior continually increases (or decreases) in strength to meet the criterion for reinforcement, a greater case for control is established.

Schloss, Sedlak, Elliott, and Smothers (1982) demonstrated the use of a changing criterion design in increasing the number of math problems correct for an 11-year-old learning-disabled student. Baseline data were collected for four days resulting in an average rate of correct responses of two. During treatment successively higher rates of performance were required to obtain tokens. Four tokens were exchanged for a positive note home to the youth's parents. The student's performance rose to meet each successively higher criterion until the youth was completing correctly ten of ten problems assigned. The functional relationship between tokens and positive notes home to parents and the number of math assignments completed correctly was established by the student's behavior improving in stepwise fashion commensurate with the changes in the criterion for reinforcement.

Concerns in Selecting the Changing Criterion Design

This design is not appropriate for behavior change procedures expected to produce a substantial change in behavior over a short period of time. A reinforcement procedure expected to rapidly increase the strength of a response will not produce a number of sessions in which behavior strength adjusts to a more stringent criterion. One or two increases in behavior that exceed the criterion for reinforcement will not clearly demonstrate the effect of treatment on the behavior. In this case a reversal or multiple baseline design would be a more effective alternative. Hartman and Hall (1976) suggest including a "mini reversal" in the changing criterion when an inconclusive demonstration exists. This procedure involves returning to a less rigorous criterion to determine if the performance will regress accordingly. This approach has the same limitations as discussed for reversal designs. The changing criterion design provides a logical, systematic, and positive framework for procedures that are expected to produce a gradual increase in the performance of an individual. The teacher can begin the program with very modest pupil expectations, thereby insuring success. Once the initial criterion is met, a slightly more demanding criterion is established. The progression from the initial to the final criterion can be sufficiently gradual to insure the adaptation of the individual to more stringent task demands without excessive frustration or failure.

CONCLUSIONS

There has been a repeated call throughout this volume for efforts to substantiate the impact of social development procedures on students' performance. Educators are encouraged to assume the role of evaluator, seeking to demonstrate the most effective intervention procedures for each student in his or her room. The collection of baseline and treatment data using systematic observation techniques begins to meet this objective. However, the case study approach fails to isolate the effect of the procedure on the student's behavior. Maturation and history are not ruled out as alternative explanations to the behavior change. The single subject evaluation designs presented in this chapter overcome the limitations of the case study technique. By employing these designs, the educator is in a position to make confident statements regarding the specific effect of the social development procedure on the target behavior. This feature assists the educator in identifying the most effective approach to meeting the objectives established for his or her student. Ineffective procedures may be quickly identified and modified or replaced.

In addition, data collected through the use of a single subject evaluation design may provide information that supports future educational efforts. Norm-referenced test data, which frequently occupy a majority of space in a student's cumulative file, report a child's or youth's current level of functioning when contrasted with the general population. At best, the data tell the educators *where* to focus their efforts. Unfortunately, this information does little to tell the educators *how* to focus their efforts. Single subject data, on the other hand, provide a precise description of techniques that have been demonstrated to have an impact on the child's or youth's performance. As a part of a cumulative file, the data provide future service agents with information regarding the student's current level of social functioning, as well as program procedures that are likely to be effective.

Finally, single case evaluation designs allow the educators to determine the exact resources required to implement an effective treatment. This feature is particularly critical in maintaining students in the "least restrictive environment." Simply knowing that a student is frequently aggressive in and of itself does not provide relevant information for placement purposes.

On the other hand, knowing the conditions and resources that are required to treat the aggressive outbursts facilitates a match between the student and setting. This placement becomes the least restrictive setting for that student. As aggressive outbursts are brought under control and the program is dismantled, the child or youth may be moved to successively less restrictive settings. The data, in this case, are used to guide placement decisions.

In summary, this chapter has described three major single subject evaluation techniques: (1) the reversal design; (2) the multiple baseline design; and (3) the changing criterion design. The practitioner can use these evaluation tools to validate a wide range of intervention/instructional procedures in school settings. Carefully matching a specific design to: (1) the response characteristics of the child; (2) the nature of the intervention procedure; (3) the number of individuals participating with similar characteristics; (4) the anticipated outcome of the intervention; and (5) the practical limitations of the classroom setting will produce an evaluation option that promotes the teacher's ability to provide socially enhancing classroom activities.

References

Abel, G.L. The blind adolescent and his needs. *Exceptional Children*, 1961, *27*, 309–310; 331–334.

Abeson, A., & Zettell, J. The end of the quiet revolution: The Education for All Handicapped Children Act of 1975. In N. West (Ed.), *Educating exceptional children*. Guilford, Conn.: Dushkin Publishing Group, 1982.

Achenbach, T.M., & Edelbrock, C.S. The classification of child psychopathology: A review and analysis of empirical efforts. *Psychological Bulletin*, 1978, *85*, 1275–1301.

Albee, B.W. Conceptual models and manpower requirements in psychology. *American Psychologist*, 1968, *23*, 317–320.

Allen, F.H., & Pearson, G.H.J. The emotional problems of the physically handicapped child. *British Journal of Medical Psychology*, 1938, *8*, 212–235.

Altshuler, K.Z. Psychiatric consideration in the school age deaf. *American Annals of the Deaf*, 1962, *107*, 553–559.

Altshuler, K.Z. The social and psychological development of the deaf child: Problems, their treatment and prevention. *Social and Psychological Development*, 1974, *8*, 365–376.

Altshuler, K.Z. Psychiatry and problems of deafness. In *Psychology of deafness for rehabilitation counselors*. Baltimore: University Park Press, 1976.

American Medical Association. Guides to the evaluation of permanent mental and physical impairments. *Journal of the American Medical Association*, 1958–1966.

American Psychiatric Association. *Diagnostic and statistical manual of mental disorders* (1st ed., DSM-I). Washington, D.C.: American Psychiatric Association, 1952.

American Psychiatric Association. *Diagnostic and statistical manual of mental disorders* (2nd ed., DSM-II). Washington, D.C.: American Psychiatric Association, 1968.

American Psychiatric Association. *Diagnostic and statistical manual of mental disorders* (3rd ed., DSM-III). Washington, D.C.: American Psychiatric Association, 1980.

Andersland, P.B. Maternal and environmental factors related to success in speech improvement training. *Journal of Speech and Hearing Research*, 1961, *4*, 79–90.

Anderson, L., Fodor, I., & Alpert, M.A. A comparison of methods for training self-control. *Behavior Therapy*, 1976, *7*, 649; 658.

Ash, P. The reliability of psychiatric diagnoses. *Journal of Abnormal and Social Psychology*, 1949, *44*, 272–276.

238 SOCIAL DEVELOPMENT OF HANDICAPPED CHILDREN

Aspy, D. The effect of teacher-offered conditions of empathy, consequence and positive regard upon student achievement. *Florida Journal of Educational Research,* 1969, *11,* 39–48.

Auerbach, A.G. The social control of learning disability. *Journal of Learning Disabilities,* 1971, *4,* 26–34.

Ayllon, T., & Rosenbaum, M.S. The behavioral treatment of disruption and hyperactivity in school settings. In B.B. Lahey & A.E. Kazdin (Eds.), *Advances in child psychology* (Vol. 1). New York: Plenum, 1977.

Azrin, N.H., & Holtz, W.C. Punishment. In W.K. Honig (Ed.), *Operant behavior: Area of research and application.* New York: Appleton-Century-Crofts, 1966.

Baer, D.M., Wolfe, M.M., & Risley, T.R. Some current dimensions of applied behavior analysis. *Journal of Applied Behavior Analysis,* 1968, *1,* 91–97.

Baird, L. Teaching styles: An exploratory study of dimensions and effects. *Journal of Educational Psychology,* 1973, *64,* 15–21.

Bandura, A. Influence of model's reinforcement contingencies on the acquisition of imitative responses. *Journal of Personality and Social Psychology,* 1965, *1,* 589–595.

Bandura, A. Behavioral Psychotherapy. *Scientific American,* March 1967, 76–86.

Bandura, A. *Principles of behavior modification.* New York: Holt, Rinehart, & Winston, 1969.

Bandura, A. Psychotherapy based on modeling principles. In A.E. Beugin & S.L. Garfield (Eds.), *Handbook of psychotherapy and behavior change.* New York: John Wiley, 1971a.

Bandura, A. *Social learning theory.* Morristown, N.J.: General Learning Press, 1971b.

Bandura, A. *Aggression: A social learning analysis.* Englewood Cliffs, N.J.: Prentice-Hall, 1973.

Bandura, A. *Social learning theory.* Englewood Cliffs, N.J.: Prentice-Hall, 1977.

Bankson, N.W. The speech and language impaired. In E.L. Meyer (Ed.), *Exceptional children and youth.* Denver: Love Publishing Company, 1978.

Barclay, J.R. Interest patterns associated with measures of social desirability. *Personality Guidance Journal,* 1966, *45,* 56–60.

Barkley, R.A., Hastings, J.E., Tousel, R.E., & Tousel, S.E. Evaluation of a token system for juvenile delinquents in a residential setting. *Journal of Behavior Therapy and Experimental Psychiatry,* 1976, *7,* 227–230.

Bartel, N.R., & Guskin, S.L. A handicap as a social phenomenon. In W.M. Cruickshank (Ed.), *Psychology of exceptional children and youth.* Englewood Cliffs, N.J.: Prentice-Hall, 1980, 45–73.

Bateman, B.D. Visually handicapped children. In N.G. Haring & R.L. Schiefelbusch (Eds.), *Methods in special education.* New York: McGraw-Hill Book Co., 1967.

Bates, P. The effectiveness of interpersonal skills training on the social skill acquisition of moderately and mildly retarded adults. *Journal of Applied Behavior Analysis,* 1980, *13,* 237–248.

Bates, P., Renzaglia, A., & Wehman, P. Characteristics of an appropriate education for severely handicapped students. *Education and Training of the Mentally Retarded,* 1981, *16*(2), 142–149.

Bauman, M.K. Group differences disclosed by inventory items. *International Journal for the Education of the Blind,* 1964, *13,* 101–106.

Beck, A.T. *Depression: Causes and treatment.* Philadelphia: University of Pennsylvania Press, 1972.

Becker, W.C., Madsen, C.H., Jr., Arnold, R., & Thomas, D.R. The contingent use of teacher attention and praise in reducing classroom behavior problems. *Journal of Special Education,* 1967, *1,* 287–307.

Begelman, D.A. Misnaming, metaphors, the medical model, and some muddles. *Psychiatry,* 1971, *34,* 38–58.

Beier, O.C. Behavioral disturbances in the mentally retarded. In H.H. Stevens & R. Heber (Eds.), *Mental retardation.* Chicago: University of Chicago, 1964.

Bensky, J.M., Shaw, S.F., Gouse, A.S., Bates, H., Dixon, B., & Beane, W.E. Public law 94-142 and stress: A problem for educators. *Exceptional Children,* 1980, *47,* 24–29.

Berlin, C.I. *A study of attitudes towards the non-influences of childhood of parents of stutterers, parents of articulatory defectives, and parents of normal-speaking children.* Doctoral thesis, University of Pittsburgh, 1958.

Berman, A., & Siegal, A.W. Adaptive and learning skills in juvenile delinquents: A neuropsychological analysis. *Journal of Learning Disabilities,* 1976, *9,* 583–589.

Bernstein, D.A., & Borkovec, T.D. *Progressive relaxation training: A manual for the helping professions.* Champaign, Ill.: Research Press, 1973.

Bialer, I. Conceptualization of success and failure in mentally retarded and normal children. *Journal of Personality,* 1966, *29,* 303–320.

Birkimer, J.C., and Brown, J.H. The effects of student self-control on the reduction of children's problem behavior. *Behavior Disorders,* 1979, *4,* 131–136.

Blackham, G., & Silberman, A. *Modification of child and adolescent behavior.* Belmont, Calif.: Wadsworth, 1980.

Blashfield, R. An evaluation of the DSM-II classification of schizophrenia as a nomenclature. *Journal of Abnormal Psychology,* 1973, *82,* 382–389.

Blatt, B. The physical, personality, and academic status of children who are mentally retarded attending special classes as compared with children who are mentally retarded attending regular classes. *American Journal of Mental Deficiency,* 1958, *62,* 810–818.

Bloom, B.S., Hasting, J.T., & Madaus, G.F. *Handbook on formative and summative evaluation of student learning.* New York: McGraw-Hill Book Co., 1971.

Blum, E. Fitting in. *Teaching Exceptional Children,* 1971, *3*(4), 172–180.

Boren, J.J., & Colman, A.D. Some experiments on reinforcement principles within a psychiatric ward for delinquent soldiers. *Journal of Applied Behavior Analysis,* 1970, *3,* 223–233.

Bower, E.M. *Early identification of emotionally handicapped children in school.* Springfield, Ill.: Charles C Thomas, Pub., 1960.

Broden, M., Bruce, C., Mitchell, M.A., Carter, V., & Hall, R.V. Effects of teacher attention on attending behavior of two boys in adjacent desks. *Journal of Applied Behavior Analysis,* 1970, *3,* 199–203.

Brookover, W. The relation of social factors to teaching ability. *Journal of Experimental Education,* 1945, *13,* 191–205.

Brown, P.A. Responses of blind and seeing adolescents to an introversion-extroversion questionnaire. *Journal of Psychology,* 1938, *6,* 137–147.

Brown, P.A. Responses of blind and seeing adolescents to a neurotic inventory. *Journal of Psychology,* 1939, *7,* 211–221.

Bruininks, R.H., & Rynders, J.E. Alternatives to special class placement for educable mentally retarded children. *Focus on Exceptional Children*, 1971, *3*, 1–12.

Bryan, T.H. Peer popularity of learning disabled children. *Journal of Learning Disabilities*, 1974a, *7*(10), 621–625.

Bryan, T.H. An observational analysis of classroom behaviors of children with learning disabilities. *Journal of Learning Disabilities*, 1974b, *7*, 26–34.

Bryan, T.H. Peer popularity of learning disabled children: A replication. *Journal of Learning Disabilities*, 1976, *9*, 49–53.

Bryan, T.H., Wheeler, R., Felcan, J., & Henek, T. Come on dummy: An observational survey of communications. *Journal of Learning Disabilities*, 1976, *9*, 661–669.

Budoff, M., & Gottlieb, J. A comparison of EMR children in special classes with EMR children who have been re-integrated into regular classes. *Studies in Learning Potential*, 1974, *3*(4), 62–68.

Buell, C.E. *Motor performance of visually handicapped children*. Berkeley, Calif.: Charles Edwin Buell, 1950.

Buscaglia, L.F. *An experimental study of the Sarbin-Hardyck Test as indexes of role perception for adolescent stutterers*. Unpublished doctoral thesis, University of California, 1962.

Butler, J. The effect of two school-based intervention programs on depressive symptoms in preadolescents. *American Educational Research Journal*, 1980, *17*, 111–119.

Butler, K.G. The Bender-Gestalt Visual Motor Test as a diagnostic instrument with children exhibiting articulation disorders. *ASHA*, 1965, *7*, 390–391.

Carr, E.G., Newsom, C.D., & Binkoff, J.A. Stimulus control of self-destructive behavior in a psychotic child. *Journal of Abnormal Child Psychology*, 1976, *4*, 139–153.

Cautela, J.R. Behavior therapy and the need for behavioral assessment. *Psychotherapy: Theory, Research and Practice*, 1968, *5*, 175–179.

Chandler, A., & Boroskin, A. Relationship of reward value and stated expectancy in mentally retarded patients. *American Journal of Mental Deficiency*, 1971, *75*, 761–762.

Chapman, R., Larsen, S., & Parker, R. *Teacher-child interaction of learning disordered students in regular classrooms: A critical review*. Unpublished manuscript, the University of Texas at Austin, 1976.

Cholden, L.S. *A psychiatrist works with blindness*. New York: American Foundation for the Blind, 1958.

Christensen, L.B. *Experimental methodology* (2nd ed.). Boston: Allyn & Bacon, 1980.

Clements, S.D. *Minimal brain dysfunction in children: Terminology and identification, phase one of a three-phase project*. U.S. Department of Health, Education and Welfare. NINDB Monograph No. 3. Washington, D.C.: U.S. Government Printing Office, 1966.

Cobb, J.A., & Hops, H. Effects of academic survival skill training on low achieving first graders. *The Journal of Educational Research*, 1973, *67*, 108–113.

Cohen, E.S., Harbin, H.T., & Wright, M.J. Some considerations in the formulation of psychiatric diagnoses. *Journal of Nervous and Mental Disease*, 1975, *160*, 422–427.

Collins, G.R. Burn-out: The hazard of the professional people-helpers. *Christianity Today*, 1977, *21*, 740–742.

Committee on Nomenclature, Conference of Executives of American Schools for the Deaf, *American Annals of the Deaf*, 1938, *83*.

Compton, P. The learning disabled adolescent. In B. Kratoville (Ed.), *Youth in Trouble*. San Rafael, Calif.: Academic Therapy, 1974.

Conger, J. *Adolescence and youth: Psychological development in a changing world.* New York: Harper & Row, 1977.

Connor, F.F., Hoover, R., Horton, K., Sands, H., Sternfeld, L., & Wolinsky, G.F. Physical and sensory handicaps. In N. Hobbs (Ed.), *Issues in the Classification of Children* (Vol. 1). San Francisco: Jossey-Bass, 1975.

Cook, T.D., & Campbell, D.T. *Quasi-experimentation: Design and analysis issues for field settings.* Chicago: Rand McNally, 1979.

Cooper, C.L., & Marshall, J. Occupational sources of stress: A review of the literature relating to coronary heart disease and mental ill health. *Journal of Occupational Psychology,* 1976, *49,* 11–28.

Coopersmith, S. *The antecedents of self-esteem.* San Francisco: W.H. Freeman, 1967.

Costin, F., & Grush, J. Personality correlates of teacher-student behavior in the college classroom. *Journal of Educational Psychology,* 1973, *65,* 35–44.

Cowen, E.F., Pederson, A., Babigian, N., Izzo, L.D., & Frost, M.A. Long-term follow-up of early detected vulnerable children. *Journal of Consulting and Clinical Psychology,* 1973, *41,* 438–446.

Coyne, J.C. Depression and the response of others. *Journal of Abnormal Psychology,* 1976, *85,* 186–193.

Craigie, F.C., & Ross, S.M. The use of a videotape pretherapy training program to encourage treatment-seeking among alcohol detoxification patients. *Behavior Therapy,* 1980, *11,* 141–147.

Creswell, D. Integration is a two-way street. *Education in Canada,* 1973, *13,* 4–7.

Cromwell, R.L. A social learning approach to mental retardation. In N.R. Ellis (Ed.), *Handbook of Mental Deficiency.* New York: McGraw-Hill Book Co., 1963.

Cromwell, R.L., Blashfield, R.K., & Strauss, S.S. Criteria for classification systems. In N. Hobbs (Ed.), *Issues in the classification of children* (Vol. 1). San Francisco: Jossey-Bass, 1975.

Cruickshank, W.M. A study of the relation of physical disability to social adjustment. *American Journal of Occupational Therapy,* 1952, *6,* 100–109.

Cruickshank, W.M. The learning environment. In W.M. Cruickshank & D.P. Hallahan (Eds.), *Perceptual and learning disabilities in children (Vol. 1) Psychoeducational Practice.* Syracuse, N.Y.: Syracuse University Press, 1975.

Cruickshank, W.M. (Ed.). *Psychology of exceptional children and youth.* Englewood Cliffs, N.J.: Prentice-Hall, 1980.

Cruickshank, W.M., & Paul, J.L. The psychological characteristics of children with learning disabilities. In W.M. Cruickshank (Ed.), *Psychology of exceptional children and youth.* Englewood Cliffs, N.J.: Prentice-Hall, 1980.

Csapo, M. Peer models reverse the "one bad apple spoils the barrel" theory. *Teaching Exceptional Children,* 1972, *5,* 20–25.

Daley, M.R. Preventing worker burnout in child welfare. *Child Welfare,* 1979, *7,* 443–450.

Darley, F.L. The development of parental attitudes and adjustments to the development of stuttering. In W. Johnson (Ed.), *Stuttering in children and adults.* Minneapolis, Minn.: University of Minnesota Press, 1955.

Davis, C.J. Development of the self-concept. *New Outlook for the Blind,* 1964, *58,* 49–51.

Deitz, S.M., Flack, D.J., Schwarzmueller, E.B., Wilander, A.P., Weatherly, T.J., & Hilliard, G. Reducing inappropriate behavior in special classrooms by reinforcing interresponse times: Interval DRL. *Behavior Therapy,* 1978, *9,* 37–46.

Deitz, S.M., & Repp, A.C. Decreasing classroom misbehavior through the use of DRL schedules of reinforcement. *Journal of Applied Behavior Analysis*, 1973, *6*, 457–463.

Dershowitz, A.M. Dangerousness as a criterion for confinement. *Bulletin of the American Academy of Psychiatry and the Law*, 1974, *2*, 172–179.

DeVault, M.V. Research and the classroom teacher. *Teachers College Record*, 1965, *67*, 211–216.

Dixon, B., Shaw, S.G., & Bensky, J.M. Administrator's role in fostering the mental health of special services personnel. *Exceptional Children*, 1980, *47*, 30–36.

Dixon, R., & Morse, W. The prediction of teaching performance: Empathic potential. *Journal of Teacher Education*, 1961, *12*, 322–329.

Domino, G., & McGarty, M. Personal and work adjustment of young retarded women. *American Journal of Mental Deficiency*, 1972, *77*, 314–321.

Doty, D.W., Mcinnis, T., & Paul, G.L. Remediation of negative side effects of an ongoing response-cost system with chronic mental patients. *Journal of Applied Behavior Analysis*, 1974, *7*, 191–198.

Dreikurs, R. The social psychological dynamics of physical disability. *Journal of Social Issues*, 1948, *4*, 39–54.

Duke, D. How administrators view the crisis in school discipline. *Phi Delta Kappan*, 1978, *59*, 325–330.

Dunn, L.M. (Ed.). *Exceptional children in the schools: Special education in transition* (2nd ed.). New York: Holt, Rinehart & Winston, 1973.

Dybwad, G. Avoiding misconceptions of mainstreaming, the least restrictive environment, and normalization. In N. West (Ed.), *Educating exceptional children*. Guilford, Conn.: Dushkin Publishing Group, 1982.

Edelstein, B.A., Elder, J.P., & Narick, M.N. Adolescent psychiatric patients modifying aggressive behavior with social skills training. *Behavior Modification*, 1979, *3*(2), 161–179.

Ellis, A.E. *Reason and emotion in psychotherapy*. New York: Lyle Stuart, 1963.

Ellis, A.E. *Humanistic psychotherapy: A rational-emotive approach*. New York: McGraw-Hill Book Co., 1973.

Elmore, P., & LaPointe, K. Effect of teaching sex, student sex, and teacher warmth on the evaluation of college instructors. *Journal of Educational Psychology*, 1975, *67*, 368–374.

Emerick, L.L. *An evaluation of three psychological variables in tonic and chronic stutterers and in non-stutterers*. Unpublished doctoral thesis, Michigan State University, 1966.

Epstein, R., & Gross, C.M. Case study: A self-control procedure for the maintenance of nondisruptive behavior in an elementary school child. *Behavior Therapy*, 1978, *9*, 109–117.

Feister, A.N., & Giambra, L.M. Language indices of vocational success in mentally retarded adults. *American Journal of Mental Deficiency*, 1972, *77*, 332–337.

Ferster, C.D. Positive reinforcement and behavioral deficits of autistic children. *Child Development*, 1961, *32*, 437–456.

Fitzgerald, D.C. Success-failure and TAT reactions of orthopedically handicapped and physically normal adolescents. *Personality*, 1951, *1*, 67–83.

Fitzgerald, D.C. A generation follow-up of some former public school mentally handicapped students. *Dissertation Abstracts*, 1968, *28a*(8), 28–92.

Foss, G., & Peterson, S.L. Social-interpersonal skills relevant to job tenure for mentally retarded adults. *Mental Retardation*, 1981, *19*(3), 103–106.

Foster, G., & Keech, V. Teacher reactions to the label of educable mentally retarded. *Education and Training of the Mentally Retarded*, 1977, *12*(4), 307–311.

Foster, G., Ysseldyke, J.E., & Reese, J.H. I wouldn't have seen it if I hadn't believed it. *Exceptional Children*, 1975, *41*(7), 469–473.

Fox, P.B. *Locus of control and self-concept in mildly retarded adolescents*. Unpublished doctoral dissertation, University of Minnesota, 1972.

Foxx, R.M., & Azrin, N.H. Restitution: A method of eliminating aggressive-disruptive behavior of retarded and brain damaged patients. *Behavior Research and Therapy*, 1972, *10*, 15–27.

Foxx, R.M., & Azrin, N.H. The elimination of autistic self-stimulatory behavior by overcorrection. *Journal of Applied Behavior Analysis*, 1973, 6, 1–14.

Frank, G. Psychiatric Diagnosis: A review of research. *Journal of General Psychology*, 1969, *81*, 157–576.

Franks, D.J. Ethnic and social status characteristics of children in EMR and LD classes. *Exceptional Children*, 1971, *37*, 537–538.

Frederick, L. v. Thomas, 408 F. Supp. 832, 835 (E. D. Pa., 1976).

Frederiksen, L.W., & Frederiksen, C.B. Teacher-determined and self-determined token reinforcement in a special education classroom. *Behavior Therapy*, 1975, 6, 310–314.

Freedman, R.D. Emotional reactions of handicapped children. *Rehabilitation Literature*, 1967, *19*, 274–282.

Freudenberger, J.J. Burn-out: Occupational hazard of the child care worker. *Child Care Quarterly*, 1977, 6, 90–98.

Froomkin, J. *Estimates and projections of special target group populations in elementary and secondary schools*. Report prepared for the President's Commission on School Finance, Washington, D.C., 1972.

Furman, W., Geller, M., Simon, S.J., & Kelly, J.A. The use of a behavioral rehearsal procedure for teaching job interviewing skills to psychiatric patients. *Behavior Therapy*, 1979, *10*, 157–167.

Gambrill, E.D. *Behavior modification: Handbook of assessment, intervention and evaluation*. San Francisco: Jossey-Bass, 1977.

Gardner, W.I. Social and emotional adjustment of mildly retarded children and adolescents: Critical review. *Exceptional Children*, 1966, *33*, 97–105.

Gardner, W.I. *Learning and behavior characteristics of exceptional children and youth: A humanistic behavioral approach*. Boston: Allyn & Bacon, 1977.

Gardner, W.I. *Children with learning and behavior problems: A behavior management approach*. Boston: Allyn & Bacon, 1978.

Gendlin, E.T. Focusing. *Psychotherapy: Theory, research and practice*, 1969, 6, 5–15.

Glynn, E.L., Thomas, J.D., & Shee, S.M. Behavioral self-control of on-task behavior in an elementary classroom. *Journal of Applied Behavior Analysis*, 1973, 6, 105–113.

Goetz, E.M., Holmberg, M.C., & LeBlanc, J.M. Differential reinforcement of other behavior and noncontingent reinforcement as control procedures during the modification of a preschooler's compliance. *Journal of Applied Behavior Analysis*, 1975, 8, 77–82.

Goldiamond, I. Self-control procedures in personal behavior problems. *Psychological Reports*, 1965, *17*, 851–868.

Goldstein, A.P., Heller, K., & Sechrist, L.B. *Psychotherapy and the psychology of behavior change*. New York: John Wiley & Sons, 1966.

Goldstein, H. Construction of a social learning curriculum. In E.F. Meyer, G.A. Virgison, & N.J. Whelan (Eds.), *Strategies for teaching exceptional children*. Denver, Col.: Love Publishing, 1972.

Gollub, W.L., & Sloan, E. Teacher expectations, race, and socioeconomic status. *Urban Education*, 1978, *13*(1), 95–106.

Goodstein, L.D. Functional speech disorders and personality: A survey of the research. *Journal of Speech and Hearing Research*, 1958, *1*, 359–376.

Gordon, T. *Parent effectiveness training*. New York: Wyden, 1970.

Gordon, T. *Teacher effectiveness training*. New York: Wyden, 1974.

Goss v. Lopez, 419 U.S. 565 (1975).

Gottlieb, J. Attitudes toward retarded children: Effects of labelling and academic performance. *American Journal of Mental Deficiency*, 1974, *79*(3), 268–273.

Gottman, J., Gonso, J., & Schuler, P. Teaching social skills to isolated children. *Journal of Abnormal Child Psychology*, 1976, *4*, 179–197.

Grossman, H.J. *Manual on terminology and classification in mental retardation*. Baltimore: Garamond/Pridemark, 1973.

Group for the Advancement of Psychiatry, Committee on Child Psychiatry. *Psychopathological disorders in childhood: Theoretical consideration and a proposed classification* (Vol. 6), Report No. 62, June 1966.

Hall, R.V., Lund, D., & Jackson, D. Effects of teacher attention on study behaviors. *Journal of Applied Behavior Analysis*, 1968, *1*, 1–12.

Hallahan, D.P., & Kauffman, J.M. *Introduction to learning disabilities: A psycho-behavioral approach*. Englewood Cliffs, N.J.: Prentice-Hall, 1976.

Hanf, C., & Kling, F. *Facilitating parent-child interaction: A two-stage training model*. Unpublished manuscript, University of Oregon Medical School, 1973.

Hardy, R.E. A study of manifest anxiety among blind residential school students. *New Outlook for the Blind*, 1968a, *62*, 173–180.

Hardy, R.E. *The anxiety scale for the blind*. New York: American Foundation for the Blind, 1968b.

Harris, A. An empirical test of the situation specificity (consistency of aggressive behavior). *Child Behavior Therapy*, 1979, *1*, 257–270.

Harter, S., & Zigler, E. The assessment of effectance motivation in normal and retarded children. *Developmental Psychology*, 1974, *10*, 169–180.

Hartman, D.P., & Hall, R.V. The changing criterion design. *Journal of Applied Analysis*, 1976, *9*, 527–532.

Harway, V.T. *Self-evaluation and reactions to success and failure experiences in orthopedically handicapped children*. Unpublished doctoral dissertation, University of Rochester, 1952.

Hasazi, J.E., & Hasazi, S.E. Effects of teacher attention on digit reversal behavior in an elementary school child. *Journal of Applied Behavior Analysis*, 1972, *5*, 157–162.

Haskett, G.J., & Lenfestey, W. Reading-related behavior in an open classroom: Effects of novelty and modeling on preschoolers. *Journal of Applied Behavior Analysis*, 1974, *7*, 233–241.

Hayes-Roth, F., Longabaugh, R., & Ryback, R. The problem-oriented medical record and psychiatry. *British Journal of Psychiatry*, 1972, *121*, 27–34.

Heber, R. Research on personality disorders and characteristics of the mentally retarded. *Mental Retardation Abstracts*, 1964, *1*, 304–325.

Hefele, T. The effects of systematic human relations training upon student achievement. *Journal of Research and Development in Education,* 1971, *4,* 52–69.

Herder, G.M. Adjustment problems of the deaf child. *Nervous Child,* 1948, *7,* 38–44.

Heron, T.E. Punishment: A review of literature with implications for the teacher of main-streamed children. *The Journal of Special Education,* 1978, *12*(3), 243–252.

Hersen, M. Historical perspectives in behavioral assessment. In M. Hersen & A. Bellack (Eds.), *Behavior assessment: A practical handbook.* New York: Pergamon Press, 1976.

Hersen, M., & Barlow, D.H. *Single-case experimental designs.* New York: Pergamon Press, 1976.

Hersen, M., Bellack, A., & Himmelhock, J. Treatment of unipolar depression with social skills training. *Behavior Modification,* 1980, *4,* 547–556.

Hersen, M., & Ollendick, T.H. Social skills training for juvenile delinquents. *Behavior, Research, and Therapy,* 1979, *17,* 547–554.

Hewett, F.M., & Forness, S.R. *Education of exceptional learners.* Boston: Allyn & Bacon, 1974.

Hobbs, T.R., & Holt, M.M. The effects of token reinforcement on the behavior of delinquents in cottage settings. *Journal of Applied Behavior Analysis,* 1976, *9,* 189–198.

Holman, J., & Baer, D.M. Facilitating generalization of on-task behavior through self-monitoring of academic tasks. *Journal of Autism and Developmental Disorders,* 1979, *9,* 429–445.

Homme, L., Csanyi, A.P., Gonzales, M.A., & Rechs, J.R. *How to use contingency contracting in the classroom.* Champaign, Ill.: Research Press, 1969.

Hops, H., & Cobb, J.A. Survival behaviors in the educational setting: Their implications for research and intervention. In L.A. Hammerlynk, L.C. Hardy, & E.J. Mask (Eds.), *Behavior Change.* Champaign, Ill.: Research Press, 1973.

Hops, H., & Cobb, J.A. Initial investigations into academic survival skill training, direct instruction and first grade achievement. *Journal of Educational Psychology,* 1974, *6,* 548–553.

Howard, S. v. Friendswood Independent School District, 454 F. Supp. 634 (S.D. Tex. 1978).

Hunt, J. Intrinsic motivation and its role in psychological development in D. Levine (Ed.), *Nebraska symposium on motivation.* Lincoln, Neb.: University of Nebraska Press, 1965.

Jacobsen, E. *Progressive relaxation.* Chicago: University of Chicago Press, 1938.

Jacobson, F.N. *The juvenile court judge and learning disabilities.* Paper presented at National Council of Juvenile Court Judges Graduate College, University of Nevada, Reno, 1974.

Jervis, F.M. The self in process of obtaining and maintaining self-esteem. *New Outlook for the Blind,* 1964, *58,* 51–54.

Johnson, D., & Johnson, F. *Joining together: Group theory and group skills.* Englewood Cliffs, N.J.: Prentice-Hall, 1975a.

Johnson, D., & Johnson, R. *Learning together and alone: Cooperation, competition, and individualization.* Englewood Cliffs, N.J.: Prentice-Hall, 1975b.

Johnson, D.J., & Myklebust, H.R. *Learning disabilities: Educational principles and practices.* New York: Grune & Stratton, 1967.

Johnson, J.L., & Mithaug, P.E. A replication of sheltered workshop entry requirements. *AAESPH Review,* 1978, *3,* 116–122.

Johnston, J.M. Punishment of human behavior. *American Psychologist,* 1972, *27,* 1033–1054.

Jones, R.L. *New labels in old bags. Research on labeling blacks culturally disadvantaged, culturally deprived, and mentally retarded.* Paper presented at annual convention of Association of Black Psychologists, Miami Beach, September 1970.

Jones, R.L. Labels and stigma in special education. *Exceptional Children,* 1972, *38,* 553–564.

Jones, R.R., Reid, J.B., & Patterson, G.R. Naturalistic observation in clinical assessment. In P. McReynolds (Ed.), *Advances in Psychological Assessment* (Vol. 3). San Francisco: Jossey-Bass, 1975.

Jones, V.F. *Adolescents with behavior problems: Strategies for teaching, counseling, and parent involvement.* Boston: Allyn & Bacon, 1980.

Jones, V.F., & Jones, L.S. *Responsible classroom discipline: Creating positive learning environments and solving problems.* Boston: Allyn & Bacon, 1981.

Kadushin, A. *Child welfare services.* New York: Macmillan Publishing Co., 1974.

Kagan, J., & Moss, H.A. *Birth to maturity.* New York: John Wiley & Sons, 1962.

Kanfer, F., & Saslow, G. Behavioral diagnosis. *Archives of General Psychiatry,* 1965, *12,* 529–538.

Kauffman, J.M. *Characteristics of children's behavior disorders.* Columbus, Ohio: Charles E. Merrill Publishing Co., 1977.

Kauffman, J.M. *Characteristics of children's behavior disorders* (2nd ed.). Columbus, Ohio: Charles E. Merrill Publishing Co., 1981.

Kauppi, D.R. The emperor has no clothes: Comments on Christoplos and Renz. *Journal of Special Education,* 1969, *3,* 393–396.

Kazdin, A.E. The effect of response cost and aversive stimulation in suppressing punished and nonpunished speech disfluences. *Behavior Therapy,* 1973a, *4,* 73–82.

Kazdin, A.E. The effect of vicarious reinforcement on attentive behavior in the classroom. *Journal of Applied Behavior Analysis,* 1973b, *6,* 71–78.

Kazdin, A.E. Unobtrusive measures in behavioral assessment. *Journal of Applied Behavior Analysis,* 1979, *12*(4), 713–724.

Kazdin, A.E. *Behavior modification in applied settings.* Homewood, Ill.: Dorsey Press, 1980a.

Kazdin, A.E. *Research design in clinical psychology.* New York: Harper & Row, 1980b.

Kazdin, A.E. *Single case research designs: Methods for clinical and applied settings.* New York: Oxford University Press, 1982.

Kazdin, A.E., & Klock, J. The effect of nonverbal teacher approval on student attentive behavior. *Journal of Applied Behavior Analysis,* 1973, *6,* 643–654.

Kelley, T.J., Bullock, L.M., & Dykes, M.K. Behavior disorders: Teacher's perceptions. *Exceptional Children,* 1977, *43,* 316–318.

Kelly, J.A. *Social-skills training: A practical guide to intervention.* New York: Springer Publishing Co., 1982.

Kelly, J.A., & Drabman, R.S. The modification of socially detrimental behavior. *Journal of Behavior Therapy and Experimental Psychiatry,* 1977, *8,* 101–104.

Kennedy, A.E. The effects of deafness on personality: A discussion based on the theoretical model of Erik Erikson's eight stages of man. *Journal of Rehabilitation of the Deaf,* 1973, *6,* 22–33.

Kent, R.N., O'Leary, D.K., Dretz, A., & Diament, C. Comparison of observational recordings in view, via mirror and via television. *Journal of Applied Behavior Analysis,* 1979, *12*(4), 517–522.

Keogh, B.K., Cahill, C.W., & MacMillan, D.L. Perception of interruption by educationally handicapped children. *American Journal of Mental Deficiency*, 1972, *77*, 107–108.

Kerlinger, F.P. Influence of research on education. *Educational Researcher*, 1977, *6*(8), 5–12.

Kidd, J.W. The "adulterated" mentally retarded. *Education and Training of the Mentally Retarded*, 1970, *5*(2), 71–72.

Kirk, S.A. The Illinois Test of Psycholinguistic Abilities: Its origin and implications. In J. Hellmuth (Ed.), *Learning disorders* (Vol. 3). Seattle, Wash.: Special Child Publications, 1968.

Kirk, S.A. *Educating exceptional children* (2nd ed.). Boston: Houghton-Mifflin Co., 1972.

Knapp, P. Emotional aspects of hearing loss. *Psychosomatic Medicine*, 1968, *10*, 203.

Knowles, L. Successful and unsuccessful rehabilitation of the legally blind. *The New Outlook for the Blind*, 1969, *63*, 129–169.

Koegel, R.L., & Rincover, A. Treatment of psychotic children in a classroom environment: Learning in a large group. *Journal of Applied Behavior Analysis*, 1974, *7*, 45–59.

Krathwohl, D.R. Improving educational research and development. *Educational Researcher*, 1977, *6*(4), 8–14.

Land, S.L., & Vineberg, S.E. Locus of control in blind children. *Exceptional Children*, 1965, *31*, 257–260.

Lange, P. Frustration reactions of physically handicapped children. *Exceptional Children*, 1959, *25*, 355–357.

Law and Behavior. *Quarterly analysis of legal developments affecting professionals in human services*, 1976, *1*, 1.

Lawrence, E.A. Locus of control: Implications for special education. *Exceptional Children*, 1975, *41*, 483–490.

Lawrence, E.A., & Winschel, J.F. Self-concept and the retarded: Research and issues. *Exceptional Children*, 1973, *39*, 310–319.

Lefkowitz, M.M., Eron, L.D., Walder, L.O., & Huesmann, L.R. *Growing up to be violent: A longitudinal study of the development of aggression.* New York: Pergamon Press, 1977.

Leland, H., Nihira, K. Foster, R., Shellhaas, M., & Kagin, E. *Conference on measurement of adaptive behavior*, III. Parsons, Kan.: Parsons State Hospital and Training Center, 1968.

Leland, H., Shellhaas, M., Nihira, K., & Foster, R. Adaptive behavior: A new dimension in the classification of the mentally retarded. *Mental Retardation Abstracts*, 1967, *4*, 359–387.

Lerea, L., & Ward, B. The social schema of normal and speech-defective children. *Journal of Social Psychology*, 1966, *69*, 87–94.

Lerner, J.W. *Children with learning disabilities: Theories, diagnosis, and teaching strategy.* Boston: Houghton Mifflin Co., 1971.

Levy, J. Social reinforcement and knowledge of results as determinants of motor performance among EMR children. *American Journal of Mental Deficiency*, 1974, *78*, 752–758.

Lewandowski, L.J., & Cruickshank, W.M. Psychological development of crippled children and youth. In W.M. Cruickshank (Ed.), *Psychology of exceptional children and youth.* Englewood Cliffs, N.J.: Prentice-Hall, 1980.

Lewin, K. *Resolving social conflict.* New York: Harper, 1948.

Libet, J.M., & Lewinsohn. Social skills of depressed persons. *Journal of Consulting and Clinical Psychology*, 1973, *40*, 301–312.

Lindsley, O.R. Technical note: A reliable wrist counter for recording behavior rates. *Journal of Applied Behavior Analysis*, 1968, *1*, 77–78.

Lorr, M. (Ed.). *Explorations in typing psychotics*. New York: Pergamon Press, 1966.

Lovaas, O.I. Interactions between verbal and nonverbal behavior. *Child Development*, 1961, *32*, 329–336.

Lovaas, O.I. Control of food intake in children by reinforcement of relevant verbal behavior. *Journal of Abnormal and Social Psychology*, 1964, *68*, 762–778.

Lovaas, O.I., & Koegel, R.L. Behavior therapy with autistic children. In. C.E. Thoresen (Ed.), *Behavior modification in education*. Chicago: The University of Chicago Press, 1972.

Lovaas, O.I., Schaeffer, B., & Simmons, J.O. Building social behavior in autistic children by use of electric shocks. *Journal of Experimental Research in Personality*, 1965, *1*, 99–109.

MacMillan, D.L., Jones, R.L., & Aloia, G.F. The mentally retarded label: A theoretical analysis and review of research. *American Journal of Mental Deficiency*, 1974, *79*, 241–261.

Mahoney, M.J. *Cognition and behavior modification*. Cambridge, Mass.: Ballinger, 1974.

Mahoney, M.J., & Thoresen, C.E. *Self-control: Power to the person*. Monterey, Calif.: Brooks/Cole, 1974.

Malkin, S.F., Freeman, R.D., & Hastings, J.D. Psychosocial problems of deaf children and their families. A comparative study. *Audiology and Hearing Education*, 1976, *2*, 21–29.

Marholin, D., II, & Steinman, W.M. Stimulus control of the classroom as a function of the behavior reinforced. *Journal of Applied Behavior Analysis*, 1977, *10*, 465–478.

Martin, G., & Pear, J. *Behavior modification: What it is and how to do it*. Englewood Cliffs, N.J.: Prentice-Hall, 1978.

Maslach, C. Job burnout: How people cope. *Public Welfare*, 1978, *36*, 56–58.

Maslach, C., & Pines, A. The burn-out syndrome in the day care setting. *Child Care Quarterly*, 1977, *6*, 100–113.

Maslow, A. *Toward a psychology of being*. New York: D. Van Nostrand, 1968.

Mattie, T. v. Holladay, No. DC-75-31-S (N.D. Miss., 1977).

Mattingly, M. Sources of stress and burn-out in professional child care work. *Child Care Quarterly*, 1977, *6*, 127–137.

Mayadas, N.S. Role expectations and performance of blind children: Practice and implication. *Education of the Visually Handicapped*, 1972, *4*, 45–52.

Mayadas, N.S., & Deuhn, W.D. The impact of significant adults' expectations on the lifestyle of visually impaired children. *New Outlook for the Blind*, 1976, *70*, 286–290.

McAndrew, H. Rigidity in the deaf and the blind. *Journal of Social Issues*, 1948, *4*, 72–77.

McCarthy, J.M., & Paraskevopoulos, J. Behavior patterns of learning disabled and average children. *Exceptional Children*, 1969, *36*, 69–74.

McKeachie, W., & Lin, Y. Six differences in student responses to college teachers: Teacher warmth and teacher sex. *American Educational Research Journal*, 1971, *8*, 221–226.

McKenzie, T.L., & Rushall, B.S. Effects of self-recording on attendance and performance in a competitive swimming training environment. *Journal of Applied Behavior Analysis*, 1974, *7*, 199–206.

McLaughlin, T.F., & Malaby, J.E. Elementary school children as behavior engineers. In E. Ramp & G. Semb (Eds.), *Behavior analysis: Areas of research application*. Englewood Cliffs, N.J.: Prentice-Hall, 1975.

McMichael, J.K. *Handicap: A study of physically handicapped children and their families.* London: Staples Press, 1971.

Meadow, K.P. Personality and social development of deaf persons. *Journal of Rehabilitation of the Deaf,* 1976, *9,* 3–16.

Meichenbaum, D.M., Bowers, K., & Ross, R.R. Modification of classroom behavior of institutionalized female adolescent offenders. *Behavior Research and Therapy,* 1968, *6,* 343–353.

Meichenbaum, D.M., & Goodman, J. Training impulsive children to talk to themselves: A means of self-control. *Journal of Abnormal Psychology,* 1971, *77,* 115–126.

Meighan, T. *An investigation of the self concept of blind and visually handicapped adolescents.* New York: American Foundation for the Blind, 1971.

Menolascino, F.J. Emotional disturbance and mental retardation. *American Journal of Mental Deficiency,* 1965, *70,* 248–265.

Menolascino, F.J. *Challenges in mental retardation: Progressive ideology and services.* New York: Human Science Press, 1977.

Mercatoris, M., & Craighead, W. Effects of nonparticipant observation on teacher and pupil classroom behavior. *Journal of Educational Psychology,* 1974, *66,* 512–519.

Mercer, C.D., & Snell, M.E. *Learning theory research in mental retardation.* Columbus, Ohio: Charles E. Merrill Publishing Co., 1972.

Michelson, L., & Wood, R. Behavioral assessment and training of children's social skills. In M. Hersen, P.M. Miller, & R.M. Eisler (Eds.), *Progress in behavior modification* (Vol. 9). New York: Academic Press, 1980.

Miller, E.A. Cerebral-palsied children. *Exceptional Children,* 1958, *24,* 298–302.

Miller, L.K., & Feallock, R. A behavioral system for group living. In E. Ramp & G. Semb (Eds.), *Behavior analysis: Areas of research and application.* Englewood Cliffs, N.J.: Prentice-Hall, 1975.

Miller, N., & Dollard, J. *Social learning and imitation.* New Haven, Conn.: Yale University Press, 1941.

Miller, R.L. Childhood schizophrenia: A review of selected literature. *International Journal of Mental Health,* 1974, *3*(1), 3–46.

Miller, S.R., & Schloss, P.J. *Career-vocational education for handicapped youth.* Rockville, Md.: Aspen Systems Corp., 1982.

Miller, W.H. Manifest anxiety in visually impaired adolescents. *Education of the Visually Handicapped,* 1970, *2,* 91–95.

Millon, T. *Modern psychopathology.* Philadelphia: W.B. Saunders, 1969.

Millon, T., & Millon, R. *Abnormal behavior and personality.* Philadelphia: W.B. Saunders, 1974.

Moncur, J.P. Symptoms of maladjustment differentiating young stutterers from non-stutterers. *Child Development,* 1955, *26,* 91–96.

Moore, B.L., & Bailey, H. Social punishment in the modification of a preschool child's "autistic like" behavior with a mother as therapist. *Journal of Applied Behavior Analysis,* 1973, *6,* 497–507.

Morse, W.C. The education of socially maladjusted and emotionally disturbed children. In W.M. Cruickshank and G.O. Johnson (Eds.), *Education of exceptional children and youth.* Englewood Cliffs, N.J.: Prentice-Hall, 1967.

Moustakas, C.E. *Children in play therapy.* New York: McGraw-Hill Book Co., 1953.

Moustakas, C.E. The frequency and intensity of negative attitudes expressed in play therapy. *Journal of Genetic Psychology*, 1955, *86–87*, 309–325.

Muma, J.R. Peer evaluation and academic performance. *Personality Guidance Journal*, 1965, *44*, 405–409.

Muma, J.R. Peer evaluation and academic achievement in performance classes. *Personality Guidance Journal*, 1968, *46*, 508–585.

Myklebust, H.R. *Psychology of Deafness*. New York: Grune & Stratton, 1960.

Nagera, H., & Colonna, A.E. Aspects of the contribution of sight to ego and drive development: A comparison of the development of some blind and sighted children. In *The psychoanalytic study of the child*. New York: International Universities Press, 1965.

National Society for the Prevention of Blindness. *NSPB fact book: Estimated statistics on blindness and visual problems*. New York: NSPB, 1966.

Nelson, R.D., Kapist, J.A., & Dorsey, B.L. Minimal reactivity of overt classroom observations on student and teacher behaviors. *Behavior Therapy*, 1978, *9*, 695–702.

Neuhaus, E.E. Training the mentally retarded for competitive employment. *Exceptional Children*, 1967, *33*, 625–628.

Nussbaum, J. An investigation of the relationship between the self-concept and reality orientation of adolescents with cerebral palsy. *Dissertation Abstracts*, 1962, *22*, 4410–4411.

Offord, D.R., Abrams, N., Allen, R., & Proushinsky, M. Broken homes, parental psychiatric illness, and female delinquency. *American Journal of Orthopsychiatry*, 1979, *49*, 252–264.

O'Leary, S.G., & Dubey, D.R. Applications of self-control procedures by children: A review. *Journal of Applied Behavior Analysis*, 1979, *12*, 449–465.

Ollendick, T., Balla, D., & Zigler, E. Expectancy of success and the probability of learning of retarded children. *Journal of Abnormal Psychology*, 1971, *77*, 275–281.

Overall, J.E., & Gorham, D.R. A pattern probability model for the classification of psychiatric patients. *Behavioral Science*, 1963, *8*, 108–116.

Patterson, G.R. The aggressive child: Victim or architect of a coercive system? In L.A. Hamerlynch, L.C. Handy, & E.J. Mash (Eds.), *Behavior modification and families*. New York: Brunner/Mazell, 1975.

Patterson, G.R., & Cobb, J.A. A dyadic analysis of "aggressive" behaviors. In J.P. Hill (Ed.), *Minnesota symposia on child psychology* (Vol. 5). Minneapolis, Minn.: University of Minnesota Press, 1971.

Payne, J.S., Polloway, E.A., Smith, J.E., & Payne, R.A. *Strategies for teaching the mentally retarded*. Columbus, Ohio: Charles E. Merrill Publishing Co., 1981.

Pendergrass, V.E. Timeout from positive reinforcement following persistent, high-rate behavior in retardates. *Journal of Applied Behavior Analysis*, 1972, *5*, 85–91.

Perrin, E.H. The social position of the speech defective child. *Journal of Speech and Hearing Disorders*, 1954, *19*, 250–252.

Perry, M.A., & Cerreto, M.C. Structured learning training of social skills for the retarded. *Mental Retardation*, 1977, *15*(2), 31–33.

Phillips, E.L. Achievement place token reinforcement procedures in a home-style rehabilitation setting for pre-delinquent boys. *Journal of Applied Behavior Analysis*, 1968, *1*, 213–223.

Phillips, L., Draguns, J.G., & Bartlett, D.P. Classification of behavior disorders. In N. Hobbs (Ed.), *Issues in the classification of children* (Vol. 1). San Francisco: Jossey-Bass, 1975.

Piaget, J. *Play, dreams, and imitation in childhood*. New York: Norton, 1952a.

Piaget, J. *The origins of intelligence in children* (2nd ed.). New York: International Universities Press, 1952b.

Poremba, E. As I was saying. In B. Kratoville (Ed.), *Youth in trouble.* San Rafael, Calif.: Academic Therapy, 1974.

Porterfield, O.V., & Schlicting, G.F. Peer status and reading achievement. *Journal of Educational Research,* 1961, *54,* 291–297.

Premack, D. Reinforcement theory. In D. Levine (Ed.), *Nebraska symposium on motivation, 1965.* Lincoln, Neb.: University of Nebraska Press, 1965.

Proctor, P. How to survive today's stressful jobs. *Parade Magazine,* June 17, 1979, pp. 4–5.

Public Law 93-112, *Vocational Rehabilitation Act of 1973,* Section 504, July 26, 1973.

Public Law 94-142, *Education for All Handicapped Children Act,* November 29, 1975.

Quay, H.C. Patterns of aggression, withdrawal and immaturity. In H.C. Quay & J.S. Werry (Eds.), *Psychopathological disorders of childhood.* New York: John Wiley & Sons, 1972.

Quay, H.C. Classification in the treatment of delinquency and antisocial behavior. In N. Hobbs (Ed.), *Issues in the classification of children* (Vol. 1). San Francisco: Jossey-Bass, 1975.

Quay, H.C. Classification. In H.C. Quay & J.S. Werry (Eds.), *Psychopathological disorders of childhood.* New York: John Wiley & Sons, 1979.

Quay, H.C., Morse, W.C., & Cutler, R.L. Personality patterns of pupils in special classes for the emotionally disturbed. *Exceptional Children,* 1966, *32,* 297–301.

Rainer, J.D., & Kallmann, F.J. *Family and mental health problems in a deaf population.* Springfield, Ill.: Charles C Thomas Pub., 1969.

Raths, L.E., Harmin, M., & Simon, S.B. *Values and teaching.* Columbus, Ohio: Charles E. Merrill Publishing Co., 1966.

Reese, E.P., Howard, J., & Reese, T.W. *Human operant behavior: Analysis and application.* Dubuque, Iowa: William C. Brown, 1978.

Rehm, L., Fuchs, E., Roth, D., Kornblith, S., & Romano, J. A comparison of self-control and assertion skills treatments of depression. *Behavior Therapy,* 1979, *11,* 429–442.

Reiss, S.R., Levitan, G.W., & Szyszko, J. Emotional disturbance and mental retardation: Diagnostic overshadowing. *American Journal of Mental Deficiency,* 1982, *86,* 567–574.

Reivich, S.R., & Rothrock, I.A. Behavior problems of deaf children and adolescents: A factor-analytic study. *Journal of Speech and Hearing Research,* 1972, *15,* 93–104.

Research Utilization Branch, Division of Research and Demonstration Grants, Office of Research, Rehabilitation Service, Department of Health, Education and Welfare. A special program to place mentally retarded persons in federal employment. *BRIEF,* 1969.

Reynolds, M.C., & Balow, B. Categories and variables in special education. *Exceptional Children,* 1972, 38, 257–366.

Rhodes, W.C. The disturbing child: A problem of ecological management. *Exceptional Children,* 1967, *33,* 449–455.

Rimland, B. *Infantile autism.* New York: Appleton-Century-Crofts, 1964.

Risley, T.R., & Hart, B. Developing correspondence between the nonverbal and verbal behaviors of preschool children. *Journal of Applied Behavior Analysis,* 1968, *1,* 267–291.

Risley, T.R., & Wolf, M. Establishing functional speech in echolalic children. *Behavior Research and Therapy,* 1967, *5,* 73–88.

Rivers, L.W., Henderson, D.M., Jones, R.L., Lodner, J.A., & Williams, R.L. Mosaic of labels for black children. In N. Hobbs (Ed.) *Issues in the classification of children* (Vol. 1). San Francisco: Jossey-Bass, 1975.

Robinson, N.M., & Robinson, H.B. *The mentally retarded child.* New York: McGraw-Hill Book Co., 1976.

Rodda, M. Behavioral disorders in deaf clients. *Journal of Rehabilitation of the Deaf,* 1974, *6,* 1–13.

Roff, M. Childhood social interactions and young adult bad conduct. *Journal of Abnormal Social Psychology,* 1961, *63,* 333–337.

Roff, M., Sells, B., & Golden, M. *Social adjustment and personality development in children.* Minneapolis, Minn.: University of Minnesota Press, 1972.

Rogers, C.R. *Client-centered therapy.* Boston: Houghton Mifflin Co., 1965.

Rogers, C.R. *On becoming a person.* Boston: Houghton Mifflin Co., 1961.

Rogers, C.R. *Freedom to learn.* Columbus, Ohio: Charles E. Merrill Publishing Co., 1969.

Rosenberg, S. *Interpersonal processes in the perpetuation and reduction of language retardation: Some speculations and some data.* Paper presented at the meeting of the American Association on Mental Deficiency, Milwaukee, May 1959.

Rosenthal, R., & Jacobson, L. *Pygmalion in the classroom: Teacher expectation and pupils' intellectual development.* New York: Holt, Rinehart & Winston, 1968.

Ross, D.M. Effect on learning of psychological attachment to a film model. *American Journal of Mental Deficiency,* 1970, *74,* 701–707.

Rotter, J. *Social learning and clinical psychology.* Englewood Cliffs, N.J.: Prentice-Hall, 1954.

Rotter, J. Some problems and misconceptions related to the construct of internal versus external control of reinforcement. *Journal of Consulting and Clinical Psychology,* 1975, *43,* 56–67.

Russo, D.C., & Kuegel, R.L. A method for integrating an autistic child into a normal public school classroom. *Journal of Applied Behavior Analysis,* 1977, *10,* 579–590.

Rutter, M.L. Psychiatry. In J. Wortis (Ed.), *Mental retardation: An annual review* (Vol. 3). New York: Grune & Stratton, 1971.

Rychtarik, R.G., & Bornstein, P.H. Training conversational skills in mentally retarded adults: A multiple baseline analysis. *Mental Retardation,* 1979, *17,* 289–293.

S-1 v. Turlington, No. 78-8020-Civ-CA-WPB (S.D. Fla., 1979).

Sabatino, D.A. Revolution: Viva resource rooms. *The Journal of Special Education,* 1972, *6*(4), 389–395.

Sabatino, D.A., & Miller, T.L. (Eds.). *Describing learner characteristics of handicapped children and youth.* New York: Grune & Stratton, 1979.

Sabatino, D.A., & Schloss, P.J. Adolescent social-personal development: Theory and application. In D.A. Sabatino, C. Schmidt, & T. Miller (Eds.), *Learning disabilities: Systemizing teaching and service delivery.* Rockville, Md.: Aspen Systems Corp., 1981.

Sali, J., & Amir, J. Personal factors influencing the retarded person's success at work: A report from Israel. *American Journal of Mental Deficiency,* 1971, *76,* 42–47.

Salvia, J.E., Schultz, W., & Chapin, N. Reliability of Bower Scale for screening of children with emotional handicaps. *Exceptional Children,* 1974, *41,* 117–118.

Sanders, D.A. Psychological implications of hearing impairment. In W.M. Cruickshank (Ed.), *Psychology of exceptional children and youth.* Englewood Cliffs, N.J.: Prentice-Hall, 1980.

Sandifer, M.G., Pettus, C., & Quade, D. A study of psychiatric diagnosis. *Journal of Nervous and Mental Disease*, 1964, *139*, 350–356.

Schlesinger, H.S., & Meadow, K.P. *Deafness and mental health: A developmental approach.* San Francisco: Langley Porter Neuropsychiatric Institute, 1971.

Schloss, P.J. Developing positive social responses with hearing impaired children and youth. *Journal of Rehabilitation of the Deaf*, 1982, *16*(1), 6–13.

Schloss, P.J. Verbal interactions patterns of depressed and non-depressed institutionalized mentally retarded adults. *Applied Research in Mental Retardation*, 1982, *3*, 1–12.

Schloss, P.J., & Johann, M. A modeling and contingency management approach to pacifier withdrawal. *Behavior Therapy*, 1982, *13*, 254–257.

Schloss, P.J., Kane, M.S., & Miller, S.R. Truancy intervention for behaviorally disordered adolescents. *Behavioral Disorders*, 1981, *6*(3), 175–179.

Schloss, P.J., & Miller, S.R. The effects of the label "institutionalized" vs. "regular school student" on teacher expectations. *Exceptional Children*, 1982, *48*, 263–264.

Schloss, P.J., Sachs, J.J., Miller, S.R. & Schloss, C.N. Increasing work production of a mentally retarded student through the systematic analysis of continuous data. *Journal of Industrial Teacher Education*, 1982, *19*(3), 20–26.

Schloss, P.J., & Sedlak, R.A. Behavioral features of the mentally retarded adolescent: Implications for the mainstream educator. *Psychology in the Schools*, 1982, *19*, 98–104.

Schloss, P.J., Sedlak, R.A., Elliott, C., & Smothers, M. Application of the changing criterion design in special education. *Journal of Special Education*, 1982, *16*(3), 359–367.

Schloss, P.J., Sedlak, R.A., Wiggins, E.D., & Ramsey, D. A stress reduction approach for professional and paraprofessional persons working with severely behaviorally disordered adolescents. *Exceptional Children*, 1983, *49*(4), 349–354.

Schumaker, J.B., Havell, M.F., & Sherman, J.A. An analysis of daily report cards and parent managed privileges in the improvement of adolescents' classroom performance. *Journal of Applied Behavior Analysis*, 1977, *10*(3), 449–464.

Scott, R.A., *The making of blind men.* New York: Russell Sage Foundation, 1969.

Seligman, M.E.P. Depression and learned helplessness. In R.J. Friedman & M.M. Katz (Eds.), *The psychology of depression: Contemporary theory and research.* New York: Winston-Wiley, 1974.

Seligman, M.E.P., & Groves, D. Nontransient learned helplessness. *Psychonomic Science*, 1970, *19*, 191.

Seligman, M.E.P., Maier, S.F., & Solomon, R.L. In F.R. Bush (Ed.), *Aversive conditioning and learning.* New York: Academic Press, 1971.

Sergeant, R.L. *An investigation of responses of speech defective adults on personality inventories.* Unpublished doctoral thesis, Ohio State University, 1962.

Sheehan, J., Hadley, R., & Gould, E. Impact of authority on stuttering. *Journal of Abnormal Psychology*, 1967, *72*, 290–293.

Sirvis, B. The physically disabled, In E. Meyer (Ed.), *Exceptional children and youth: An introduction.* Denver, Col.: Love Publishing, 1978.

Skinner, B.F. *Science and human behavior.* New York: Free Press, 1953.

Smith, J.E., & Payne, J.S. *Teaching exceptional adolescents.* Columbus, Ohio: Charles E. Merrill Publishing Co., 1980.

Solomon, A.L. Personality and behavior patterns of children with functional defects of articulation. *Child Development*, 1961, *32*, 731–737.

Solomon, R.R., & Wahler, R.G. Peer reinforcement control of classroom problem behavior. *Journal of Applied Behavior Analysis*, 1973, *6*, 49–56.

Sommers, V.S. *The influence of parental attitude and social environment on the personality development of the adolescent blind.* New York: American Foundation for the Blind, 1944.

Sowers, J.A., Rusch, F.R., & Hudson, C. Training a severely retarded adult to ride a city bus to and from work. *AAESPH Review*, 1979, 15–25.

Spence, S.H., & Marzillier, J.S. Social skills training with adolescent male offenders: Short-term effect. *Behavior, Research, and Therapy*, 1979, *17*, 7–15.

Spitzer, R.L., Endicott, J., Cohen, J., & Fliess, J.L. Constraints on the validity of computer diagnosis. *Archives of General Psychiatry*, 1974, *31*, 197–203.

Springer, N., & Roslow, R. A further study of the psycho-neurotic responses of the deaf and hard of hearing child. *Journal of Educational Psychology*, 1938, *29*, 590–596.

Sternlicht, M. Issues in counseling and psychotherapy with mentally retarded individuals. In I. Bialer & M. Sternlicht (Eds.), *The psychology of mental retardation: Issues and approaches.* New York: Psychological Dimension, 1977.

Sternlicht, M., & Deutsch, M.R. *Personality development and social behavior in the mentally retarded.* Lexington, Mass.: D.C. Heath, 1972.

Stevenson, H.W. *Children's learning.* New York: Appleton-Century-Crofts, 1972.

Strain, R., Shores, R., & Kerr, M. An experimental analysis of "spellover" effects on the social interaction of behaviorally handicapped preschool children. *Journal of Applied Behavior Analysis*, 1976, *9*, 31–40.

Stuart v. Nappi, 443 F. Supp. 1235 (D. Ct. 1978).

Sulzer-Azaroff, B., & Mayer, G.R. *Applying behavior-analysis procedures with children and youth.* New York: Holt, Rinehart & Winston, 1977.

Swap, S. Disturbing classroom behaviors: A developmental and ecological view. *Exceptional Children*, 1974, *41*, 163–172.

Szasz, T.S. The myth of mental illness. *American Psychologist*, 1960, *15*, 113–118.

Taplin, P.S., & Reid, J.B. Effects of instructional set and experimenter influence on observer reliability. *Child Development*, 1973, *44*, 547–554.

Telford, C.W., & Sawrey, J.M. *The exceptional individual* (2nd ed.). Englewood Cliffs, N.J.: Prentice-Hall, 1972.

Thomas, C.M., Sulzer-Azaroff, B., Lukeris, S., & Palmer, M. Teaching daily self-help skills for "long-term" maintenance. In B. Etzel, J. LeBlanc, & D. Baer (Eds.), *New developments in behavioral research: Theory and application.* Hillsdale, N.J.: Erlbaum Associates, 1977.

Thomas, D.R., Becker, W.C., & Armstrong, M. Production and elimination of disruptive classroom behavior by systematically varying teacher's behavior. *Journal of Applied Behavior Analysis*, 1968, *1*, 35–45.

Thomas, D.R., Nielsen, L.J., Kuypers, D.S., & Becker, W.C. Social reinforcement and remedial instruction in the elimination of a classroom behavior problem. *Journal of Special Education*, 1968, *2*, 291–302.

Thompson, G., Iwata, B., & Poynter, H. Operant control of pathological tongue thrust in spastic cerebral palsy. *Journal of Applied Behavior Analysis*, 1979, *12*, 325–333.

Thoresen, C.E., & Mahoney, M.J. *Behavioral self-control.* New York: Holt, Rinehart & Winston, 1974.

Tofte-Tipps, S., Mendonca, P., & Peach, R. Training and generalization of social skills: A study with two developmentally handicapped, socially isolated children. *Behavior Modification*, 1982, *6*, 45–71.

Trap, J.J., Milner-Davis, P., Shirley, J., & Cooper, J.O. The effects of feedback and consequences on transitional cursive letter formation. *Journal of Applied Behavior Analysis*, 1978, *11*(3), 381–394.

Trapp, E.P., & Evans, J. Functional articulatory defect and performance on a nonverbal task. *Journal of Speech and Hearing Disorders*, 1960, *25*, 176–180.

Truax, C.B., & Mitchell, K.M. Research on certain therapist interpersonal skills in relation to process and outcome. In A.D. Bergin & S.L. Garfield (Eds.), *Handbook of psychotherapy and behavior change*. New York: John Wiley & Sons, 1971.

Turner, A.S., Hersen, M., & Bellack, A.S. Social skills training to teach prosocial behaviors in an organically impaired and retarded patient. *Journal of Behavior Therapy and Experimental Psychiatry*, 1978, *9*, 253–258.

Twardosz, S., & Sajwaj, T. Multiple effects of a procedure to increase sitting in a hyperactive retarded boy. *Journal of Applied Behavior Analysis*, 1972, *5*, 73–78.

Ullman, E.A. Teachers, peers, and tests as predictors of adjustment. *Journal of Educational Psychology*, 1957, *48*, 257–267.

Ullman, L.P., & Krasner, L. *A psychological approach to abnormal behavior*. Englewood Cliffs, N.J.: Prentice-Hall, 1969.

Varni, J.W., & Henker, B. A self-regulation approach to the treatment of three hyperactive boys. *Child Behavior Therapy*, 1979, *1*, 171–191.

Vernon, M. Sociological and psychological factors associated with hearing loss. *Journal of Speech and Hearing Disorders*, 1969, *12*, 541–563.

Von Isser, A., Quay, H.C., & Love, C.F. Interrelationships among three measures of deviant behavior. *Exceptional Children*, 1980, *46*, 272–276.

Walker, H.M., & Hops, H. Increasing academic achievement by reinforcing direct academic performance and/or facilitative nonacademic responses. *Journal of Educational Psychology*, 1976, *68*, 218–225.

Walker, J.J. The gifted and talented. In Meyen (Ed.), *Exceptional children and youth: An introduction*. Denver, Col.: Love Publishing, 1978.

Wallace, G., & Kauffman, J.M. *Teaching children with learning problems*. Columbus, Ohio: Charles E. Merrill Publishing Co., 1978.

Warner, R.W., & Swisher, J.D. Drug-abuse prevention: Reinforcement of alternatives. In J.D. Krumboltz & C.E. Thoresen (Eds.), *Counseling Methods*. New York: Holt, Rinehart & Winston, 1976, 510–517.

Watson, D.L., & Tharp, R.G. Self-directed behavior: Self-modification for personal adjustment. Monterey, Calif.: Brooks/Cole, 1977.

Wehman, P., Abramson, M., & Norman, C. Transfer of training in behavior modification: An evaluative review. *The Journal of Special Education*, 1977, *11*, 11–16.

Weiskopf, P.E. Burnout among teachers of exceptional children. *Exceptional Children*, 1980, *47*, 18–23.

Wepman, J.M., Cruickshank, W.M., Deutsch, C.P., Morency, A., & Strother, C.R. Learning disabilities. In N. Hobbs (Ed.), *Issues in the classification of children* (Vol. 1). San Francisco: Jossey-Bass, 1975.

Werry, J.S. Childhood psychosis. In H.C. Quay & J.S. Werry (Eds.), *Psychopathological disorders of childhood*. New York: John Wiley & Sons, 1972.

White, G.D. The effects of observer preferences on the activity levels of families. *Journal of Applied Behavior Analysis*, 1977, *10*(4), 734.

White, R.W. Competence and the psychosexual stages of development. In M.R. Jones (Ed.), *Nebraska symposium on motivation*. Lincoln, Neb.: University of Nebraska Press, 1960.

Whitehill, M., Hersen, M., & Bellack, A.S. Conversation skills training for socially isolated children. *Behavior Research and Therapy*, 1980, *18*, 217–225.

Whitman, R.L., Mercurio, J.R., & Coponigri, V. Development of social responses in two severely retarded children. *Journal of Applied Behavior Analysis*, 1970, *3*, 133–138.

Wilson, C.W., & Hopkins, B.L. The effects of contingent music on the intensity of noise in junior high home economics classes. *Journal of Applied Behavior Analysis*, 1973, *6*, 269–275.

Wiltz, N.A., & Gordon, S.B. Parental modification of a child's behavior in an experimental residence. *Journal of Behavior Therapy and Experimental Psychiatry*, 1974, *5*, 107–109.

Wingate, M.E. Behavioral rigidity in stutterers. *Journal of Speech and Hearing Research*, 1966, *9*, 626–629.

Wolfensberger, W. Differential rewards as motivating factors in mental deficiency research. *American Journal of Mental Deficiency*, 1960, *64*, 902–906.

Wolpe, J. *Psychotherapy by reciprocal inhibition*. Stanford, Calif.: Stanford University Press, 1958.

Wood, K.S. *Parental maladjustment and functional articulatory defects in children*. Unpublished doctoral thesis, University of Southern California, 1946.

Wood, K.S. Parental maladjustment and functional articulatory defects in children. *Journal of Speech and Hearing Disorders*, 1949, *11*, 255–275.

Wysocki, B. Body image of crippled children as seen in Draw-a-Person Test behavior. *Perceptual and Motor Skills*, 1965, *21*, 499–504.

Ysseldyke, J.E. Diagnostic-prescriptive teaching: The search for aptitude-treatment interaction. In L. Mann & D.A. Sabatino (Eds.), *The first review of special education*. Philadelphia: Journal of Special Education Press, 1973.

Ysseldyke, J.E., & Foster, G.G. Bias in teacher observations of emotionally disabled children. *Exceptional Children*, 1978, *45*, 18–26.

Zigler, E.F. The retarded child as a whole person. In D.K. Routh (Ed.), *The experimental psychology of mental retardation*. Chicago: Aldine, 1973.

Zigler, E.F., & Harter, S. The socialization of the mentally retarded. In P.A. Goslin (Ed.), *Handbook of socialization theory and research*. Chicago: Rand McNally, 1969.

Zimmerman, E.H., & Zimmerman, J. The alteration of behavior in a classroom situation. *Journal of the Experimental Analysis of Behavior*, 1962, *5*, 59–60.

Zinzer, O. *Imitation, modeling and cross-cultural training*. Aerospace medical research laboratories. Wright-Patterson Air Force Base, Ohio: Aerospace Medical Division, September 1966.

Index

257